THE DEVELOPMENT OF AUSTRALIAN BASKETBALL

MORMON YANKEES

GIANTS ON AND OFF THE COURT

THE DEVELOPMENT OF AUSTRALIAN BASKETBALL

MORMON YANKEES

GIANTS ON AND OFF THE COURT

FRED E. WOODS

FOREWORD BY

SHAWN BRADLEY

CFI

AN IMPRINT OF CEDAR FORT, INC.

SPRINGVILLE, UTAH

TO THE MORMON YANKEES AND ALL THE AUSTRALIANS WHO EMBRACED THEM

ISBN 13: 978-1-4621-1059-9 (with DVD)
ISBN 13: 978-1-4621-2019-2 (without DVD)

Published by CFI, an imprint of Cedar Fort, Inc.
2373 W. 700 S., Springville, UT, 84663
Distributed by Cedar Fort, Inc., www.cedarfort.com

THE LIBRARY OF CONGRESS HAS CATALOGED THE FIRST EDITION AS FOLLOWS:

Woods, Fred E., author.
Mormon Yankees : giants on and off the court / Fred E. Woods.
pages cm
ISBN 978-1-4621-1059-9
1. Mormon Yankees (Basketball team)--History. 2. Mormon missionaries--Australia--History. 3. Church of Jesus Christ of Latter-day Saints--Australia--History. 4. Mormons--Australia--History. 5. Basketball--Australia--History. I. Title.

GV885.42.M67W66 2012
796.3570994--dc23

2012002120

Cover design by Brian Halley

Edited and typeset by Kelley Konzak

Printed in the United States of America

10 9 8 7 6 5 4 3 2 1

Printed on acid-free paper

CONTENTS

Acknowledgments ix

Foreword xi

Introduction 1

Interviews 51

- Betty Benson 51
- Gunars Esins Berzzarins (GEB) 54
- Delmar Bjork 58
- Gary H. Blacker 62
- Ronald L. Bouck 66
- Gary D. Bouma 69
- Roger L. Bown 71
- Shawn Bradley 74
- Betty Brooks 76
- Keith Brooks 79
- Colin J. Burdett 81
- Cliff Burns 83
- Rodney Burt 85
- Bishop H. David Burton 91
- Richard D. Christensen 93
- DeLyle H. Condie 96
- Marie Cray 103
- Lorna Cullis 105
- George Dancis 107
- Mike Dancis 109
- Percival William Frederick Davis 110
- Sherm Day 113

Heather Dodd 117
Jessie L. Embry 121
Arthur Emery 124
Ray Feeney 126
Charles Bruce Flick 129
Inga Freidenfelds 133
Lolita Freidenfelds 135
Mark J. Frodsham 137
James Nyle Garn 139
Lindsay Gaze 142
Paul G. Grant 151
Gayle Hampson 156
Ted E. Haynes 157
Geoff Heskett 161
Gordon Holt 165
Owen Hughan 168
Dr. Donald F. Hull 170
Eldon J. Huntsman 172
Edward A. (Ted) Johnson 177
Dr. David A. Kimball 179
Dr. Richard Ian Kimball 182
Eric Leivesley 184
Pat Leivesley. 186
James William Lundahl 188
Elspeth Lyon 190
Carl McGavin 192
Joan McNair 194
Mervyn Moy 196
Denise Mutton 200
Peter G. Mutton. 202
Dennis O'Riordan 204
Allan Pascoe. 207
Neville Pearse. 209
Robert G. Pedersen 211
Don Pemberton 214
James Richard (Rich) Rampton 216

Harold (Hal) Reeb 218
Denis Ryan 220
Bob Skousen 224
Robert (Bob) Steck 228
Raymond Arthur Steen 233
Keith Stringer 236
Harold E. Turley Jr. 239
Dell Tuttle 242
Garwood Walton 246
Kay Watts 249
Norman L. Weitzeil 252
Wilburn West 255

Endnotes 259

Bibliography 279

Index 287

MORMON YANKEES (1956). COURTESY OF RODNEY BURT.

ACKNOWLEDGMENTS

THIS COMBINED BOOK and documentary (DVD) was made possible through the assistance of a number of individuals and several institutions. Gratitude is expressed to Corey Lindley (former president of the Australia Melbourne Mission) and many Mormon Yankees who donated funding for the documentary. Special thanks are also extended to the College of Religious Education at Brigham Young University for its financial support and resources rendered via transcriptions made from oral history interviews transcribed by student employees in the Joseph Smith Building Faculty Support Center. I am also grateful for the competent staff employed at the Brigham Young University Harold B. Lee Library and the Church History Library of The Church of Jesus Christ of Latter-day Saints as well as the University of Melbourne Library and the State Library of Victoria.

I wish to also thank my former BYU student research assistant, Candice Bellows, and my current TA, Suzie Davis, for editing this document as well as emeritus BYU English professor Don Norton. Executive editor Devan Jensen was also helpful in proofreading the text as well as students under his tutelage at the BYU Religious Studies Center. I am thankful to my daughter Addie R. White for improving the manuscript, and I am especially grateful to my wife, JoAnna Woods, who made substantial changes to the writing style of this manuscript. Thanks is also extended to Kelley Konzak and Jennifer Fielding of Cedar Fort, who have provided professional direction throughout the editorial process and have been delightful to work with.

Sincere gratitude is extended to Ben Watson for initially envisioning this compelling story and for compiling historical data and contact information. Thanks also to Dennis O'Riordan for sharing materials concerning Australian Mormon history in the twentieth century. Heartfelt thanks is expressed to Shawn Bradley for writing the excellent foreword to this book. I am particularly grateful to the film director, Martin L. Andersen, with whom I had the pleasure of working closely to produce this documentary. We enjoyed several trips to Australia, capturing scores of oral history interviews. Martin also carefully read the manuscript and gave useful feedback as well as providing most of the images.

In addition, appreciation is expressed to the Mormon Yankees for sharing their journals, scrapbooks, photos, and newspaper clippings and for permitting us to record priceless oral history interviews. The interviews capture the unique experience these Latter-day Saint missionaries had in the mid-twentieth century "down under." Gratitude is also expressed to the many others willing to be interviewed, who interacted with these young men and watched them play the game they love. Further, appreciation is extended to Trevor Evans for help with early film work and to Graeme and David Cray, who assisted with arranging interviews and scanning images.

Finally, appreciation is expressed to my family, who have always been a constant support to my diverse projects. This one was especially dear to me since I served an LDS mission to Australia from 1977–79 and fell in love with the land and more especially with the great people of Australia.

FOREWORD

BY SHAWN BRADLEY

I SAT NERVOUSLY EXCITED in a foreign airport awaiting the final flight of the trip. "Auckland, New Zealand, to Sydney, Australia" couldn't come soon enough. What was Australia going to be like? How are the people? What about the food, the driving, the language? Who is my new companion, and will he be able to handle all my stuff? Actually, I was more worried if I could handle his. I wasn't going on a mission anymore, I was *on* one. Do I talk to that person over there? Will she wait for me? What about that family? Where's my companion? I had just traveled almost halfway around the world to serve as a missionary for The Church of Jesus Christ of Latter-day Saints, and I felt so anxious.

I then had a thought as I was walking to board the plane. The people weren't just looking at me because I was seven feet six inches tall; they were now looking because of this big name badge on my coat. Though I didn't realize it at that time, my challenge was going to be how I could use the two to work together and fulfill my purpose more fully as a missionary.

I had been a pretty good kid, growing up in a small farming and mining community in central Utah. My parents had raised me the best they could and provided a great life for my siblings and me. Having grown up on a small ranch, we learned many great principles of work and dedication. Though at the time when I was milking the cow, any benefit other than the milk was very hard to see. Grandpa and I were once digging a ditch at the top of one of our fields, and it started to rain—a slow, big-drop kind of rain. The kind where I wondered what was moving in the brush until one of the big drops hit me and sent shivers down my back because of the cold shock of it all. I said under my breath, "I hate the rain." My grandfather turned to me and let me know that I was not allowed to "hate the rain." He explained that we don't get it very often, and when we do, we should be grateful and welcome it with open arms. Literally, he made me stand there with open arms looking up into the sky trying to catch a drop with my mouth. From that moment I've always been grateful for the rain, and I was thankful for the change in perspective.

I saw more rain on my first day in Australia than I did the entire previous year back home. This was much different than the ranch in Castle Dale, Utah, but it was how it was supposed to be. Not too long into my mission, I had someone ask me if I knew who the Mormon Yankees were and if they were going to start up again. I didn't and kind of dismissed it, though the conversation did come up a couple of times during my two years in Australia. I learned they were a traveling basketball team that played exhibition games to help people gain positive exposure to the Church. It wasn't until many years later, when I met Dr. Fred Woods, that I learned more about the Mormon Yankees and my perspective changed again. I learned they were Latter-day Saint missionaries who played basketball on a team that traveled all over Australia. The Mormon Yankees were around for over twenty years and beat some pretty good basketball teams along the way. They played exhibition games prior to the 1956 Olympics against teams preparing for the Olympics. Missionaries like Elder Loren C. Dunn, Bishop H. David Burton, Bob Skousen, and many others used their skills in basketball to break some of the barriers of misunderstanding and to help others come to know a little more about The Church of Jesus Christ of Latter-day Saints. They did this over thirty years before I was serving in the same area, and their influence was still being felt. I know it worked, for I've never had a negative conversation concerning the Mormon Yankees.

Dr. Woods has used his skill and brought to light stories of young Latter-day Saint missionaries. He has helped change our perspective of them and helped us come to know them better. They used their gifts to be great examples. Dr. Woods has helped us see how the Mormon Yankees serve as a guide in using what we all have to help others come to know Christ. He has helped us learn that through the Mormon Yankees' sportsmanship, exemplary behavior, and dedication, they've proven to be giants both on and off the court.

INTRODUCTION

THE CHRISTIANIZING OF BASKETBALL

IT WAS JAMES Naismith's job at the Young Men's Christian Association (YMCA) to lure boys to the Christian fold and shape them into responsible, God-fearing citizens. He succeeded by inventing a simple physical competition involving a soccer ball and two peach baskets affixed to opposing walls. The game was enough to bring boys in from the streets of Springfield, Massachusetts, during the cold days of December 1891. The game of basketball was born.[1]

The YMCA invented the phrase *muscular Christianity* to describe the use of recreation for religious purposes. Late nineteenth-century churches were quick to copy the YMCA's phenomenal success in this enterprise. By 1905, basketball in America was deeply embedded in churches, high schools, and colleges.[2] The Church of Jesus Christ of Latter-day Saints was among the many participants in this movement.[3] Throughout the Roaring Twenties, the Church's Young Men's Mutual Improvement Association (YMMIA) hosted basketball tournaments in Salt Lake City, bringing in teams from Utah, from the Intermountain West, and eventually from throughout the United States. But the Mormons coined their own term for this type of religiously motivated sports

JAMES NAISMITH, INVENTOR OF BASKETBALL. COURTESY OF MEADE PUBLIC LIBRARY, MEADE, KANSAS.

participation: *spiritualized recreation*.[4]

By the 1930s, full-time Latter-day Saint missionaries were using basketball to build bridges in various countries and communities, which led to some being converted to the Church. A high-profile example of this occurred when missionaries serving in Germany were asked to help train the German national basketball team for the 1936 Olympic Games, the first Olympics to include basketball. The Mormon elders[5] were not only asked to coach the German team but were also invited to officiate during the first Olympic basketball competition; ultimately, Germany did not even place.[6]

Spiritualized Recreation Down Under

Perhaps the most notable instance of spiritualized recreation in Latter-day Saint history took place when Mormon missionaries began playing basketball in Australian YMCA competitions. Before World War II, the 1937 annual report of the Melbourne YMCA noted "a group of Mormon players [missionaries]" who were participating in the chapter's basketball games.[7] In 1938, the "visiting group of American Missionaries" not only won the Melbourne YMCA championship but also went undefeated throughout the season.[8] During the 1939 season,

LDS basketball team (1938). Courtesy of Church History Library, The Church of Jesus Christ of Latter-day Saints.

LDS BASKETBALL TEAM (1947). COURTESY OF BETTY BROWN.

the Mormon elders representing the YMCA won championships in both the city of Melbourne and the state of Victoria.[9] This accomplishment was newsworthy enough to be covered in the Latter-day Saint periodical *Improvement Era*.[10]

More coverage appeared in a Melbourne newspaper, giving credit to these Mormon visitors for stimulating public interest in basketball and for improving Australian standards of play. The missionaries organized clinics and played with Australia's best in order to popularize the game. At a banquet held in Victoria to promote basketball, world-famous cyclist Hubert Opperman said,

> Basketball being a secondary sport of mine, I naturally admired the consistent success of the Mormon teams and felt that there must be a specific reason for such outstanding displays of speed and stamina. It was gratifying, if not surprising, therefore, to discover after their match at Fitzroy stadium that their general mode of living and training as demanded by the Word of Wisdom [the Latter-day Saint health code] confirmed views to which I have been gradually converted during years of cycle racing. The balanced diet which they favored—the elimination of tea, alcohols, coffee, and tobacco from their regime—and their strong preference for raw fruits and steamed vegetables provided an excellent example for both athlete and general citizen to follow as a basis for health and fitness.[11]

This glowing endorsement of the Latter-day Saint lifestyle shows that the missionaries were having success on and off the court. With their basketball play, missionaries were bringing the Church out of obscurity and displaying Mormon standards. Their exemplary behavior and hard work continued to bear fruit; the Melbourne YMCA's 1940 annual report recounted that the Mormon missionaries had secured another championship.[12] The *Improvement Era* again ran an article in the spring of 1941 featuring the 1940 Latter-day Saint Victorian championship team. This team went undefeated in 1940 and had won each championship since 1938. The players were listed as Elders Sam Francis (captain), Paul Francis, Donald Hogan, Ray Walker, Ray Walton, Jack Decker, Harold Goddard, Delwyn Wilde, Heber Gilbert, Ray Bryan, and McMullin.[13] The *Improvement Era* also showcased a contemporary team known as the Mormon Colts from Sydney, New South Wales; this team was composed of Mormon missionaries and local young men. "The club lost the local championship in a close final match but staged a comeback later by decisively winning the highest title of the region."[14]

PLAYING RESUMES IN POSTWAR YEARS

During World War II, Latter-day Saint international missionaries returned to their homelands. But this temporary setback didn't curtail the spread of basketball. Postwar years saw a great rise in the popularity of basketball in Australia. The *Austral Star* provides evidence that by the late 1940s both the local young men and the American missionaries were again playing basketball.[15] By this time, the game had spread to a greater extent in the Tasmanian District and to Church branches in Hurstville, New South Wales; and Adelaide, South Australia.[16]

"Extra, Extra! Read all about it! Mormons win New South Wales Championship" read a headline in the August 1947 issue of the *Austral Star*. This Mormon team included six elders and two local Church members. They beat the Moore Park basketball team 45–44 with only five seconds remaining in the game, to win the championship.[17]

The Mormon basketball players continued their influence year after year, generating great publicity for the Church. In the spring of 1949, the University of Sydney hosted a field day of sports and invited the Mormon basketball team to join in the play.[18] This goodwill was reciprocated six months later when the Victorian Basketball Association and the Latter-day Saints collaborated to throw a dinner dance at the

Latter-day Saint Tingey Hall in Melbourne.[19] The event was reported in the *Austral Star*, and all were said to have "had a very enjoyable evening."[20]

Another article printed in 1950 quotes an elder describing a good-will basketball game: "The Elders accepted an offer to play basketball with a Bendigo team—no money attached, but much friendship is extended and a trip to Castlemaine given. The exhibition game in Castlemaine proved a victory for our team. We were introduced to the audience, and after the game met the mayor."[21] This same year, the "Historical Record of [the] Victorian District" observed several victories won by the "B Grade Elders basketball team" and specifically noted that on September 11, 1950, "This is the last game our missionary team plays this year. Several worthwhile contacts have been made through our basketball games this season."[22]

Throughout this period, the Mormons expanded game playing into other regions and different levels of play. June Trost, representing the Brisbane Branch in Queensland, wrote, "The Brisbane L.D.S. basketball team on June 27th [1950] won the 'B' grade Y.M.C.A. League Championship. . . . Elder Petersen particularly distinguished himself . . . by being the highest individual scorer in the league. The Church's other team[,] the 'Seagulls[,]' is also on top, being at present the only undefeated team in the 'B' grade Central Basketball league."[23] It is also evident that both Church members and missionaries were thoroughly involved with championship play in the Brisbane region, though they played on different teams. Trost also reported, "Eight members of the Church, five missionaries and three local brethren, took part in this year's basketball championship played in Brisbane. Four

RELIEF SOCIETY SISTERS AT TINGEY HALL (1930). COURTESY OF MARIE CRAY.

LDS BASKETBALL TEAM (EARLY 1950S). COURTESY OF DENNIS O'RIORDAN FROM COLLECTION OF RON CUTTS.

of these men . . . played in the final—two on both teams."[24]

Determined, young, Mormon players were competing in Tasmania at this time as well. Nancy Mitchell of the Hobart Branch described the M-Men as being on the "warpath to victory." The team consisted of several members as well as Elders Weaver and Payne.[25] In addition, the missionaries in New South Wales were having success playing as a team in the Sydney Basketball Association. In fact, although they were labeled as a "dark horse" when the season commenced, they ended up "making a name for themselves." By the time the season was half over, they were undefeated and therefore were invited by the Association to withdraw from the "B league." The Association reasoned, "This would not only better qualify them [the missionary team] to play in the New South Wales Open-state championship at the end of the season, but would increase the spirit of competition in the 'B' league. The Elders obligingly complied."[26] As the year came to a close, occasionally the elders played against each other. For example, the Toowoomba Branch in South Queensland noted that four of their local elders had played four visiting elders in an exhibition match "before a large audience." Win or lose, the publicity continued to be useful for the Church.[27]

In 1951, victories expanded. The Bankstown (New South Wales) Branch observed, "Several of the Elders have been active in the Basketball competition. . . . Elders Anderson, Gregson, and Hintze were selected for the N. S. W. [New South Wales] team which defeated New Zealand Universities on May 22nd."[28]

In Melbourne, the missionaries finished a five-month season by winning the 1951 YMCA championship. The *Austral Star* noted that during this period, "the fruits of Mormonism were on display," as the elders had "created a very honorable impression; receiving many tributes, not only for their skill in playing the game but also their example of clean living and sportsmanship which they have continually displayed." The article further noted that Elder Graydon Calder, captain of the missionary team, received an award for being the most outstanding player in the league. Additionally, the article observed that "through such an exhibition of talents he has been able to do much in preaching the gospel and acquainting more people with what it means to be a Latter-day Saint."[29]

More exposure and success continued into the fall of 1951 as "the Brisbane and Ipswich Elders journeyed up to compete in a basketball match against the Toowoomba team. This event, which was staged in the street, drew a large crowd. Once again success attended the Mormons."[30] In November, the Brisbane Branch reported that the missionaries played a championship YMCA game against a local team called the Triangles and had a victory in double overtime, "with the cheering support of the onlookers."[31]

AUSTRAL STAR (OCTOBER 1954). COURTESY OF PERRY SPECIAL COLLECTIONS, LEE LIBRARY, BRIGHAM YOUNG UNIVERSITY.

Fans multiplied as they observed the missionaries' impressive skill and clean living. Peggy Whitehead, writing for the Melbourne Branch in early 1952, informed the *Austral Star* that the Melbournian Saints "were very proud to see our local Elders win the Melbourne

Y.M.C.A. 'A' Grade basketball championship recently. The final game was a joy to witness, when they fought extremely hard and came from [behind]."[32] Midway through the year, Whitehead again wrote that the Melbourne Saints were "pleased to see the missionary Elders in second place on the basketball ladder, which is played at the Y.M.C.A."[33]

However, 1953 proved to be an off year. By spring, Charles V. Liljenquist was serving as the "editor advisor" for the *Austral Star* and president of the Australian Mission, which had its office in Melbourne. Although several 1953 *Austral Star* articles discuss basketball, they do not have the scent of victory that previous decades had brought, though the writers apparently tried to stay optimistic. Ruth Nash, representing the Bankstown Branch, noted, "Though the basketball team has not yet come out on top in a match, we hear that they are learning fast. Keep at it, boys."[34] The same month, Mary Bellott from the Melbourne Branch reported, "Our basketball players have not been winning so well lately—they admit to a couple (or so) defeats, but an evening of Square Dancing rapidly restores their spirits."[35]

Marie Cray, an Australian who joined The Church of Jesus Christ of Latter-day Saints as a teenager, remembered that in the early 1950s, basketball had not yet supplanted Australia's favorite pastime. "Australian

MORMON YANKEES IN ADELAIDE (1954). COURTESY OF TED JOHNSON.

HARLEM GLOBETROTTERS OFFICIAL PROGRAM (1954). COURTESY OF GEORGE AND MIKE DANCIS.

football was the sport you heard most about, and that was a man's game; whereas basketball seemed to be more of a sissy game." She further noted, "Real men played football out in the elements, rain, hail, or shine, sliding around in the mud, running up and down on the grassy ovals. Whereas, for the missionaries inside, it was a little more refined and civilized inside, away from the cold and the rain, [and they] played it on nice, polished boards, not too far to run either way."[36]

Arthur Emery, another convert and the only native Australian who played on the elite 1954 Mormon elders' basketball team in Adelaide, remembered that the Aussies of this era were "sports crazed." However, Emery also explained the feeling toward the American game of basketball and the American Mormon athletes who were coming onto the courts at this time: "'Why do we need the Yanks here?' That would be the general attitude. . . . Women's netball was already in existence, and well entrenched, but not men's basketball, so people weren't interested in basketball in that era."[37]

THE MORMON YANKEES HIT THE COURT

The organization of a highly skilled, handpicked Latter-day Saint team called the Mormon Yankees ushered in a new era of accelerated interest in both the Church and basketball.[38] This team consisted of tremendous talent, especially in their player-coach, Elder Loren C. Dunn. The timing for forming an elite team was just right, since the Harlem Globetrotters had just come through Australia in early 1954 and had spurred an interest in basketball, which was noticed by Australian mission presiden, Charles V. Liljenquist.

Elder Dunn recalled, "After they visited Adelaide, President Liljenquist held a press conference" and, referring to the superstar Dunn, told

EARL MCBRIDE (LEFT), LOREN C. DUNN (CENTER), AND TED JOHNSON (RIGHT). COURTESY OF BOB STECK.

the reporters, "We've got somebody coming who's better than the Globetrotters." He later told Elder Dunn, "I'm going to send you to Adelaide. We haven't been able to make much headway in Adelaide, but they're a great sports town." Elder Dunn responded, "If I wanted to play basketball, I would have stayed home." President Liljenquist quickly remarked, "Elder Dunn, you're going to Adelaide and play basketball. . . . We'll give you any missionary you want, but organize a team there and establish a good reputation for the Church." The team Dunn put together won the South Australian basketball title.[39]

Elder Dunn not only put a great missionary team together, but shortly after his arrival in Adelaide, he also immediately commenced to help local Latter-day Saint boys on two youth basketball teams of the Prospect Branch, and it was soon reported they were "improving fast."[40] In June 1954, the *Austral Star* recalled the genesis of the team and their purpose:

> In February and early March, President C. V. Liljenquist visited Adelaide for the purpose of ascertaining possibilities of missionary participation in basketball play in the State [of South Australia], and after preliminary discussion with newspaper and radio officials the decision was made to send a group of top-flight basketball players to represent the Church in the sport, *with the main objective being to gain publicity for the Church.* Elder Loren C. Dunn was sent to prepare the way for the rest of the team, and is now coaching the group of Elders for tournament play.[41]

The article further noted that the Mormon Yankees were members of the United Amateur Basketball Association "A" Grade League. There were six other teams in the league, and the tournament schedule allowed the Mormon Yankees to play each team three times. Concerning the makeup of the team, Dunn provided the following description: "Our first five are Elder Ted Johnson, at one forward, and at the other forward, Elder Norman Weitzeil. Both these men have proved to be high scorers and very good rebounders. I am at the centre." Dunn continued, "One guard is Elder Ted [E.] Haynes, and the other is Elder Robert Steck. Both these Elders are good dribblers and they are about the best in the league on defense. One of our substitutes is Brother Arthur Emery, the only local player on the team. He plays forward and is fast, a good rebounder and accurate with his shots."[42]

Emery recalled that Dunn was "a very compassionate man,[43] . . . a wonderful man, and a great example to the team. I remember we always had a word of prayer before the actual game." Emery also thought that he was selected as a member of the Mormon Yankees team "probably because I was the captain/coach of the local [Adelaide] LDS team. We played in the local competition. And I was number-seven [man] in the Mormon Yankee team."[44]

Elder Ted Johnson, a former high school and college basketball player and a student sportswriter at Brigham Young University (BYU) before his mission, remembered that at the time the Mormon Yankees were being launched in Adelaide, the Harlem Globetrotters had just passed through the city and "lit everybody's fire." The Mormon Yankees copied the Globetrotters' routine of warming up for their games to the song "Sweet Georgia Brown."[45] The Harlem players helped the Australians to see a much higher level of basketball skill, and thus when the American missionaries arrived on the Adelaide courts, the timing was right for an upgrade of performance.

The Mormon Yankees had ample experience playing both on the high school and collegiate levels before their missions, and these players caught the attention of many people. Johnson recalled, "The thing which really lit the fire of the [local Church] members was that they had something to cheer about. It was a focus, and the focus was absolutely delightful."[46] The missionary team also brought pride to the local Saints, who had been pegged for

ABOVE: TED JOHNSON. LEFT: TED JOHNSON, OLDER. COURTESY OF TED JOHNSON.

decades as members of "the church that practiced polygamy." Now they could hold their heads high as fans of a popular team with outstanding players.

Led by Dunn, the Mormon Yankees had phenomenal success throughout the year. Dunn, a native of Tooele, Utah, taught his teammates many of the same techniques and plays that he had learned while playing for the exceptional BYU basketball coach Stan Watts before Dunn's mission. What is most impressive is that the Mormon Yankees were also willing to pass on these same skills to the Australians.[47]

HARD WORK, HARD FLOORS

Johnson, a mission companion to Dunn, also recalled that many of the Mormon Yankee games in Adelaide were played in a building known as the OBI, or "Our Boys Institute." The OBI, an organization similar to the YMCA, arranged sports competitions for young men, although the surface they played on was very hard. Mikelis Dancis, a Latvian basketballer who, with his brother George (the Latvian giants), played against the Mormon Yankees in Adelaide, explained that the games at the OBI were played on a former roller-skating rink, which had a

Stan Watts (top row, far left) and Loren C. Dunn (bottom row, third from left) with 1950 BYU basketball team. Courtesy of Perry Special Collections, Lee Library, Brigham Young University.

LATVIAN GIANTS GEORGE DANCIS (LEFT) AND MIKE DANCIS (RIGHT). COURTESY OF MARTIN L. ANDERSEN PRODUCTIONS.

concrete floor.[48] Colin J. Burdett, a 1956 basketball Olympian for Australia, recalled that floor "was pretty hard to fall on, believe me." Because the playing surface was so rough, Burdett noted that players' "basketball boots . . . would only last two or three games before we had a hole in the bottom of them."[49] Johnson remembered, "Sometimes the benches were filled, standing room only, and it was a great day when we could do that and the members were just out there cheering. . . . Many, many, many were touched by the fact that we were there to do our work, and then to do our proselyting as well."[50]

Hard work on and off the court led to conversions and long-lasting friendships that continue to this day. One young married couple that Johnson fondly remembered was Peter G. and Denise Helen Mutton, to whom Dunn and Johnson finally had a chance to teach the restored gospel after several unsuccessful attempts to find them at home. Denise was contacted first and requested that the elders return when her husband was home. Johnson described the Muttons as "very, very, receptive, extremely receptive." "When we left on our bicycles after teaching them together for the first time," he noted, "we floated home."

DENISE AND PETER MUTTON (2010). COURTESY OF MARTIN L. ANDERSEN PRODUCTIONS.

Although Denise and Peter were receptive to the gospel message, their extended family was not as enthusiastic. Denise recounts:

MISSIONARIES ON BIKES (1950S).

> I was excited with the missionaries, so I decided to tell my family and my mother-in-law, and they said, "Oh, be careful, because the Mormons come and take the girls away, because they have polygamy." I became a little bit frightened, so then the missionaries came another time and knocked on the door, but I didn't answer it, and then they came back at night-time and my husband was home, and then they gave us the first discussion.[51]

Several months later, Peter and Denise were baptized in Adelaide and have remained stalwart Church members who kept in touch with these elders for many years.[52]

In the sports world, newspaper writer Gunars Esins Berzzarins (better known as "GEB") furthered the Mormon Yankees' exposure by writing numerous positive articles about the Yankees in the *Adelaide Advertiser* in 1954. He remembered that at the time the Mormon Yankees came to Adelaide, it "was the greatest thing that could happen to Australian basketball, particularly Adelaide, of course, by extension to Australian basketball as well. . . . There were these great teams, the Lithuanians, the Latvians, the Mormon Yankees as they were called, and the best Australian teams. There was a great, great competition." GEB took particular notice of the Mormon Yankees' exemplary play and the impact they had both on and off the court:

> The first thing that would impress us would be how disciplined they were—as a team, as an individual player; and then the next thing, how complete, if you like, the individual players were in their particular field, whether it was guard playing guard or playing forward or the center; and of course, the team cohesion. As far as the game plan, if you like, in my recollection, they could do all sorts of things. They could play man to man, could play zone, could play press, depending on the circumstances. Of course in many cases, they didn't have to ride a press because they were far too good anyway. . . . They were gentlemen on and off the court, and . . . I can't remember any instance of a case of pushing, shoving, or name calling

and rolling [by] any of the Mormon players, and of course that made an impression. That affected the other teams as well. . . . I remember them passing out some literature and the Book of Mormon around [to] the players and the public.[53]

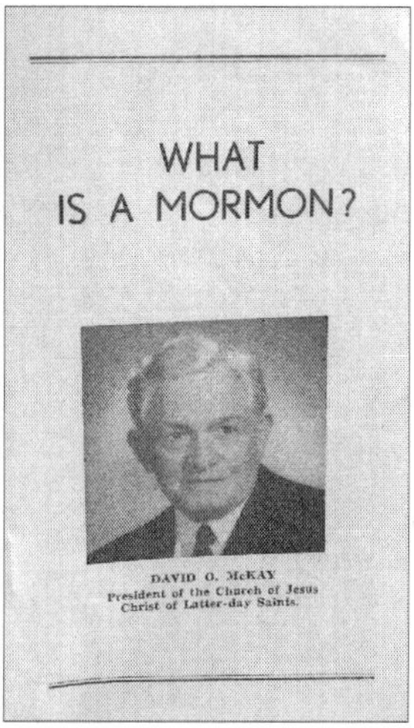

"What Is a Mormon" missionary tract. Courtesy of Bob Steck.

Building a Reputation

The Mormon Yankees had great success for the 1954 season; not only did they win the annual South Australian basketball title, but they also claimed a victory over the Australian all-star team. In addition, their South Australian District led the Australian Mission in number of baptisms, and they won the hearts of many Australians.

The Mormon Yankees' success and popularity even led to an invitation by the Australian Tennis Association to have the Yankees put on an exhibition in Adelaide before a crowd of nearly 9,000 spectators prior to matches played by well-known world-champion tennis players.[54] The Mormon Yankees were also invited to perform as part of the "world[-] famous professional tennis troop at Adelaide" in the late fall, where an estimated crowd of 6,000 watched the Yankees play. The head of the local Amateur Basketball Association, Mr. Vern Thomas, noted that the Mormon Yankees "will always be remembered in Adelaide, not only for the high caliber of play they brought with them, but also the outstanding team spirit, sportsmanship and unity they displayed," which, he said, "had never been seen on the basketball courts of South Australia before."[55]

Mormon Yankees with tennis stars (1955). Courtesy of Bob Steck.

As part of their winning season, the Mormon Yankees were invited to travel to a number of

MORMON YANKEES S. AUSTRALIA CHAMPIONS (1954). COURTESY OF BOB STECK.

cities to play exhibition games, with all expenses paid for each performance. The *Church News*, published out of Salt Lake City, reported, "They [the Yankees] had many opportunities for radio and newspaper interviews as well as for speaking engagements before youth organizations, and were encouraged to discuss the Gospel as well as basketball." The Mormon Yankees' exposure and success was multiplying such that the mission revised the pamphlet then in circulation, "What Is a Mormon?" A section on basketball was added, along with a photo of the Mormon Yankees. Elders found crowds waiting after each game to have copies of the tracts autographed. Such success and interest caused President Liljenquist to divide the original team that had made its mark in Adelaide and create two Mormon Yankees teams in 1955, with one team playing in Brisbane and the other in Sydney.[56]

UNPRECEDENTED OPPORTUNITIES

The year 1955 continued to be a year of success and exposure for the Mormon Yankees teams. Some of the individual missionaries were invited to play in an Australian state competition. Inasmuch as the Mormon Yankees players were not Australian citizens, they could not compete as a team in the Australian Basketball Championships. However, a program outlining the championship play for 1955 reveals that Elders T. Bushnell, R. (Robert) Steck, and N. (Norman) Weitzeil played for the Queensland team, and Elders Dunn, Smith, and North were on the New South Wales state team roster.[57]

Charles Bruce Flick, a scrappy member of the New South Wales team who played on the Australian Olympic team in 1956, observed, "[The year 1955] really was a turning point as I saw it. For the first time in Australian basketball history, Mormon missionary members

CHARLES BRUCE FLICK. COURTESY OF BRUCE FLICK.

were actually members of a state team; the New South Wales state team had three members. . . . And so that was a breakthrough."[58]

Mervyn Moy, captain of the New South Wales team, recalled that in 1955, every Australian state "was allowed to have two or three Mormon players invited, to play with that state, for the purposes of the championships. I think this was only a one-off situation, I don't think it ever happened before or after. . . . We had Elder Dunn, and we had Elder North, and Elder Day [Elder Smith], on our team as honored guests, guest players." Moy further noted, "They were so prominent, and so benevolent, in showing us the standard of play that would be required in '56 for the Olympics."[59]

Another noteworthy event for the newly created Mormon Yankees team in Sydney occurred when they played a team from Lithgow, a mining town in the Blue Mountains west of Sydney, in New South Wales. The *Church News* noted, "Tracts entitled 'What Is A Mormon?' and 'Mighty People of the Rockies' were eagerly accepted by everyone except the local minister. . . . In Lithgow, the hand-bills were captioned with 'Yankee Mormons' (Capt. by World's best Amateur Basketballer, ELDER DUNN)."[60]

MERV MOY CARRYING OLYMPIC TORCH (2000). COURTESY OF MERV MOY.

HALFTIME ENTERTAINMENT

To contribute to the Mormon Yankees' success on and off the court, the elders put together halftime entertainment, which became quite a crowd pleaser. A quartet of missionaries sang for the audience, but the real showstopper was a hilarious and stunning routine developed by Elder Ronald L.

RON BOUCK IMITATING A SEAL DURING A HALFTIME SHOW. COURTESY OF RON BOUCK.

Bouck. Before his mission, Bouck had been a cheerleader at West High School and the University of Utah, both in the vicinity of Salt Lake City, Utah.[61] Bouck explained, "Because of my build, I have short legs and a long torso, so I can run like a monkey on all fours. . . . I would stun the crowd. . . . They were absolutely flabbergasted that a religious elder would have the gumption to do that in front of a crowd."[62] Australian Ray Feeney, who watched from the stands, remembered that Bouck "would wear a white track suit and entertain the crowd and cheer on the players, doing flip flops up and down the court. We had never seen this sort of thing in Sydney and it really got the crowd going."[63] In addition to his physical antics, Bouck could imitate a seal, parody famous comedians of the day such as Stan Freberg and Jerry Lewis, and twirl a cane while imitating Charlie Chaplin.

SIGNIFICANT CHANGES

In 1955, missionary work was significantly reorganized in Australia, and the changes facilitated expanded influence for the Mormon Yankees. In early February, Church president David O. McKay visited Australia, the first Church president to do so. Elder Loren C. Dunn recalled the visit of President McKay and the impact of his tour of the mission:

DAVID O. AND EMMA RAE MCKAY ARRIVE IN AUSTRALIA (1955). COURTESY OF DENNIS O'RIORDAN.

> When he got to Adelaide, he held a press conference, as he did at each stop on his trip. One of the people in the press started asking him about the Mormon Yankees. This was unsolicited. The newspaper reporter praised the group of boys who were playing basketball. President McKay didn't know anything about it and answered what questions he could. President Liljenquist answered a few other questions. After the press conference, President Liljenquist said to President McKay, "It's been a good program, but it's too bad we're going to have to end it." President McKay asked, "Why?" And President Liljenquist said, "We don't get enough missionaries who can play basketball. Elder Dunn and some of these others will be going home." President McKay said, "You keep the program going. We'll see that the basketball players come." For years after that, some of the most talented basketball players who were on missions were assigned to Australia because of the attention the basketball program was getting there.[64]

Not only did President McKay make the decision that talented basketball players would continue to be assigned to Australia, but during his visit, he also decided to soon divide the Australian Mission into two missions so that missionary work could be managed more effectively.[65] Marjorie Newton explained that a few months later, Church apostle Elder Marion G. Romney was sent by President McKay to arrange the division so that both missions had about half of the roughly one hundred missionaries serving in Australia at the time. "The new Southern Australian Mission, based in Melbourne, covered the states of South Australia, Tasmania, Victoria and Western Australia and contained just under 50 percent of the Australian population of nine million. The Australian Mission, with headquarters in Sydney, covered New South Wales, Queensland and the Northern Territory."[66] This decision opened

CHARLES V. LILJENQUIST SITTING TO DAVID O. MCKAY'S RIGHT. COURTESY OF RODNEY BURT.

up an opportunity to create more Mormon Yankees teams to accommodate play in both missions.

Marion G. Romney (left) and Charles V. Liljenquist (center). Courtesy of Ted Johnson.

A CLOSE CALL

However, the Mormon Yankees were initially in danger of extinction with the arrival of a new South Australia Mission president. President Thomas S. Bingham called four missionaries into his office one night in the fall of 1955 after two of them had just finished playing a championship game for that season. "I hope you . . . all know that this will be the last basketball we play," he said. "We didn't come here on our missions to play basketball." Elder DeLyle H. Condie, one of those four missionaries, had just arrived in Australia. He was picked up at the train depot and asked by Elders Christensen and Johnson, who were members of a recreational team, if Condie and his companion, Elder Benson, would like to watch Christensen and Johnson play in the championship that evening. After the elders' Victoria team finished the game, the missionaries were admonished by President Bingham that basketball playing was over. Condie recalled, "I felt fine about that. I hadn't expected to play basketball; it wasn't the reason I went on a mission."

Conventional missionary work resumed for several months, but when Condie was sent to serve in Melbourne in early 1956, the position on basketball playing was suddenly reversed. Condie explained, "I was asked to pick out missionaries who would be part of a team of missionaries who would be willing to participate in this recreation league that had been going on for years in Melbourne. I was surprised of course, having heard, and remembered what [President Bingham] had said."

Condie discovered that the decision had been approved by the Church's First Presidency and Quorum of the Twelve Apostles, and the South Australia Mission was to have a basketball team.[67] Fifty years later, Condie was visiting with Lindsay Gaze, an Australian basketball player who had played against Condie and competed in seven Olympic Games as both a player and a coach. As the two men discussed why the Mormon missionaries had been allowed to play again, Gaze told Condie that Ken Watson, coach of the Australian Olympic basketball team, "had gone to President Bingham . . . and suggested that the Olympic games were on the schedule, and were coming up . . . and that they would appreciate the opportunity to have some competition, some players who maybe had some talent and some experience, like the [Mormon] Yankees did." Watson "told President Bingham that it would be a great proselyting tool for the Church, a benefit for the Church, and that he saw that it would be a great benefit to them [the Australian team] when they were getting ready for the Olympic Games."[68]

COACH KEN WATSON. COURTESY OF KEN WATSON FAMILY.

Elder Rodney Burt, who in 1956 was serving as a missionary in the South Australia Mission and as second counselor in the mission presidency to President Bingham in Melbourne, recalled a similar explanation of the basketball position:

> At this time Ken Watson, who was the executive secretary of the Victoria Basketball Association and who would later become the Olympic coach for the Australian Olympic team, came to President Bingham and asked him if the Church would be willing to sponsor a team in the local league in Victoria, and he stressed that they wouldn't ask the missionaries to interfere with their work, but they just wanted their expertise. They would like help in coaching. They would like help in instruction. They just wanted to develop basketball in Victoria, and President Bingham came to me and said, "It looks like we're going to play basketball." So we started organizing a team, and by April we had formed a team, calling ourselves the Mormon Yankees.[69]

This shift in thinking had an impact on various regions of Australia. By April 1956, the *Austral Star* noted that there would be several Mormon Yankees teams playing in Australia throughout the year: "The 'Mormon Yankee' basketball teams . . . will be participating in Queensland, New South Wales, Victoria and West Australia." However, the Mormon Yankees in Victoria garnered the most success and notoriety. The *Star* noted, "The Victorian team's starting five consists of Elders Condie, Hull, Kimball, Garn and Bjork. Two of these players, Elder Condie and Hull[,] have had previous experience playing basketball at the University of Utah and the Utah State University respectively." Condie led the team as coach and player. He had played varsity basketball under Coach Jack Gardner at the University of Utah. As with player-coach Dunn, Condie used superior plays and techniques that Gardner had drilled into him before his mission.[70]

Other players on the team (pictured in the article with the entire team) were Elders Ford, Meldrum, Davis, Leishman, and Burt. An *Austral Star* article stated that during the spring, the Mormon Yankees would be playing against the Latvian Daina (a local team), the YMCA, and the Church of England, as well as the Australian Olympic team, and mentioned that "all games will be played at the Hall of Industries on the Melbourne Showgrounds . . . at 7:00 p.m."[71]

Mormon Yankees Play Olympic Teams

Later issues of the *Austral Star* reveal that the Victorian Mormon Yankees won the Latvian "Riga" Basketball Championship[72] and also beat the Australian Olympic team. The Bentleigh Branch of Victoria reported in the *Austral Star*, "Most of our branch attended the basketball game between the Elders['] 'Mormon Yankees' team and the 'Australian Olympic Team.' It was all worth the sore throats [the] next day to see them defeat the Aussie team."[73]

Apparently the Victorian Mormon Yankees team not only won more publicity for the Church but also raised funds for needed Church buildings. The timing was fortuitous because in 1956 a multimillion-dollar Church building program was initiated for the Saints "down under." This project was an outgrowth of President McKay's visit the year before. "Nineteen large, modern meetinghouses were built in the first phase of the program in Australia (1956–1959), each containing a chapel, a large recreational hall with a stage, a kitchen, offices and classrooms."[74] Zita Margaret Gage, representing the Prospect Branch, noted her appreciation: "The missionary team from Melbourne proved to be a successful draw for those interested in basketball and we in Adelaide and Prospect were very pleased to see them and grateful also because of the monetary gain for our Building Fund."[75]

Burt recalled what occurred when he and his companion went to Melbourne to visit the director of planning for the Victoria region to discuss their interest in building Latter-day Saint chapels:

> In Australia we had an extreme amount of red tape, government regulations, and it took three weeks just to get a title cleared for the Bentleigh Branch. Well, we were getting more and more frustrated by the red tape. We just couldn't get started, and we went to our solicitor, our lawyer, and he said, "Well that's just the way it is. It takes time." And when we asked him if there was any way that we could expedite it, he said, "I can't." He said, and I don't know why he said it, but he said, "I think you three could probably have an influence." So he gave us a name and we went into Melbourne and met with this fellow. He was the director of planning, overseeing what went on in the cities, in Victoria, and we explained that we were from The Church of Jesus Christ of Latter-day Saints and that we were interested in building chapels, and we asked him what we could do to expedite it. And he said, "Nothing, there's just rules and regulations you've got to follow, and that's the way it's got to be and it takes time."

The director then stopped and asked if the visitors were Mormons, because his son had played against the Mormon Yankees the week before. The missionaries said yes, and the director then said, "'Your missionaries come out at their own expense, they come out with no expectations of rewards, and spend two years teaching your message.' . . . He said, 'Come back next week, I think I can help you.' And boy, things just started to open up, and we really got going with the church building program in Victoria."[76]

The Church buildings certainly helped the missionaries in their proselytizing efforts, but the Mormon Yankees became the catalyst for Church recognition and growth because of their exposure and expanding reputation. One of their greatest opportunities to be spotlighted by the sporting press occurred in the fall of 1956, when news spread that the Mormon Yankees would play in exhibition contests to help prepare the Australian national team for the Olympics.

The *Sporting Globe All-Sport Magazine* (published out of Melbourne) carried a full-page article with a picture of Condie and the words "Condie Is Colossal" in large print. The article noted that "in one short, and all too brief, season, Condie has given many electrifying performances which have served to whet Australian appetites for this big man game. And they'll certainly have this taste satisfied when the Yanks turn out with their seven-footers and 'little' six foot four players in the [exhibition] Games." Further, "these giants zoom through the air over the tiny ten foot high basket and smash the ball through the net. They turn on speed that leaves even the midgets gasping as they try to catch up with the fast strides that eat up the court."

Speaking of Condie, the *Sporting Globe* credited,

> The big man acts as a point duty policeman as he sets up screens for the other players to go zipping around to cut and drive at the basket. On his own Condie has brought all this to Victorian and Australian basketball this year. It has given large crowds a thrill just to watch this champion in action. He defeated Australia virtually on his own in one Olympic trial with a display that made it appear that the Australians weren't trying—it was just too easy. Now Condie is to help the Australian Olympic squad's preparation in the three weeks' intensive training period prior to the actual start of the Games. His experience and knowledge will be of inestimable value.

The *Sporting Globe* also pointed out Condie's prior basketball experience and his plans to practice medicine after his mission was completed. Condie was described as a "quiet-speaking young man who is thoroughly enjoying his short stay in Australia. He is here as a church missionary." In addition, the article noted that "the Mormons have done much to lift the standards of Australian basketball. . . . The Mormons go out of their way to help players and teams hit good standards, and Condie is one of a long line of star performers who have appeared here since the 1930's. Basketball and the Mormons seem to go hand in hand."[77]

Lindsay Gaze, a seven-time Olympian as both player and coach, spoke of Condie's impressive coaching: "His behavior and the way in which he was able to impose discipline on his team without an authoritarian approach was very, very impressive. The message of being able to teach by persuasion rather than by dogmatic demand was one of those characteristics that he displayed which I admired and I hoped that I might be able to achieve as well."

Gaze also commented on how the Mormon Yankees would readily assist the Australian athletes in developing their skills on the court. He related how "their willingness to share with their opposition was so important to us."[78] Inga Freidenfelds, the then twenty-one-year-old Latvian captain of the Australian Olympic team, noted, "They'd offer their help."[79] Geoff Heskett, who played with Freidenfelds in the 1956 exhibition games against the elders, remembered that Condie "even assisted me . . . whereas a normal thing, if you're playing against somebody, you don't tell them [what not] to do or what to do." Heskett vividly recalled a time when Condie complimented him in a game by saying, "Gee, that was a good shot!"[80] Mormon Yankee Elder Don Hull remembered, "We would say to them [the Australian Olympic team], 'Look, when you get the ball, fake to the right and go to the left.' . . . We really coached them as we went along. . . . We tried to help them, because we liked them."[81] The Mormon Yankees' sportsmanship did not go unnoticed. Moy remembered, "They'd be the first to put their hand down and pick you up."[82]

INGA FREIDENFELDS IN HIS OLYMPIC COAT AND TIE. COURTESY OF MARTIN L. ANDERSEN PRODUCTIONS.

Near the end of 1956, the *Austral Star* reported the scores of the year's exhibition games between the Mormon Yankees and the teams of various nations soon to be competing in the Olympics:

> Nov. 7—Mormon Yankees 62; Australia 52.[83]
> " 10—Russia 101; Mormon Yankees 69.
> " 14—Mormon Yankees 61; France 59.
> " 17—Russia 87; Mormon Yankees 78.
> " 19—France 66; Mormon Yankees 63.
> " 20—Philippines 74; Mormon Yankees 60.
> " 21—Mormon Yankees 74; Chile 62.[84]

MORMON YANKEES TEAM (1956). COURTESY OF RODNEY BURT.

This showing was impressive: a group of missionaries practicing only one day a week could beat several Olympic teams and lose in one game to the Russians by only nine points. Elder Delmar H. Bjork recalled that the Russians played very rough; they "'held' a lot, 'pulled uniforms,' and ran 'moving screens.' More than once when on a break-a-way, or steal, I had my green and gold shorts pulled down towards my knees. They played with 'heavy arm lock/fouls.' . . . My fellow Mormon Yankee team members all received their share of 'dirty tricks' playing those two games."[85] Russia secured the silver medal at the Melbourne Olympics, with America clinching the gold.[86]

But the Mormon Yankees' success was no coincidence. Apparently, some of the players, who had a wealth of high school and collegiate basketball experience, were handpicked by the Missionary Department of the Church. Elder Mark J. Frodsham related, "When I went on a mission to Australia, I came to find out later that they had considered college players to go there for the specific reason that they had the Olympic team there."[87] Elder Paul Grant, a member of a Mormon Yankees team at this time, noted, "There was Delyle [DeLyle H. Condie] and myself from the U. of U. [University of Utah], and there was Mark Frodsham from BYU, and Don Hull had played at Utah State, and then Nyle [James Nyle] Garn had played Junior College up at Ricks."[88]

OLYMPIC GAMES PROGRAM (1956). COURTESY OF GEORGE AND MIKE DANCIS.

The Mormon Yankees were apparently in high demand that season inasmuch as the World Olympic Committee had ruled that the national teams could not play each other before the official Olympic Games began.

Immediately following the exhibition play in Melbourne, the Victorian Mormon Yankees traveled to Tasmania with the Nationalist Chinese team to play exhibition games against each other for three days in the cities of Devonport, Launceston, and Hobart. The Yankees won two games and lost the third game by only six points.[89] Concerning the trip, Condie recalled, "We went on the plane together, and we went on the train from place to place, and had an absolutely enjoyable time. I think it was Elder Garn who happened to become very, very close to one of the Chinese players. . . . They were just delightful people."[90] Grant remembered, "We got along with the coaches . . . very well. They were very friendly, most spoke English reasonably well. We stayed at the same hotels. . . . It was a fine experience, and by the time it was over, we were all friends. Chatted about everything, except the political circumstances. . . . That was not wise."[91]

FORMOSA CHINA PLAYING IN OLYMPIC GAMES (1956). COURTESY OF DELYLE CONDIE.

These exhibition games brought great publicity to the Church and made proselytizing a bit easier. Elder Garn recalled, "Our success rate . . . after the Olympics . . . was good. Those of us on the Mormon Yankee basketball team kind of changed our approach a bit. Some of us, rather than say[,] 'We're missionaries from the Church[,]' . . . would [say,] . . . 'We're members of the Mormon Yankee basketball team,' . . . and that got us into some homes."[92] Condie remembered, "We found people who had read about us in the newspaper as we knocked on doors. . . . We found that even more people knew about the Mormon Yankees, and they became friendlier to us, as we approached them."[93] Hull, Condie's companion at this time and a fellow member of the team, remembered, "DeLyle and I were interviewed on the radio, and so when we went tracting, people would say, 'Oh yeah, Elder Hull, I heard you on the radio the other day.'"[94]

MORMON YANKEES 1957–58

The hard-won reputation of the Mormon Yankees also favorably affected their proselytizing activity for 1957. President Bingham reflected on the impact these young basketball-playing elders had on the Australians: "We know that basketball in and of itself does not convert people to the gospel, nor has it brought outstanding and immediate results, but in a country where Mormonism is not generally accepted[,] we feel it can do an immeasurable amount of good in breaking down prejudice and hatred against the Church."[95]

HAL REEB AND UNIVERSITY OF MELBOURNE BASKETBALL TEAM. COURTESY OF HAL AND JANICE REEB.

Elder Harold Reeb was even invited to help coach the University of Melbourne basketball team from February 1957 to February 1958. At the university's invitation, Reeb came onto the court to raise the basketball team's level of play. Reeb recalled that in mid-February 1957,

> President Bingham called me in and asked me if I'd coach University of Melbourne basketball, . . . said they'd had a request from the university for somebody to come and do that. So that was when I started working with those kids, and it was a great experience. It was a lot of fun, and they treated me very well, and I'd take whoever my companion was, . . . and we'd go out and practice with them, and then we had games, at least one game during the week. So I got a double dose of basketball. I got to play with the Mormon Yankees, and I got to play with, or practice and play with, some kids from the university.[96]

Excerpts from Reeb's journal shed further light on his work as a Mormon Yankee and his yearlong coaching experience, an effort that paid off after much hard work:

> February 12, 1957: "Went into the M. H. [Mission Home] & talked to Pres. Bingham for about 2 Hrs. . . . Well[,] it looks as if I'm to coach the B-Ball team at the U of Melb. beginning Sat."
>
> February 16, 1957: "The practice went fair this morning. They aren't very good players, have much to learn, but have the potential. They treat me fine."
>
> February 18, 1957: "Just got in from our 1st B-Ball game. We lost 37-26 but all concerned feel there are great possibilities in the team. They've sure got a lot of improving to do but it'll take time."
>
> February 23, 1957: "Coached the U of M & practiced with the [Mormon] Yankees this AM."
>
> February 27, 1957: "President Bingham said I should spend more time with the B-Ball team; good chance to spread the gospel. . . . Pres B. complimented me highly for the good work coaching. . . .

March 6, 1957: "The U of M won their [first] game Mon. nite & all are quite happy."

March 18, 1957: "U of M won a game tonite."

March 20, 1957: "Norm Longmuir [one of Reeb's players] typed up a very good report on the B-Ball club for me & also said everyone was pleased & had learned more in the past few weeks than all their previous years of B-Ball. After today I sure feel I[,] we got much to learn."

April 2, 1957: "The U played ball last nite at 10PM and won easily against a bunch of midgets. Everyone played good ball for a change."

April 18, 1957: "The Uni played the Aust. [Australian] Army [team] & won 50–22."

April 23, 1957: "The U of M. beat the New Zealand Army [team] 33–16."

May 1, 1957: "Played ball tonite—won 58–39 over Bus. Houses. I slopped in over 20 [points]. We played better ball. Was chosen . . . to play against a U. S. Naval team.

May 2, 1957: "Well the Uni won their 1st league game 45–19. They really looked good & it seems that all concerned were happy & pleased, even me."

June 22, 1957: "Practiced this AM with the Yankees & coached the Uni in the afternoon. They scrimmaged some of the elders & looked very good, as [a] matter of fact beat them by 3 pts. They sure have a good spirit amongst them."[97]

Don Pemberton, who played under Reeb for Reeb's full year of coaching, recalled, "We all called him Elder Reeb. No one was calling him by his first name, . . . that was a level of respect. He was the coach." Pemberton recounted a memorable day after practice when Reeb spoke frankly to the team: "Look, playing basketball is one thing, but how you live your life is another. I'm just saying to you guys, if you're smoking, if you're drinking, if you're wasting your bodies, you're wasting your lives." Pemberton concluded, "My sense of Harold Reeb, . . . he was a guy I looked up to tremendously. He was so clean cut, he was so good at his basketball moves, but he was just an exemplary human being, and . . . I thought he was just a magnificent person."[98]

Under Reeb's coaching, the University of Melbourne basketball team had a magnificent year in 1957. In June they tied for first place with the University of Sydney in the Australia University Tournament in Perth. Reeb was a supervising elder in the Melbourne region and therefore was unable to accompany the team to the tournament because President Bingham felt that traveling the lengthy distance to Perth was unwise for Reeb.[99] However, in the fall of the year, the University of Melbourne basketball team held a banquet in which Reeb was recognized for his great coaching efforts. He wrote, "The Uni had a nice dinner tonite; paid me a lot of swell compliments & gave me a rug, book, pennant and a group picture. It was really great of them. I'm sure thankful for the chance to work with them."[100] At the conclusion of an eventful year of coaching and prior to a mission transfer to Perth, Reeb wrote his last journal entry about the University of Melbourne team: "Feb. 25, 1958 . . . The Uni ball team practiced last nite & then had a little party afterwards for me. They're really swell guys."[101] Reeb felt content as a Mormon Yankee player and satisfied to have served the community by coaching the university team.

Other elders playing on Mormon Yankee teams also experienced much success. In 1957, the *Austral Star* observed:

> The missionaries of the South Australian Mission have taken advantage of the basketball season and are using it as another method of proselyting the gospel. This endeavour has proved very successful in the past and this year should be no exception. Throughout the mission there has [*sic*] been four teams formed by the elders and each team carries the name, "Mormon Yankees." Teams are in Western Australia, South Australia, Victoria, and Tasmania.

The *Star* also mentioned the success of the South Australian Mormon Yankees team, led by Condie. Among other things, it was observed that this team had again beaten many other teams by a large margin, including the Australian Olympic team before a crowd of about a thousand. The explanation given for these repetitive victories was the Mormon Yankees' "considerable experience." The article noted Condie's familiarity with the game from his playing for the University of Utah and also mentioned that "other team members have also had considerable hoop experience. Elder Don Hull, Elder Mark Frodsham and Elder Paul Grant have all played basketball at different universities before coming to Australia."[102]

In 1957, with the introduction of Australian television, the Mormon Yankees had significantly increased exposure. Elder G. LaMont Christensen wrote:

> "Mormonism" and basketball have been introduced simultaneously to many thousands in Sydney and its suburbs through the medium of television during the past year. Television, which was initiated in Australia just prior to the Olympic Games last November, is steadily gaining in popularity here, as is the American sport of basketball and the Elders of the Church of Jesus Christ of Latter-day Saints. In fact, it has been estimated . . . that there are more basketball players in Australia today than there are active participants in any other sport. Five members of the regular Sydney "Mormon Yankee" basketball team were selected to represent the City of Sydney Amateur Basketball Association in the first inter-district Basketball Competition conducted in the city. This was initiated by ATN-Television Studios. . . . There are 100,000 television sets in the Sydney area and approximately 75,000 are turned to ATN during game-time Saturday with an average of 4 viewers per set. This means the missionaries perform before an audience of about 300,000 each week.[103]

The year 1958 proved victorious for Mormon Yankees teams both in New South Wales and in Victoria. The New South Wales Mormon Yankees again claimed the state championship, playing at the Sydney Boys' High School.[104] Two months later, the Victorian Mormon Yankees team defeated the Melbourne YMCA team at the Melbourne Showgrounds to claim the Victorian state basketball championship.

MORMON YANKEES BASKETBALL TOURS, 1959–60

In 1959, two elders ushered in a whole new era of Mormon Yankees basketball with the inception of traveling tours. This enterprise commenced when Zelph Y. Erekson, president of the Australian Mission (covering New South Wales, Queensland, and the Northern Territory), asked Elder Sherman Day to be in charge of the Mormon Yankees in Sydney, the city that was also home to mission headquarters.[105] After accepting the assignment, Day approached President Erekson with an idea:

> [I said,] "Are you willing to explore taking this Mormon Yankee thing to even greater heights, to assist us in proselyting?" and he said, "Absolutely. What do you have in mind?" And I said, "I think we ought to go to a couple of cities that surround here where we've got missionaries, or where we want to put missionaries, and we ought to have the Mormon Yankees play their town team and leave these missionaries, or introduce these missionaries, and I think we can generate a lot of goodwill off of the goodwill that the Mormon Yankees have." And he said, "Elder Day, that's a pretty bold plan. How many cities do you think we should go to?" and I said, "Two," and it later turned out to be far more than that, but that's as big as I could think of at that time. He said, "Flesh it out, I'm going to be released as mission president, a new mission president will be coming in a couple of months [Weldon V. Moore], and we can present the idea and see how it goes." So that was the genesis. That happened, the new mission president [Weldon V. Moore] liked the idea, by that time we had sponsors lined up, and it was basically a go, and we started notifying towns that we were available, and one thing led to another, and pretty soon we were riding around Australia.[106]

Day said that while contemplating the financial costs relative to touring, he enlisted some help. "I went to my good friend and sometime companion Bob [Elder Robert G. Pedersen] and said, 'We need to raise some money if we're going to do this tour for the Mormon Yankees and go to all these sites,' and Bob said, 'I can do it.'" Pedersen had experience selling products as a student prior to his mission.

ZELPH Y. EREKSON AND HIS WIFE. COURTESY OF SHERM DAY.

> He'd been a pots and pans salesman, so he didn't know that you [could] say no, he was very optimistic, he said, "We'll do it." So we set some goals; . . . we asked . . . [a] company for three pairs of shoes for each

> player, we asked another company for basketballs, four new basketballs, and the big one was Bob asked Volkswagen to provide us a Kombi [van] that we could drive around, and also, they came in and said, "We'll not only provide you the Kombi van, we'll provide the publicity in each town. As you come we'll advertise it in the papers." So . . . really I'd have to say that my stroke of luck was finding good people to help who knew how to do that.[107]

Pedersen remembered, "I said, 'Sherm, you get us the places to play, and I'll get us there.' And so I arranged with Volkswagen of Australia, and they furnished us a brand new, current 1959 Volkswagen, and then Stokes McGown . . . furnished us gear and clothes and basketballs, and shoes, so the Mormon Yankees looked as classy as . . . any professional team."[108]

Recalling the success the Mormon Yankees encountered on their tours in such towns as Forbes (near Sydney), Day explains,

> We went there in the usual way with our Kombi [VW] van, we had clinics at school, there were great advertisements in the paper; after the game the articles in the paper were very nice about the Mormon Yankees and the thrilling game, and the style of ball we

PRESIDENT WELDON V. MOORE AND M. Y. TEAM (1959). COURTESY OF SHERM DAY.

MORMON YANKEES TOUR TEAM (1959). COURTESY OF SHERM DAY.

played, and the media and the deputy mayor and receiving the keys to the city, and then there was another article that was about a quarter of a page, and in that article it said that Elders So-and-so and So-and-so were being left behind to acquaint this town with Mormonism, and so as they knock on your door, welcome them to our city. And they reported to us later that they got in almost every door. Now they didn't convert all the people, but people would say, "Oh, your guys were here last week," and their names were in the paper, and I think, we had a lot of anecdotal kind of things about, it eased the proselyting in these towns, and it also destroyed a lot of the stereotypes that these small towns had about the Mormons. . . . Polygamy, we addressed it head on with our program, . . . that we don't practice polygamy. So yes, there's no question it improved the proselyting in those towns.[109]

Pedersen noted the publicity that the Mormon Yankees received in every town due to sponsorships:

We found enormous support . . . from Volkswagen, because every city we went to, . . . they were excited to have us come to their towns, because every Volkswagen dealer in every town that we went to, would arrange with the local mayor, the local news, the local radio stations, and they would greet us and meet us on the town hall steps, because we were the American Mormon Yankees, coming to town. They got a lot of benefit out of it, but it also cost us as missionaries, and as the Church of Jesus Christ of Latter-day Saints, not one penny we expended to pay for the tour. It was because of outside sponsorships that Sherman [Day] and I obtained, to make sure that the Church didn't have to expend any funds.[110]

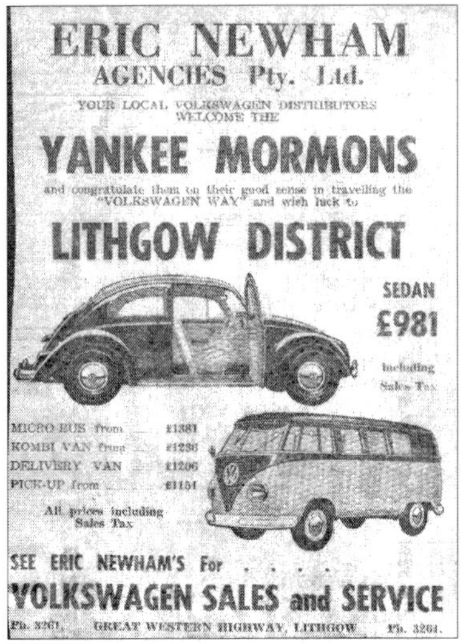

MORMON YANKEES PROGRAM WITH VW AD (1959). COURTESY OF SHERM DAY.

Pedersen did most of the driving on primitive roads and felt that the elders worked hard on the tours: "We had extra Books of Mormon we put under the seat, we put our gear in the back, and . . . on top of the Volkswagen, . . . but this was not a fraternity trip. This wasn't a bunch of guys roaming around the country. We worked hard. We would travel, oftentimes after our game at night, if we did not stay there in the town, with members or locals."[111]

According to G. LaMont Christensen, who compiled statistics for the June 1959 tour, the Mormon Yankees passed through twelve county centers in New South Wales and traveled "2,087 miles, playing 19 games in 16 days, establishing all-time attendance and scoring records in more than a dozen cities, being mobbed by autograph hunters, selling 186 copies of the 'Book of Mormon' and giving away dozens more and directly affecting approximately 200,000 persons."[112]

ELDER BOWN ENTERTAINS

Another component of this very successful tour was the unique talent of Elder Roger L. Bown, who technically traveled with the team as one of the eight players. But like Bouck's role in 1955, Bown's primary responsibility was entertaining crowds, announcing the games, and doing halftime shows.[113] These performances included professional and hysterical impersonations of such people as Billy Eckstine, Jerry Lewis, the Everly Brothers, and Winston Churchill.[114] Pedersen and James Richard Rampton, fellow members of the traveling Sydney team,

SHERM DAY (LEFT), RICH RAMPTON (CENTER), AND BOB PEDERSEN (RIGHT). COURTESY OF SHERM DAY.

remembered that Bown also impersonated Jack Benny, Satchmo (Louis Armstrong), Elvis Presley, and Mr. Magoo. To add a bit of humor to the game, Bown would sometimes call out the plays for the Mormon Yankees before they actually occurred, so as to direct the team what to do next.[115] Bown recalled:

> Many times I would call a play and our players weren't even in that and then they'd look at me and say, "Oh, okay," and then they'd pass the ball that I designated to someone and we used to have a lot of fun doing that. Our team in many instances was so good that we could have won by 100 points, but we let them stay with us and keep with us and . . . the fun of it was, sometimes you'd have to throw the ball in back and our players would throw them [the ball] back like the globe trotters [Harlem Globetrotters] that throw the ball under their arms or between their legs. I mean, on a tight game, no, but in a game where we could really run the score up, they kind of played along. The crowd enjoyed this. We were playing to the crowd. We wanted to make the crowd accept us as Mormon Yankees and as missionaries for our Church.

BOB PEDERSEN (LEFT), SHERM DAY (CENTER), AND RICH RAMPTON (RIGHT). COURTESY OF MARTIN L. ANDERSEN PRODUCTIONS.

Bown had honed his talents while serving in the army from 1954 to 1955. During that time he teamed up with another military man, and they did impersonations at the United Service Organizations (USO) building. Bown remembered that in the early days, "I did Jerry

THE ENTERTAINER

(Sounds of drums, trumpets, things like that.)

Tonight we shall hear from the lips of the man himself — THE BOWN — (low-muffled into a whisper). I have worked in radio for four years. I had my own record show called "The Modern Sounds", which featured Rock and Roll, plus modern tunes. I then worked on television for a few months before being featured in Uncle Sam's Army in Special Services for two years. I was lucky to take second place in my category in trying out for the Ed Sullivan TV show. I have graduated from Brigham Young University in Provo, Utah, with a Bachelor of Science degree in Radio, Speech and Television.

My act consists of singing and impersonations of well-known singers and movie stars. I expect to return to radio and TV work in my home town of Provo, Utah, U.S.A.

Until later, we say "Ta Da" to the talented lad from U.S.A. (same as above, drums, trumpets, things like that!)

ELDER ROGER BOWN

MORMON YANKEES PROGRAM WITH ROGER BOWN (1960). COURTESY OF SHERM DAY.

Lewis's part, and he did Dean Martin's part. All-Army Talent Contest [competition] in Arizona, traveled to San Francisco, trying out for the Ed Sullivan Show, took second place." This training led to other impersonations that Bown did while traveling and performing with the Mormon Yankees. Bown was comfortable impersonating Joe Louis, Peter Lorre, James Cagney, and President Franklin Roosevelt, but he thought that the Australian audience responded best to his Winston Churchill impersonation. Some of Bown's experience also derived from several years of working with radio broadcasting. Bown related, "I had my own show from six to midnight: rock and roll, modern sounds; I did jazz, classical music."[116] This prepared him for announcing the basketball games.

A PERSONAL ACCOUNT

Another Mormon Yankees team commenced a tour in the spring of 1960 to the Queensland region; this tour lasted for two weeks and included Bown as entertainer. One of the players, Elder Harold Turley, wrote a day-by-day account of the tour in his journal. These highlights provide a sense of the planning, the challenges of travel, the clinics held in a number of cities, and the overall excitement of this basketball excursion:[117]

> Friday, April 22nd. We had our last basketball practice today before our tour. . . . We are going to play on TV tomorrow. . . . A lot of missionary work will be accomplished by it. We took care of more tour arrangements today in getting things set up for the tour. We are going to buy a car (Volkswagen Micro Bus) for two weeks and then sell it back. I never knew that there was so much to planning a tour such as this. . . .

Saturday, April 23rd . . . We were like chickens with their heads cut off in trying to get everything completed. We had to get jumpers that have been made for us, plus a record "When the Saints Come Marching In[,]" which we'll use in our tour as we come out onto the basketball court. Everything was a race against time. The money for the Microbus came only *minutes* early. . . . We rushed over to get the 58 Microbus. . . . It is costing us 850 pounds. We then rushed out to Yeronga to get the car rack to put the luggage in on top. We then rushed clear back across town to our flat, then off to the Valley to pick up our 8,000–9,000 programs. . . .

Monday, April 25th. We were up at 4:30a.m., which is mighty early. . . . We've really got a full load, but we really are looking forward to a wonderful and successful tour. We stopped off in Red Hill to pick up our signs (banners) for the front and back of the Microbus[118] (we can sit 9 comfortably). We finally left Brisbane for Rockhampton at 7:30am. There are eight of us at present and we'll pick up Elder Bown, our entertainer, in Rocky [Rockhampton]. The team is as follows: Elders Blacker, Macdonald, Stoker, Tuttle, Butler, Jorgensen, Snow, Bown and I. We are all good friends. Rocky is 500 miles away, but it has taken us 20 hours to get there. We really had troubles and for a while I was beginning to wonder if we'd ever get there. We had 3 flat tires, plus taking the wrong road, which cost us 100 extra miles. We all received nicknames [from Elder Bown] on the tour, and this is where Elder Macdonald received his because he was the one driving when we got lost, so he was named Percy Pathfinder. Elder Bown is a tremendous entertainer and he used these nicknames in his calling the games. We finally arrived in Rocky [Rockhampton] at 4:00a.m. and the Lord had his arms around us because two of the tires were blowouts and we had just patched the tires with old pieces of tube. I'll never know how we finally made it. What a day!!![119]

Tuesday, April 26th. We were up at 7:00a.m. and off to get a couple of tires plus get to Mckay [Mackay] at 3:00p.m. for three clinics there. . . . We had more trouble on the way to McKay [Mackay] with one more flat or blowout. . . . The roads are really terrible. . . . It was 275 miles to McKay [Mackay] and we didn't make it until 6:00p.m. They met us outside the city and escorted us in to town. They had over 100 people waiting for basketball clinics and we disappointed them. . . . We've got to do some good here because this is the town

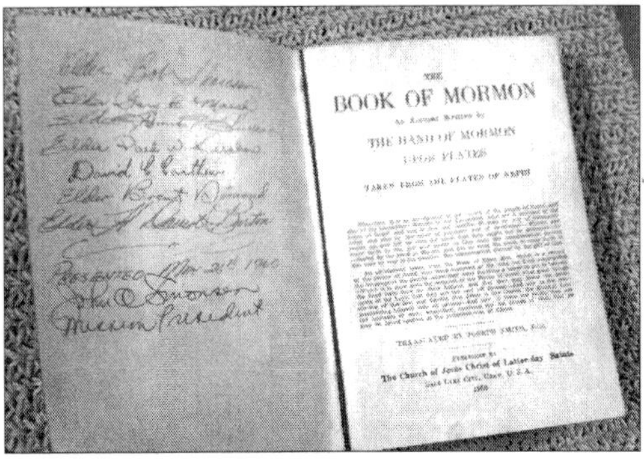

SIGNED COPY OF THE BOOK OF MORMON. COURTESY OF OWEN HUGHAN.

where they kicked the missionaries out. We stayed at the best hotel in town[,] which was the Paradise Private Hotel. Everything was on the house. . . . We were escorted to the game. It was just packed with . . . about 700 people there. For our warm-up drill, we came in to the tune, "When the Saints Come Marching In" by Louis Armstrong. We played a good game and we won 57–36 points. . . . When the game was over, we were mobbed by the people wanting our autographs. We were just like movie stars to them. We were there an hour and a half signing autographs and giving out Books of Mormon. It was something fantastic! Before each game as we are introduced, we present the opposing team with a Book of Mormon autographed by the team. They can't refuse it and if nothing else, it is a souvenir to them from us. This went over very well. Our prime purpose of this tour is to establish better relationships in these towns for the next Elders into the town. . . . [120]

Wednesday, April 27th. We were up and off again by 8:00a.m. this morning for Charters Towers. We had more trouble . . . and had to get another new tire. We were on the road all day long. Sometimes it seems like we travel all the time. Elder Bown keeps us laughing all the time. He's really a terrific fellow and very talented. . . . We beat them [Charters Towers] 44 to 25. . . . We gave out quite a few Books of Mormon . . . and really established a good feeling in the town which will really help the Elders in the future. . . .[121]

Thursday, April 28th . . . Elders Blacker, Butler, Snow and I gave a clinic in Charters Towers in the morning before we parted for Townsville. . . . We finally got away for Townsville by noon. . . . We beat them 46 to 40. . . . We had 2500 people watch the game which was really a fabulous crowd for Townsville, especially for basketball. We signed programs for better than an hour at a constant pace all the time, and we gave out quite a few Books of Mormon besides all this. . . .[122]

Friday, April 29th . . . We made a store appearance before making our way to Ingham that afternoon. . . . The publicity manager for the Ingham Basketball Association, met us at the outskirts of the town at 3:00p.m. . . . We then went and met Mr. Carey[,] who is the Ingham Basketball Association President. . . . Ingham is a really wonderful little town and we were treated like royalty. . . . Elder Bown had a very good half time show that night and the girls really wanted him to do Elvis Presley for them in his impersonations and he wouldn't do it mainly because he didn't know it, so after the game he told these girls that I could really do Elvis well. They all rushed me and I was quite embarrassed because they wouldn't believe me that I couldn't do it. I gave them all Books of Mormon, so it was some advantage after all. It was really quite an experience that I shan't forget very easily. We won the game by the score of 62 to 28. In the second half we really clowned around in playing football and baseball on the basketball court during the game and the fans really liked it very much, and we really had a ball at the same time, too! . . .[123]

Saturday, April 30th . . . We don't have a game tonight so . . . we played some beach football. . . . The Juniors took on the Seniors and we [the juniors] beat them [the seniors] pretty bad—15 touchdowns to their 9 touchdowns. It was sure a lot of fun besides relaxing. About 3:00p.m. we left Ingham and headed south back to Townsville. . . .

Sunday, May 1st. We had a very enlightening Sunday here in Townsville with the Saints. . . . All of us spoke in the evening service and it was really a very good meeting. . . .

May 2nd, Monday . . . We traveled all day again over those terrible roads, but we made it just on time for tea [dinner] at the Paradise Private Hotel [in Mackay]. . . .

Tuesday, May 3rd . . . We are back in McKay [Mackay] again. . . . At noon we were off to our best store appearance of our tour which was held at T. C. Biernes, the

MORMON YANKEES PROGRAM (1960). COURTESY OF SHERM DAY.

largest store in town, and we really did some good and a lot of proselyting. . . . We passed out programs to everyone in the store and told them about the Church at the same time. . . . At 3:00p.m. we had our first clinic with all the high school kids and it was quite a success. . . . At 5:00p.m., we had a clinic for the men and women players. Before each clinic began, we had talks on: Origin of Basketball, Desire, Teamwork, and Word of Wisdom. A lot of the players are really thinking of giving up smoking, etc., because of our examples. . . .[124] At night we had another very successful game and there were even more people there this time than last time—approximately 900 people. Jim [Connolly], who was in charge of the McKay [Mackay] Basketball Association, had it very well organized. . . . After the game, one of the players had a party over at his beautiful home for both teams. It really turned out tremendously well. They had enough food to feed an army. . . . I was very impressed by the sincerity and hospitality of these fine people. . . . I would really love to be one of the Elders that is going to open McKay [Mackay] when it is reopened.[125]

Wednesday, May 4th. We got to bed at 2:30a.m. this morning and then we were up at 5:30a.m. to get on our way to Rockhampton for the clinic and the game this evening. . . . We beat them . . . 37 to 30. . . . We again signed many, many autographs and gave out a lot of Books of Mormon. . . . Harvey Halftime [Elder Bown] did another fine job.

JIM CONNOLLY. UNKNOWN SOURCE IN MACKAY, QUEENSLAND, AUSTRALIA.

Thursday, May 5th . . . We traveled 300 miles today from Rockhampton to Maryborough. . . . We stayed at one of the nicest hotels. . . . Elders Tuttle, Butler, Snow, Jorgensen gave the clinic that afternoon. We had a wonderful night in that we beat them 76 to 30 and we did a lot of playing around with our clowning tactics. . . . Here there are 5 girls to every boy and the girls really mobbed us afterwards and we signed an awful lot of programs and gave a lot of Books of Mormon out that night. . . . We made a very good impression in the town. . . .

> Friday, May 6th . . . The Elders ought to get a tremendous reception the next time that they are back through the town [of Maryborough]. We finally made it into Kingaroy at 6:00pm. . . . As a team, we really clicked well in beating them 89 to 65. . . . Elder Bown put on a superb performance. We had a ball with him calling our nicknames over the loudspeaker. . . . They had a party for us after the game. . . .
>
> Saturday, May 7th. The last day of our tour and it just seems like we got started. We've had such a great time together that the time has just flown by. I went with Elder Blacker to visit the Sports Stores and visit the managers in spreading good-will. . . . During Elder Bown's half time performance, a drunk tried to break it up, but Elder Blacker came to his rescue. Most of the people thought it was part of their act. They seemed to all enjoy it. . . . It was really hilarious watching Elder Bown try to take care of the drunk—it was quite a climax to everything. We left after the game for Brisbane. . . .
>
> Saturday, May 8th. In a way it was good to get back because we were really exhausted. We spent about 97 hours both weeks of the tour doing some type of proselyting.

This same year, the Mormon Yankees defeated the 1960 Australian Olympic basketball team prior to the Games. Lindsay Gaze, then a member of the Australian team, remembered a number of the Mormon Yankees, including BYU star basketball player Bob Skousen. Gaze remembered that Skousen was recognized widely at the time "as probably the best pure shooter that we saw, particularly in that era. . . . I still remember him beating us with a shot that he literally said, the moment before he released the ball, 'I have never done this before.' . . . We had

MORMON YANKEES TOUR TEAM (1960). COURTESY OF GARY H. BLACKER.

BOB SKOUSEN. COURTESY OF BOB SKOUSEN.

him double teamed in the corner with his back to the basket and we were a point ahead. So he did a turnaround jump shot with his back to the basket from the corner . . . nothing but net."[126]

During the year, the elders played much and worked hard in their proselytizing efforts off the court. The Australian Saints also donated hundreds of hours in planning for the development of the first Church stakes "down under." These stakes, organized in the same areas in which the Mormon Yankees had opened so many hearts and doors (Sydney, Melbourne, and Brisbane), had a great impact on the development of the Church in Australia after 1960.[127]

MORMON YANKEES EXPAND

In 1961, missionary work expanded into distant places whose inhabitants had never before seen Latter-day Saint missionaries, let alone a Mormon Yankee. Eight elders were sent thousands of miles north of Sydney to open up four new areas in Darwin; Thursday Island; Papua New Guinea; and Lae, New Guinea. Turley and his companion, Elder Reed, had the assignment to open Lae. When Turley and Reed first arrived, the natives feared them and thought that the elders had come to take their women. Relying on earlier success, the elders quickly began coaching three basketball teams of young women ages fifteen to twenty. Turley noted, "We trained them so well, that they were beating other teams from Papua, and other places. . . . The negativeness just melted away. And all of a sudden, we were heroes in this small town because of what we were doing for the basketball program."[128]

Basketball teams were also formed to build bridges on Thursday Island, which Elder Gary H. Blacker and Elder Gordon Holt traveled three thousand miles north by train, boat, and plane to open. Soon after their arrival on January 26, 1961, Blacker, a former collegiate basketball player and Mormon Yankee player-coach, had the idea to organize basketball teams for both the young men and the young women. Holt recalled that the girls were just as interested in the game as the boys were.[129]

Later, Elder James William Lundahl replaced Holt as Blacker's companion. As was typical, Lundahl observed that playing basketball resulted in opportunities to teach the Latter-day Saint health code.

> The Word of Wisdom would come up . . . as we were playing basketball and they were getting tired and they just kept playing and kept working, [and] it would come up there, when we'd go to these parties. At first, they would come up and say, "Would you like a drink?" And we'd explain, "No, we don't [drink alcohol]." And then we'd explain to them about the Word of Wisdom and after that, after a period of time, they didn't ask us anymore, they respected it.[130]

The elders spent much time coaching the various youth teams and selecting top competitive teams. They called the select teams "the Saints." Both the male and the female teams consisted of nine players ranging from age sixteen to age twenty-five. After working hard to develop the skills of these youth and to get the players in top shape, Blacker arranged for the teams to travel to the mainland of Australia to compete in the Cairns basketball tournament, an unprecedented event for Thursday Island. This opportunity was the most significant that had ever been presented in the players' young lives, and the community rallied to support the teams. The female players made their own skirts as part of their uniforms, and other community members had bake sales to support the teams. After all was said and done, the two teams each placed second at the Cairns tournament.[131] The elders left a lasting legacy for the Church on Thursday Island.[132]

GARY BLACKER (LEFT), GORDON HOLT (CENTER), AND JAMES LUNDAHL (RIGHT) (1961). COURTESY OF JAMES WILLIAM LUNDAHL.

JAMES LUNDAHL AND GARY BLACKER WITH THURSDAY ISLAND WOMENS TEAM. COURTESY OF GARY H. BLACKER.

END OF AN ERA

About the same time Blacker was bidding farewell to his players and many island friends in the summer of 1961, a monumental decision was being made at the general level of the Church: no more using sports as a vehicle to preach the gospel of Jesus Christ. Apparently this policy change was announced at the first general meeting for the training of mission presidents. At this time, a uniform system of preaching the gospel was introduced, a system that standardized proselytizing throughout the world. During this period of transition, Elder Bruce R. McConkie of the Church's First Council of the Seventy was called to serve as the president of the South Australian Mission (he ultimately served from 1961 to 1964), and he disbanded the Mormon Yankees. Melbourne Stake mission president Keith Stringer remembered:

> When the Mormon Yankees were abolished by the order given by Bruce McConkie, I felt a little bit disappointed, because I thought it was a great promotional situation, where we could be seen not only as preachers of the gospel, but as preachers of the good rules in basketball. . . . He just said, "Oh, it's got to stop." And that's all there was to it. It was explained to us that it was from Salt Lake,

from the General Presidency, and so as we learned in the early stages of being totally obedient to everything that's said from Salt Lake, we just accepted it and went on with life just the same.[133]

When Stringer's teenage daughter, Kay Watts, heard about the closure of the Mormon Yankees era, she "was devastated." Watts felt that the Mormon Yankees gave Church members "something to be proud of, they gave us an identity, they gave us a purpose, to be Latter-day Saints at school, to be proud of who we were."[134] She also recalled, "I remember President McConkie when he announced it, he didn't want to stop it either, but he was teaching us to be obedient to the leaders and as a fledgling church and fledgling members."

She later reflected that "obedience and sacrifice were part of growing up in the Church and that's what the members needed to learn then." Watts explained that one thing that helped ease this painful transition was the formation of local teams. She noted, "We were encouraged in the youth program to move out, get going into basketball teams." She said that in her local ward, "We formed a basketball team. . . . We called ourselves the Blackburn MGs, the Blackburn Mormon Girls, and we registered at Albert Park, and we had a really smart uniform. . . . Elder [H. David] Burton . . . became our coach, and he is now the presiding bishop [of the Church,] and he had a huge impact on us girls."[135]

MORMON YANKEES FIFTY YEARS AFTER A MISSION (2009). COURTESY OF MARTIN L. ANDERSEN PRODUCTIONS.

ELDER BRUCE R. MCCONKIE. © BY INTELLECTUAL RESERVE, INC.

Generally, Church members and the sports communities of various other faiths and cultures were disappointed by the dissolution of the Mormon Yankees teams. Gaze tried his best to wield his influence: "I still remember meeting with the president [Bruce R. McConkie] here in Victoria trying to convince him that we should be the exception." Gaze told President McConkie that there were "still benefits for the Church to have their missionaries assembled here and participating and doing the things that have been done in the past."[136]

Although the era of the Mormon Yankees had come to a conclusion, the Church in Australia continued to progress. The missionaries had simply used basketball to lay the groundwork for greater Church acceptance and growth. At the time of transition in proselytizing efforts, Elder Gordon B. Hinckley counseled the attendees of the 1961 mission presidents' seminar that they should never disparage the methods used by earlier missionaries, which would certainly include the valuable work accomplished in Australia by the Mormon Yankees.[137]

Bishop H. David Burton, a former Mormon Yankee and currently the presiding bishop for The Church of Jesus Christ of Latter-day Saints, reflected that for Australia, the Mormon Yankees "certainly opened a lot of doors in the formative years of the growth of the Church. Many . . . individuals . . . came into the Church at that time." Bishop Burton later reflected,

BISHOP H. DAVID BURTON. COURTESY OF MARTIN L. ANDERSEN PRODUCTIONS.

> If I were a historian writing the history of Australia, one thing I would include would be a chapter on the value of basketball as a proselyting tool for the [Mormon] missionaries. It wasn't an end of all ends, and not everybody participated, but the teams were selected, based on the talent that was available, and used to help the Church come out of obscurity in that part of the world. . . . It wasn't just a fling, it wasn't just a use of a gimmick. It was genuinely used to bring good publicity to the Church and introduce individuals to the gospel of Jesus Christ.[138]

CONCLUSION

Between 1937 and 1961, basketball was used by many Mormon elders "down under" to build bridges and win friends for the Church and to teach countless Australians a higher level of the emerging American game. The Mormon Yankees' successful playing sparked hundreds of positive newspaper articles and favorable radio broadcasts that reached millions of homes. This media coverage paved the way for missionaries to introduce the restored gospel, overcome negative stereotypes about polygamy and other issues, and gain entrance into homes. These opened doors in turn led to more converts, the construction of many chapels, and, in 1960, the organization of several stakes.

FRED E. WOODS AND LINDSAY GAZE. COURTESY OF TREVOR EVANS.

LEGACY OF MORMON YANKEES (2009). COURTESY OF MARTIN L. ANDERSEN PRODUCTIONS.

Although the Mormon Yankees basketball program was discontinued in 1961, it surely served a great purpose in early missionary work in Australia. In fact, since The Church of Jesus Christ of Latter-day Saints was introduced to Australia in 1840, it has probably never received as much positive publicity in one decade as it obtained from the Mormon Yankees in the 1950s. Much textual material from journals, magazines, newspapers, mission minutes, and oral history interviews demonstrates that the Church benefited greatly from the Mormon Yankees' exemplary behavior, diligent proselytizing labors, and athletic abilities.[139]

It is remarkable that although it has been over fifty years since the Mormon Yankees played the game "down under," hundreds of Australian sports fans, writers, athletes, and citizens from various regions still remember not only the name of the team but often the names of the players whom they have not seen since the mid-twentieth century. Not only did the teams demonstrate superb skill on the court, but by their sportsmanship and exemplary behavior, the Mormon Yankees also proved to be giants both on and off the court. It is therefore appropriate, as former Olympian Lindsay Gaze has suggested, that they be remembered.[140]

INTERVIEWS

OF THOSE WHO KNEW ABOUT THE MORMON YANKEES

IMAGES COURTESY OF MARTIN L. ANDERSEN PRODUCTIONS

BETTY BENSON

SYDNEY, NEW SOUTH WALES, AUSTRALIA
JUNE 26, 2010

I REMEMBER THAT knock on the door. There were two ladies knocking on my door and saying they were Mormons. I didn't know what a Mormon was, and I couldn't hear them properly because my husband was playing drums in the room where they knocked, so I brought them in, and we went into another room and closed the door, and they taught me the first discussion of the Church. They taught me about what the Church was trying to tell me. So I was impressed with that, and my husband and also my three children listened to that gospel message. It took us about eight months, but we were baptized in December of that year. During that time, we went with other members of the Church to various things, and one of the things I really remember is seeing the missionaries playing basketball and wondering just how they got to be so good at it. Then I found out that they were top basketball players who had come over here on missions, and the elder that I particularly remember is Harold Turley, and I think he came from El Paso. . . . Before the missionaries knocked on my door, I knew nothing about Mormons. The word *Mormon* wasn't in my vocabulary, and so it was interesting to me to find out about them. I've always been a curious person, curious about different things. I wanted to know what they were about, which is why they got invited into my house. . . .

While we were still looking at whether we wanted to join the Church or not, we were invited to a basketball game that the Mormon Yankees were playing. . . . And the whole family, the three kids and John and I, went to that game. The missionaries would come over in breaks, between the game[s], and talk to us. And when they were making what we thought were good plays and they were looking very physical, we would be . . . cheering for them and making a lot of noise; our kids would be too. They were very enthusiastic about the Mormon Yankees. . . .

I'm pretty well sure that they were doing a lot of proselytizing between the game area[s]. They were talking to people, and lots of members had brought friends along, and we were kind of friends in a way because we were not members of the Church at that time. We did have a lot of things to talk about. I believe that some of the investigators, whatever you call them, and we were too, were having some discussions with the missionaries between games, especially before the game started, and after the game finished, there was a lot of social activity where the missionaries talked to us and gave us pamphlets and things like that, and they had their scriptures tucked away, hidden under a seat or something while they played the game, but when they finished the game, they came out. . . .

Bringing the Mormon Yankees here as a basketball team—I think their legacy has been that they were able to relate to the people at just a personal level, and people got to know them and got to admire them for the wonderful way they looked, to start with. They looked so healthy and so good, and to be able to meet with us and talk to us about family things. Our friends, a lot of their friends came and sat in with us when we were talking to those missionaries, and many of them were impressed and loved the missionaries.

GUNARS ESINS BERZZARINS (GEB)

ADELAIDE, SOUTH AUSTRALIA, AUSTRALIA
JUNE 18, 2010

NOTE: *GEB, a native Latvian, was a sportswriter for the Adelaide Advertiser who wrote articles about the Mormon Yankees during the 1950s. At the time of this interview, he was eighty-five years old and had been writing for the* Latvian Weekly *for the past thirty-seven years.*

I'VE HEARD IT said that there are three stages in Adelaide basketball, and the first was, obviously, before the Mormons arrived. Basketball was being played in Australia. In those days it was called five-a-side for international rules because the girls played a sort of basketball which, they said, became netball; [it was] renamed netball. And then when the Latvians and Lithuanians particularly, to a lesser extent Estonians, came, they had already their skills from Europe and from the DP [Displaced Persons] camps in Germany because [while] waiting for immigration, there was plenty of spare time, and the most people could do was sport, and basketball was sort of the favorite. So they took up basketball in a—well, not in a big way because we were so many in numbers, but in Adelaide, the Lithuanians set up a team. The Latvians joined the YMCA, which was . . . from Europe, from Latvia, and then here it was later. We got a chance and we founded our own club and started our team in the competition, and that was in the early fifties.

And they were doing really well, the two teams: Lithuanians and Latvians were normally the favorites. And then we arrived to, if you are to call [it], the third stage, when the Mormons arrived, and from memory, the very first one was Elder Dunn, Loren Dunn. And I believe for a while he played for one of the Australian teams, being on his own. Then the others followed, and they set up their own team. That was the greatest thing that could happen to Australian basketball—particularly Adelaide, of course, [and] by extension to Australian basketball as well. So there were these great teams, the Lithuanians, the Latvians, the Mormon Yankees as they were called, and the best Australian teams. There was a great, great competition. . . .

The first Mormon basketballer I can remember is Loren Dunn. One of the key points in that one was that prior to that, George Dancis was the giant, both in Adelaide, and [he] was on the Australian team. And then Loren Dunn appeared, and he was about the same size as Dancis, and I would say that he had even more skills than Dancis because he had been skilled in the American basketball school. That, of course, the Latvians had to adjust their game to cope with him, and there was some great duels, if you like, between George and Elder Dunn, and sometimes one would come out on top, and sometimes it was the other. Depending how that went, it [the game] might finish also; the results would be depending upon that one. Looking at the old records, they can see that one game . . . the Latvians would win by a few points; next time, the Mormons would win. But then, of course, he had the great support, and the first thing that comes to mind, or the two things that come to mind talking about the Mormon team, that they were great sports, gentlemen, and great players. That was really one of the turning points, and the Australians also woke up to what really basketball [was when] played at the highest level, at least in our terms, and it's a sporting conduct at the highest level [that] would be shown by the Mormons. . . .

The first thing that would impress us would be how disciplined [the Mormon Yankees] were—as a team, as an individual player, and then the next thing, how complete, if you like, the individual players were in their particular field, whether it was guard playing guard or playing forward or the center. And of course, the team cohesion. As far as the game plan, if you like, in my recollection, they could do all sorts of things. They could play man to man, could play zone, could play press, depending on the circumstances. Of course, in many cases they didn't have to ride a press because they were far too good anyway. They only had some of the tough matches against the Latvians. But that was my impression. They were gentlemen on and off the court, and there was never a—I can't remember any instance of a case of pushing, shoving, or name calling and rolling [by] any of the Mormon players, and of course that made an impression. That affected the other teams as well, because he [Elder Dunn] had a team as gentlemen as you like in play, regardless how good they are and how they outscore you. You kept into check yourself, and you don't really do the wrong thing. . . . Helping a player that was knocked down would probably be just natural to them. . . .

Loren Dunn, of course, was the first that comes to memory, but he had all this support, and they were actually more than support. . . . Each one had its own role, and they would perform whatever they were asked to do. And there were these two guards, Elder [Bob] Steck and Elder [Hal] Christensen. . . . Christensen, he's probably the best guard that we have seen, or I have seen, in playing in Adelaide, very solidly, always best to do all the things that you expect them to. And then there was a forward, Elder [Ted] Johnson, who was a dynamic player under the board, helping Loren Dunn. There were others, like Haynes. . . .

I think there's no doubt that their abstinence from alcohol and from smoking would make an effect. Anybody who could do that or not do that would naturally be a better player in whatever sport you did play, basketball or anything; of course it's natural. With Latvians it sometimes wasn't quite so easy, and they might celebrate after a great win or after a great tournament, but they still kept within limits, I would say. . . .

There never was any question of a conflict, if you like, as far as religion. I don't think that our basketball—it's the Latvian basketball's sphere, particularly, of religious—and the Mormons, although [they] were always happy to explain what their faith was all about, I don't think they would try to push it. I know they never did. But if any [person] was interested, they would go out of their way to explain. I remember just one of the Australian basketballers that converted and played for the Mormons. I think it was Rex Holmes. But that's the only one that comes to mind. Otherwise, religion, if you'd like, never interfered one way or the other. . . . I remember them passing out some literature and the Book of Mormon around the players and the public, of course. Because when the Mormons played the Latvians, it was a full house, a thousand. . . . I would say that the Mormon Yankees were accepted as basketballers, regardless whether they were Americans or Englishmen or whatever. It was just basketball. . . .

I'm sure the Mormons were accepted just like any people of any religion, I would think, or at least the common [religions] like Anglicans or Catholics or Lutherans. I don't think there was ever any strong feelings one way or another, particularly not in basketball. The people came to watch them. They came to see good basketball, and that's all they were interested in, particularly, as I said earlier, good sportsmen and good players. . . .

There is no question that whoever watched them play, and we watched them play against some of the top teams, couldn't help but be influenced and try to emulate them. After all, that's how many players learn: what the coach tells them, and what they see of the good players who play better than them performing on the court, and they try to emulate them. And I think in Adelaide, anyone of, say, my age, if you speak to them in the street, who has been watching basketball, they'll remember the Mormons. They remember Loren Dunn and [Hal] Christensen and [Bob] Steck. . . . I've watched basketball in Australia from day one, if you like, and so many teams have been and gone, and many of them I couldn't place; I couldn't recollect what they were like. The names may ring a bell, but that's about all. When you talk about the Mormon Yankees, then that's a team that immediately brings to mind all those names that I mentioned earlier and that already gives me a picture. That's how basketball should be played, and that's how basketball will be played in the future, although basketball today is no longer what it was twenty, thirty, fifty years ago.

DELMAR BJORK

TAYLORSVILLE, UTAH, USA
APRIL 16, 2011

I WAS BORN in Salt Lake City in 1934, a time where the Depression was just starting to ease up. . . . Everybody was trying to come through a depression. I saw a sign on the Eighth Avenue meat and grocery store that said, "Looking for butcher help—young man." At that time, I said, "That's for me." I was age fourteen and felt like I could learn to be a butcher, which would help the family. . . . Five years later, I became a journeyman butcher. . . . Because I was working in the evenings after school and on weekends, my experience in getting basketball training was limited. . . . I received my mission call in the latter part of November 1954. . . . In January 1955, in San Francisco, I boarded the HMS [SS] *Orcades*, a British ship in the Matson lines. . . . Our next stop was Hawaii, where we spent time. . . . We left there for Fiji, and in the Fiji Islands—that was a marvelous experience, which everyone should go to the Fiji Islands. From Fiji, went to New Zealand, then finally to Sydney, Australia. . . . Upon leaving the SS *Orcades*, I caught an old train headed to Melbourne, at which time I finally met the [mission] president, . . . President Liljenquist. . . .

A few days after in the mission, after being called to the mission home, and my first assignment was to work in another old home to the rear of the mission home. I was told that a meeting would begin at eight o'clock in the morning and that everyone had to be up by about five o'clock to be ready. It was a house full of missionaries: thirty-four of us, to be exact. Upon eating breakfast and shortly thereafter, as we finished, one of the leaders said, "We need one person to stay behind and clean up after this meal of breakfast." Guess who won the toss, which was not my will. Nevertheless, there I stood looking by myself at a pile of dishes about fifteen inches high and six foot long, and I was trying to get old soaps and cleaners to work. I was doing the dishes, complaining, really, maybe discussing or possibly cussing a bit about my assignment. When all of the sudden I saw some wonderful hands enter the picture from my right, large hands. And the hand belonged to someone who picked up a dish towel and dried off a dish and then another one. I said, "Never mind, I can do it." Then I thought, "Oh boy, I better see who that is." So I looked to the right, and it was the prophet of the Church . . . helping me do the dishes, which was rather startling—caused me to tremble, even shed a tear like I am now. And in so doing, my memory was flooded with all kinds of thoughts, and I didn't really know how to react. I felt weak in the knees, and yet we finished the dishes together. Upon finishing the dishes, the prophet said, "I think now we can go and complete our assignment." And I said, "Well, thank you very much." . . .

I got a call from . . . our supervising elder, whose headquarters was in Sydney, New South Wales, Australia. He invited me to come to Sydney and consider playing on the Mormon Yankee ball team based in Sydney. I thought that would be really interesting, and I certainly volunteered. We met and played ball together the first time in Bankstown, which is a suburb of Sydney. We were playing against local teams. . . . We met some of the players who were eventually to become Australian players on the Australian Olympic team. . . .

Winning the Australian championship in 1955 was really a benefit to us and for the Church. . . . The Church began to grow as the name *Mormon* or *Yankee* began to touch the newspapers. In fact, there was a time when the Mormon Yankee team was brought south to Wollongong, where again we played, and this was done with locals from Wollongong and Unanderra. Yet the newspapers gave us great writings, and we thought that was a wonderful accomplishment. Little by little, doors were open. Mormons didn't only wear funny hats, but they also could play ball. It was something that we learned as we were in that field. There was a lot of blessings. Should we have won all those games? I think it was nice, but I'm sure we had the Lord's help a number of times. . . .

In 1956, the . . . Olympic tournaments were held in Melbourne, Australia. . . . In this particular time, as the Olympics were brought forth from—people from other countries were bringing their teams to Melbourne, Australia, expecting to play one another [in] preparation games. But the World Olympic Committee had said, "No, you don't play another Olympic team until the day you play them for real." Suddenly the Mormon Yankees' name became very important. Whoever was in charge at the Church headquarters authorized us to play two games each of each team by contract that we would play at least two. When that was done, it became a bit of a challenge because we played teams from France, Italy, Brazil, Russia—there were South American teams, there were teams from Germany, Scandinavia, but I don't remember all of them at this time. . . . It's interesting to me that the Church authorities, wherever they be, had called players that seemed to fit and work together. DeLyle Condie was our player-coach; he played for the University of Utah. . . .

As we played the games against the Russians, we knew we were up against a tough team. It was not uncommon to see armlocks as you see maybe in the professionals today. We learned that real quickly from the Russians. I myself, being a guard, was on breakaways quite a bit. I tried to steal the ball; when I got a chance to steal the ball, I always felt this hand on my shorts in the back, grabbing me and holding me back. Sometimes they would call a foul, but rarely. I said to myself, "Why are they so desperate to win those games?" Then I began to think about it. These were people whose livings were made under the Communist regimes by doing nothing but playing basketball. Had they lost a game to a Mormon Yankee team, it could have been the end of their careers. So to this very day, I've not felt so bad to lose to those Russians. . . .

I felt so blessed to be able to play with the Mormon Yankees, and I was a starter most of the time. I could not really understand that because there were too many other wonderful ball players the Church had in positions to play. As I look back upon it across the years, some of the things that have been important to me were this opened the doors to some wonderful membership into the Church. . . . It was wonderful to have companions with us who would go out and lead cheers and hope people would catch on. They were making appointments with people. . . .

Not long after the Mormon Yankees played and received coverage in Melbourne, . . . our missionaries would go out into the field. Doors were opened. People began to ask about the Church. . . . The Church began to grow in numbers while I was still there.

From the time that the ship that I was on docked at Sydney Harbor, I could not be more pleased with the people I met. I felt like I was at home. The people were kindly, very courteous; they looked at us carefully. At the time we were asked to wear hats, which turned out to be all right because the sun in Australia's very strong, and probably they kind of kept us from going bald a little quick in those days. But I really enjoyed the people. Never before, having traveled halfway around the world by that time, had I met people that were scholastic; they were very energetic, and sports meant a lot to them, all the way from the racetrack of horses to the man running down the street for his exercise and for the chances of being in races. . . . When in Melbourne, where we happened to be able to play a little basketball, the members of the Mormon Yankee team also were very well accepted. . . . We found people cheering for the Mormon Yankees. Although, when it was a game against the Australian Olympic team, they didn't cheer for us very often. . . . To the people of Australia, you are wonderful and great. Thank you for your caring and concern with us, the Mormon Yankees—The Church of Jesus Christ of Latter-day Saints.

GARY H. BLACKER

NORTH OGDEN, UTAH, USA
JULY 8, 2010

I LOVE SPORTS; I've played since I was a young man. Any spare time, I'd go to the neighbors'; even on dirt grounds, I'd play basketball. . . . But I love football, I love baseball, I love tennis—I love them all. After graduating from Ontario High School, I got a college basketball scholarship to play at Boise Junior College. . . . I went [on a mission] . . . in July of 1959 and got to Australia. And right at the beginning, I just got into the mission home in Sydney, and they told me they had heard that I had played some ball, and they said, "An American aircraft carrier just came in the Sydney harbor. Would you like to play? We're going to play their team that's on the aircraft carrier." I got introduced to basketball nearly the first couple days that I arrived in that country. From there on, it was a story of me traveling to different parts of Australia and having a wonderful time teaching the gospel but also being able to use my abilities as a basketball player to preach the gospel. . . .

It seemed like the sports pages always had articles about the Mormons. We were always in there because wherever we played ball as a team, the publicity was tremendous. We always got headlines or pictures of one of us in the newspapers telling us how we did, because at that time Australia was still a little bit in awe of Americans and our abilities; we were ahead of them a bit. That's why we probably did as well as we did, is because we'd had more training, more coaching. We were just above them in basketball, although they started having some tremendous players even while I was there. . . . Mr. Gaze was one of their greatest athletes that came out of Australia. We had lots of publicity—we knew the sports people. They interviewed us; they knew about our background. They knew about us. It seemed like another elder would come into town, and they would grab us. It was news for them because sports and basketball was beginning to take its place in Australia. . . .

Why was I chosen? Why did I get selected? We had a very good mission president, President Moore. He was [asking], "What can we do to help the missionary program besides knocking on doors?" The Australians were sports minded. . . . They loved their sports, their athletics. I think President Moore felt that we had an opportunity here. For some reason, when I was sent, there were also some college basketball players that were called on missions at that time. It was a wonderful experience. . . . Being able to play basketball on our mission is the greatest tool that we had, because there were lots of missionaries that at least had played high school basketball. A lot of them were probably better than most of the Australian men at the time. We were able to make an impact in nearly every town that the missionaries were sent to and where there was a bigger city, where there was a few of us in one area. When we ever joined to have a team, then we really got recognition, and we had recognition since then. We even had tours where we traveled all over Australia playing the representatives, a town's best players. We'd play in front of big crowds, and yes, we opened doors because of basketball. . . .

I have forgotten lots of details, but I want you to know that we did lots of planning . . . because we had to have sponsors help us pay for this trip or the mission would . . . never have let us do it. I don't remember all the details, but I met with Qantas, the airline company; they helped fund the program. Hardy tennis shoes was one of the big Australian brands at the time; they did and a few more. I had to have those people sign contracts that they would help us and fund us before we could ever even get started, and that meant printing. We had to print programs. [On one basketball tour] we gave away over six thousand printed programs to fans that attended the games, and we also gave away 188 Books of Mormon. We were playing basketball, but we were doing Church work all the time. I had to many times introduce ourselves when we started the game, and then we'd tell them where we're from, a little bit about the Church, but the program told them a lot of things about the Church and the chapels in Australia and then explained about the players and explained about our mission as missionaries. . . .

Going into a new foreign town, not knowing anybody, and we would start warming up, and we'd play "When the Saints Go Marching In." We'd have music, and Roger [Bown] did that. We warmed up to good music that made us all relax and got the people in the crowd excited, and then we'd play the first half, and then Roger would take over. We would rest at halftime, and Roger would come out and entertain, and he was a great impersonator. He impersonated many, many people, and it was amazing that Australians knew most of them although they were mostly American stars that he was impersonating. Australia loved America. . . . They still feel to this day [that] during World War II, it was such a wonderful thing that the Yanks were there to save Australia because the Japanese were getting very, very close to invading their country. . . .

As we come [came] into each stadium, and when I say *stadiums*—we played in maybe one or two wood floor[s]—[I mean a] cement basketball court. We were on cement. I think 90 percent of all the games that I ever played in Australia were on cement, which was very hard on your legs, but we played on tennis courts that were converted. We played on ice-skating rinks that were converted into playing basketball. And so they were just not up to us as far as gymnasiums. We had really a rough time. We'd come into the area, and I'd always want Roger [Bown] to play "When the Saints Come Marching In," to tie in the name of our church, so we had the Saints. Then we—they would introduce us . . . and then Roger would also introduce if I wasn't—sometimes they would ask me to say a few words before the game began—and then we would have the music come on of "Sweet Georgia Brown," which got us revved up, and we thought we were the Harlem Globetrotters, I guess, because that's what they used. We did that; it warmed and loosened us up and loosened the crowd up. . . . We had the crowd on our side every time that we played. . . .

[On Thursday Island], they wanted to practice anytime we could. We would schedule and teach the gospel. We had investigators, but as you know, the only two of us—we weren't too busy as far as Church work. . . . We got as many meetings as we could, but we also had spare time, so I think we practiced quite often, and they would get off work. We'd set time so that they could be there, but they loved practice. But sometimes they thought Elder Blacker, Coach Blacker was a little bit rough on them, just a little bit tough. . . . The kids followed us everywhere we went, but because of sports, we added another thing. So besides religion, we added athletics to the scope, and it made things so much better because they loved their sports. Australian people and Thursday Island people were very athletic. . . . I remember it was the biggest thing that ever happened to Thursday Island was that we as Thursday Island were going to send a women's team and a men's team to this big tournament in Cairns on the mainland of Australia, which also included most of Queensland that came to Cairns for this big basketball tournament. Never had Thursday Island been represented in their history; this was their first time, so we were preparing for that. I know we raised money. We had these bake sales. . . . The tournament in Cairns put Thursday Island on the map because our women . . . [placed] . . . second and we came [in] . . . second place. . . .

Sports was probably number one in their life. . . . They loved athletics, . . . and they were a very competitive people. I know that we opened many, many doors in Australia because if we could say we were a Mormon, we could also say, "Have you heard of the Mormon Yankees?" And most people in Australia by the time that we left—that I left in '61—there were thousands of people who had heard or seen the Mormon Yankees play, and so I know that was a big part of our success in Australia. . . . People saw the Church through basketball, and I was so grateful that I was a part of it.

RONALD L. BOUCK

SALT LAKE CITY, UTAH, USA
DECEMBER 27, 2010

I'M NOT VERY tall, so I'm not a basketball player. . . . I had both high school and college cheerleading experience. So I was grounded in being a gymnast, but I think I can give an interesting perspective on the Mormon Yankees because I was an entertainer for most of the games that were there for a while and saw the boys practice; they only had a chance to practice once in a while before they were called. They'd come from all over in their districts; we'd go and get on the train and go and play a basketball game, and I would be there to entertain. I did some gymnastics, handstands, some comic routines. Because of my build—I have short legs and a long torso, so I can run like a monkey on all fours, and I remember one time that a lady was expecting a baby, and I made her laugh so hard that I was afraid afterwards that she might have her baby right there. It was kind of funny. But it was part of the game—it was an exciting time for us to get together. And the guys, they had experience with high school and some college basketball, so they would play their routines and play against these teams, and I was able to mingle with the crowd, talk to them, associate with them. . . .

At that time there were two comic people who were well known. Jerry Lewis was one; the other was Stan Freberg. And I did parodies on Stan Freberg: "The Yellow Rose of Texas" to a recording, and of course

Jerry Lewis with his squeaky voice, and I would do the antics of Jerry Lewis and run around like he was—rather silly, which caught the eye of the people. And they recognized it because even in Australia, these two comedians were well known. . . . I've done imitations of Charlie Chaplin with his, that sort of thing, and his cane, twirling his cane. Again, I would do that white face, moustache, hat, and of course a dark coat, and strut around like Charlie Chaplin, and people recognized that, so we had some fun with that. I was part of this entertaining group for halftime; or when the game got kind of boring or whatever, I'd run out and do a cheer: "Come on, Yanks, let's go!" And so that's part of the fun in the experience of this. . . .

Quite often we'd get an invitation to play because the Aussies were interested in our rules, American-rules basketball, so we would then advise the members of the Church about the basketball game that was scheduled so that they could also associate with the crowd. One time in Toowoomba, the Catholic priests blocked off the streets, so we were in downtown Toowoomba with the traffic stopped and the streets blocked off; the Catholic priests were going around talking to their parishioners. We were talking to some of our members, and then we had leaflets as well—which would be a program or whatever—and then also some literature that we'd hand out after the game. Quite often we'd get them asking us for information about, "Well, what are you Yanks doing here?" And we had then an opportunity to interact with them. . . .

I think that the Australians in that particular period will remember us because, again, we had some pretty good athletes on the team, and there was a lot of respect of the Americans in that particular time, after the war, for saving their country, and so the combination of sports and history made it important for them to be a figure that they will remember. . . .

The mission president really knew who played basketball and who didn't. He got enough information through interviews and so forth, so as the assignments were made where elders would be sent to certain locations, he would have an awareness of that. Sometimes the invitation to play basketball would come with the invitation of the local people or it would come as an elder that would hear about that. So then the word would get back to the mission president, and we got clearance, and then there would be some telephone calls and coordination of that so that during the time that the elders were in certain locations, they could be pulled together to go to a certain location for a gym for practice—also for the game, where it would be in a town hall or a city or whatever. So there was some logistics to this. . . .

When I first arrived in Sydney Harbor, a little dinghy drove up to the boat; we got down a rope ladder and got in the boat and got over to the dock. The mission president met us. We went to a hotel—the mission president sized us up and said, "Elder So-and-So, you're tall; you play basketball. We'll send you up north." This . . . [was] . . . Charles Liljenquist, the first mission president. When I got there, there was only one mission president. So they sent the elders. I was sent somewhere way away; I wasn't playing basketball. Later on, I got into the mission home as a clerk, and that was when I linked up with this. President Erekson was a little more promotional in the idea of, "Well, let's use the elders. They're talented; they're good. Let's send them out!" So we did that. . . .

One observation I had of the members of the Church was that they were extremely proud of their missionary boys. Quite often they would try to get their own youth to learn to play basketball so they could play with the Mormon Yankees. Again, it was an ideal that they were looking up to, and there was something of a satisfaction of coming from a basketball game where the Mormon Yankees "drubbed" the local basketball team, and they had an opportunity to talk a little bit about it with their neighbors. . . .

I love the Australian people. They were kind; they were understanding. They were indicative of the middle class—a great group of people at that time. Open-hearted people. The men were quite masculine; the women were just so gracious about us. So I love the Australian people, and the legacy of having served a mission in Australia is very much a part of my life.

GARY D. BOUMA

MELBOURNE, VICTORIA, AUSTRALIA
JUNE 26, 2010

THERE IS A particular way of being religious and spiritual in Australia that stands out as different from other countries like Canada, the US, the UK, New Zealand even. And that—it goes back to the convict origins, where Australia was founded in a time that was at the lowest ebb of religion in the UK for centuries. And so they hadn't been churched; they hadn't been exposed to religion; they come out here as convicts, forced to go to chapel whilst they're in jail but otherwise let loose, in charge of their own spirituality. That whole business of being in charge or responsible for your own spirituality, your own religion, still hangs there, and it's also kind of low temperature—don't get too excited about it. Australians are low-temperature religion; not all, but it's not something you get excited about. But in that context is a lively spiritual openness, reflection, and it goes on. Into that context comes churches trying to Christianize this place. They came as missionaries, as church leaders, as a whole variety of things, and throughout the history of Australia since about 1840, it's been one after another coming to Australia. . . . The religion being borne by migrants, so more and more Catholics came, more and more Catholics appear, et cetera, et cetera. The various divisions in European Christianity are found here, and in the twentieth century, with some Buddhists and Hindus, a variety of

Japanese new religions, and lo and behold, Latter-day Saints. . . .

In the era, [the] end of the Second World War, through the fifties, there was a large community-building, nation-building orientation in Australia. The churches were very much part of that. Whether they were welcoming migrants, which they were, and stitching them in, the churches, as I said, produced not only the services and Sunday Schools, but they had sporting facilities as well. If you looked at where you got your entertainment, yes, there were movies and theaters, but there might be movies in the churches. There'd be dances, but they would often be run—certainly in the suburban areas and in the country towns—they would be run by the churches. So there was a great involvement of church in general social life, so if you were coming in as a new player in this, whether you were Italian Catholics who were new at that point or you were the Latter-day Saints coming in, to offer sport would be to do precisely the same thing as everybody else was doing, and not in a copycat way, but that was simply a very important way of engaging with the community. . . .

What I've encountered both in Salt Lake City and wherever I've gone—so it's not just a Salt Lake City phenomenon—when I've encountered of the Latter-day Saints, they are extremely well organized, not in an oppressive way but in a capacity-building way, that the structures are there to enable people to live a rich, full, human life. If you need a job, chances are they will find you one. If you need something or [a] food parcel or whatever else, they may be asked to work for an hour or two to get what it is. So you indeed maintain your humanity by making a contribution and getting the service. In all of the reflection, whether it was on education or social service or higher education provision, to my mind, it was always aimed at excellence, competence, and being careful. There was a bedrock of compassion, a bedrock of competence, and always being, striving for excellence and getting very close. The results are very, very strong. That once involved within the community, there will be pressures to maintain, simply the pressures that you may become dependent on it [and] whatever else; yes, but that's true of any kind of community. So that it is among those few religious organizations in Australia, and probably in many parts of the world, there [that] are actually sufficiently resourced to be able to say to somebody who comes in, "Yes, we can help you."

ROGER L. BOWN

SALT LAKE CITY, UTAH, USA
JULY 9, 2010

THE TRAINING GROUND for me was when I was in the army, '54 to '55, and I went over to the USO building, and there was a gentleman there doing an impersonations of singers. And I thought, "Well, I can do better than that. I can do the speakers." . . . And so we got together. They wrote an orchestration for us. I did Jerry Lewis's part; [my partner] did Dean Martin's part. We won the All-Army Talent Contest [competition] in Arizona—traveled to San Francisco, trying out for the Ed Sullivan Show, took second place. . . . Then I went on my mission. . . .

I was a [mission office] literature clerk, and one day we had a program, and President Joseph Fielding Smith and his wife came to visit. [The mission] president said, "We've got a presentation for you." And I said, "Well, I do impersonations." He said, "Why don't you do that, and we'll have President and Sister Smith sit there and watch this." So I did my impersonations. Sister Smith just about fell off her chair, and President Smith was just as serious as could be. I finally got him to laugh on Churchill and Roosevelt. And Churchill was, "We the British people shall never surrender. I say to you, people of America, put some money in the pot, boys!" Well, he broke down. . . .

[On a basketball tour], I remember the flat tires. The roads were not that good, and one time I think we blew through three tires . . . and on our trip that next day, we blew another one. But it was fun. We were packed in there. We always opened with a word of prayer and closed the night with a word of prayer and prayed that we'd be safe in our travels. We never had any problems, except blown tires. But it was fun. We'd eat on the bus. We were always prayerful. . . . Every time we'd stop to get something to eat, we'd always tell them who we were, or sometimes we would leave a Book of Mormon. "Who are you blokes?" "Well, we're the Mormons." Mormons was the name. Not The Church of Jesus Christ of Latter-day Saints, LDS; they didn't know that. But they knew the Mormons. This is why we called [ourselves] the Mormon Yankee from America basketball team, and that got us by. That name was known throughout Australia because we had paper coverage, news coverage of our team in Sydney, which was very good. And when we went on a tour, why, we are going to go those places, and a town that knew of us—why, it was a big deal. It was a very big deal. . . .

When we would start a game, as I recall, someone would introduce us, one of the prestigious persons that lived in that area, whether it was the chief of police or the mayor. They would announce . . . [the] "Mormon Yankee Basketball team"—[that] we were touring and they were fortunate to have us here in their town, and so here we are, the Mormon Yankee basketball and the play-by-play announcer, Elder Bown, who will do impersonations at halftime. And then I would call the game. I would have a list of the other players, and I would try and do the best on that; sometimes I would screw up the other guys' names because it's hard to pronounce some names. But many times I would call a play and our players weren't even in that, and then they'd look at me and say, "Oh, okay." And then they'd pass the ball that I designated to someone, and we used to have a lot of fun doing that. Our team in many instances was so good that we could have won by one hundred points, but we let them stay with us and keep with us. And when the fun of it was—sometimes you'd have to throw the ball in back, and our players would throw them back like the [Harlem] Globetrotters that throw the ball under their arms or between their legs. I mean, on a tight game, no, but in a game where we could really run the score up, they kind of played along. The crowd enjoyed this. We were playing to the crowd. We wanted to make the crowd accept us as Mormon Yankees and as missionaries for our church. . . . We always signed autographs.

We would sign in the Book of Mormons. Prior to the game, in our Book of Mormons, we would put our name in the back. Each one signed those Book of Mormons, and we would have numerous—how many we gave out, I don't know. In one game I think we gave out 100 or 120 or more. But if they want our autographs next, we'd flip to the front of the book and put our autograph on. I would like to find one of those books someday. . . .

I know when we do our clinics with the kids, town folk, the parents would all crowd around and watch. They were very interested to watch how we handle those children and how kind we were to them, and that was an emphasis for us, to be kind to the kids, kind to the children, pat them on the back, "Good job. Good job." If they did a lousy job, they still did a good job. The parents were so proud. I mean, how would you feel if it was your child out there, not knowing what he was doing, but learning basketball? . . .

I think it opened their doors for the missionaries because when they would contact people in the towns where we went and made our presentation and played our basketball, "Oh, you're with the Mormon Yankee blokes that came here. Well, come in, come in." We were now received with a smile instead of a question mark and a hesitation. It opened up doors. It opened up doors for the missionaries that came in after us. Hopefully we were the ones that paved the way for the people to be more responsive to us. And that led to chapels, led to temples, led to a growth in the Church from Australia, and we're grateful that we were able to be a little bit, a little part of that. . . .

One point I like to make, though. We had a Sylvester fellow in Sydney that when our players would break away on a fast break, he would try and trip them. In many cases, he did trip them. And we huddled together and called a timeout. We said, "What are we going to do with this?" . . . [Elder] Rich Rampton, ex-football player at the University of Utah, said, "Let me handle him. Let me handle him. I'll take care of it." So we were underneath the basket going up for rebounds, Sylvester was close. . . . He [Rich Rampton] came up with his fist cocked, and he came up under the jaw, opened it up, and got the rebound. If you didn't watch what was happening, you would have missed the fist. Sylvester was out . . . , and they carried him off, and he came back in later, but he never tripped—never again did he trip any of our players. I'll never forget that. We had to do something. But again, there was nothing negative written up about it.

SHAWN BRADLEY

MURRAY, UTAH, USA
MARCH 25, 2011

BASKETBALL REALLY STARTED for me when I was born. I was an infant. My father loved basketball; his father loved basketball; and they put a basketball in my crib when I was an infant. And they never pressured me to play basketball—they never did anything like that—but they loved the sport, and I grew up loving the sport as well. Although I did play many other sports; I started baseball before I was able to play in a league of basketball, when I was six, but having grown up in the places that I did, basketball and sports were one of the few things available to us to get us off the ranch for a minute. . . . Well, having grown up just a couple of hours away from BYU, that was the closest university to my hometown [of Castle Dale, Utah], the one that I followed the most, . . . so I went to BYU, and it was a great experience. . . .

I knew that by going on a mission, basketball wasn't going to be the priority. I knew that there might be opportunities for me to share my talent and break down some barriers of communication and be able to talk with people, and that's something that every missionary can establish, or to find what his niche in life is and what is unique that can touch the person that's on the other side of the door, touch the person that's on the bus or the person that's walking in the mall or someone they meet on the street or a neighbor or something like that. Everyone has uniqueness about them that they can share that, if someone will be interested in, they can start a conversation that can lead towards the gospel. And so, did I think I was going to play a lot of basketball? No. But did I think I had a talent that might be able to be utilized? Yes, and we did. We used that the best that we could while I was serving in Australia. . . .

One of the opportunities that I had while I served in Sydney, Australia—and I served there in '91 to '93—once a month, there was a lot of attention for this college basketball player who was a top prospect to leave college sports and go be a missionary, and so it was a newsworthy event. And what we tried to do was manage, about once a month, do an article or an interview as a missionary to a regional or national program in Australia, and there was a couple of times where I was able to, every few months, do a significant media piece. The Area Authorities in Australia utilized that the best that they could, and we had a plan, and we would kind of use that for positive exposure for the Church in that area. Another thing that my mission president and I thought would be wise was to do a monthly fireside, or every other month do a fireside-basketball camp. So we'd have this basketball camp, clinic—you know, we'd bring these kids in, fifty to one hundred kids, or at least promote it out there, and these kids would come, and we'd have a basketball clinic. I'd share some skills and teach them some drills and work on some things like this, and then after that the requirement was, "Well, now you've got to stop and listen to why I'm really here," and I'd share the Joseph Smith story with them, or I'd share something about the gospel. I'd share something about one of the parables of Christ, something along these lines, so they got some basketball and they got some spirituality all in one, and that was another unique way that my mission president and I thought would be beneficial, and we heard good things about it. . . .

[I had not] heard about the Mormon Yankees prior to serving my mission, but when I became a missionary and went to Australia, I did. I heard about them a lot, and many people I talked to, "Oh yeah, I remember your group. There was a group from your church that was here, and they used to play all over the country." And so there was—and I don't know how many years prior to me serving there, I know it was many, that they were in Australia—but they were talked about by a lot of people. Not hundreds or thousands, but many people when they found the connection that I was Mormon and I was a basketball player, and they were like, "Oh yeah, I remember a group that came," and they would tell me about the Mormon Yankees, so their fame had spread.

BETTY BROOKS

MELBOURNE, VICTORIA, AUSTRALIA
DECEMBER 11, 2009

I USED TO go as a teenager to the exhibition building, so I think it was the first they [the Mormon Yankees] started to play, and my mother and I went. We were the only members of the Church at that time, and we used to encourage them. Quite often there wasn't many members going in the early days, and my mother and I would go almost every week. . . . We loved to go to the basketball, and I went right up until the time I went on a mission in 1955. And then I can remember now that when I was screaming at the basketball, I ruined my voice, so consequently I don't have a good singing voice. I'd say I never had one, but I think yelling at the basketball caused me to lose my vocal cords as I strained it. I yelled, and when the boys were going for a basket, I'd say, "Box it!" and encourage them to get it in, and then if they didn't get it in, both Mom and I would give a sigh, "Oh, no!" They really loved us being there because I think even though they were playing for the Church, representing the Church, they really loved the game. They wanted to play basketball. I guess that was like their P-day [preparation day]; they wanted to be there just letting off their energies in another form and not just doing missionary work. But they were great missionaries. They were all, you know, there were the little elders that were the cheers [cheerleaders] and would run up and down and cheer us to encourage the game. They'd just run around, and not only the members of the Church were cheering them on, but the nonmembers were cheering them on as well, so they were really excited. . . .

There were quite a few girls that were there after the game to have a little chat with the missionaries, and I think quite a few came along to church, too. There were girls that joined the Church. . . . When we went to the game, we'd call in at the doughnut shop in Footscray; as we were passing to get the bus to go over to the exhibition buildings, we would go buy a dozen doughnuts, and we'd take them to the game, and we'd say to the missionaries, "Now if you don't win tonight, elders, you don't get any doughnuts." But of course, even if they didn't win, we still gave them doughnuts. I don't know whether that encouraged them any, but I think they didn't really need much encouragement, but they loved to have a doughnut after the game, that was for sure. They really loved to play the game, I think. I enjoyed watching the game, and they loved to be great showmen, I think, too. . . . The uniform said Mormon Yankees on them. . . .

I think the Church was better known through the basketball game. . . . I really do think it did have a great impact because the Church grew. We were very small up until the mid-forties [1940s], and during that period from the mid-forties to the mid-fifties, lots of people came into the Church that are still active in the Church today. Some have passed on, but there are a lot of members in the Church and their next generations, on and on, have come from those people, and they were mostly good-living LDS people. And so I guess from that, the missionaries did a wonderful job, and they were able to get the Church better known than just knocking on doors and being rejected. . . .

I was extremely proud because they always conducted themselves in an honest manner. You know, if somebody said, "You fouled," they'd say, "Right, we fouled." They never argued or contended at all, to my knowledge; I never saw any contention among the LDS basketball teams. . . . You never heard bad language, not accepting the judge's decision—the ref's decision. They were always obedient, and if they were fouled off, they were fouled off, and they knew the reason why, and they accepted it. And they did get fouled off at times. It was only because of their enthusiasm to win. . . .

They never let us down. We were proud to be part of them; we were proud to be Mormon members. And people would say, "Are you a member of the Church?" And both Mom and I would be proud to say, "Yes, we're members," because we were always there, and sometimes we were able to do missionary work with people and tell them about why they [the Mormon Yankees] were here, what they were doing, and be able to pass on our thoughts about the missionary work in the Church. So it wasn't just the missionaries; it was us being missionaries as well. We loved to do that.

KEITH BROOKS

MELBOURNE, VICTORIA, AUSTRALIA
DECEMBER 11, 2009

IN 1958, I was baptized into the Church, and the missionaries had a basketball team they called the Mormon Yankees. And they were quite tall players, . . . and they were a particularly strong team, and even when they played the Victorian basketball team, the Mormon Yankees would beat them. So this continued for a while. Then some of the missionaries left to go home from their mission, and the newer missionaries didn't seem to be quite as good, and the Victorian basketball team improved, so the Mormon Yankees didn't win so many times against the state team. But they were wonderful players. I remember there was Elder Frodsham, Elder Grant, Elder Condie, and some other particularly good players, and they were, I think, very good ambassadors for the Church. They got the Church known through their basketball. . . .

The impression I got was that the people were very inspired by them and at their athletic ability, skill on the court, and being nice-natured young men as well. They created a great impression for the Church. . . . I think as they competed on the basketball court, they gave a very good impression of sportsmanship and good-naturedness, besides their skill of the game and their athleticism. So they were a really good example for those that attended, and there was quite a few who used to attend the basketball games, and I'm sure they would have been impressed. . . .

When the decision was made to discontinue the Mormon Yankees and the missionaries playing in the basketball competition, . . . it was disappointing for the Saints because they enjoyed going to the games and watching them compete, so it was disappointing. But the Church leaders thought they should be proselyting more of the time instead of playing.

COLIN J. BURDETT

ADELAIDE, SOUTH AUSTRALIA, AUSTRALIA
JUNE 18, 2010

WHEN I REALLY get [got] into playing in the top grade, [I] was meeting all these new Australians who taught us how to play the game. The Mormon team, which was a fantastic team, I played against them for two years, and . . . I can only remember one player, . . . Elder [Loren C.] Dunn. They were so friendly, and of course they were a great, great team as well. . . . Our coach at the OBI, his wife used to put on some suppers after, and the Mormon boys would come along. They were so friendly. . . .

I can really remember Elder Dunn, mainly because of his size. He was a fairly large man, and he had an exceptional hook shot. He scored a great number of points. One of my colleagues from the Latvian team, George Dancis, used to guard him, but he had his problems, believe me. . . .

In my playing days, we were strictly amateur, and we had to go to work, and we paid for everything that, you know, boots and all our uniforms and subscriptions to the club. The only basketball boots we could get in those days, I think, came from Korea, and they would only last two or three games before we had a hole in the bottom of them. In fact, when I got selected for the Olympic team, I wrote to Abe Saperstein of the Harlem Globetrotters and told him that I'd been selected together with my club mate, Peter Sutton, who is now deceased, and I wrote to him and asked him if he could send us out a couple pairs of basketball boots. So what should arrive at the village but two pairs of Converse boots. I thought it was great on his part. . . .

We played the game fairly hard. What they do with the Sonics and the Lakers today, they used to say it's a noncontact sport, but I don't really go along with that. I can only say one thing, and that's that . . . the Mormon Yankees were real gentlemen when we played against them. . . . I know they didn't drink Coca-Cola and smoke and anything; I knew basically a little bit about their background, mainly because I ran into several of them and they'd given me their cards, which I kept for many years. . . .

They would have had a great impact, really, on not only the players but the spectators as well. The way they played, the way they conducted themselves, I couldn't speak any more highly of them, really, as a team. . . .

The OBI, which is *Our Boys Institute*, was a similar setup to the YMCA, where they conducted gymnasium sporting events. They had a skating rink there as well, which we played our basketball on, which was pretty hard to fall on, believe me. . . . Clubs were all within the OBI. We had, I think, eight teams. Most of them made up with the Mormons and Latvians, Lithuanians, Estonians, or a couple of YMCA [players].

CLIFF BURNS

MELBOURNE, VICTORIA, AUSTRALIA
DECEMBER 11, 2009

[IN YMCA BASKETBALL] I was only really conscious of eight senior teams, eight—it may have been twelve—and that was a senior teams of the best players and the best organizations, which was the only senior competition that I can remember. But it did involve the Mormons, the Latvians, the Church of England, the YCW (which is a Catholic organization), and other clubs as well. So as a senior competition, it wasn't a highly recognized sport in those days. In fact, there's—I would say probably there's only been maybe a couple thousand people playing. But once more facilities became available, the game itself absolutely expanded very, very rapidly. . . .

Prior to the Olympic Games, it was really starting to take tremendous strides, yes, and I think at that time they built a stadium which had nine courts, and . . . Lindsay Gaze, he was the manager of the center at that time, and once it developed, it gave enormous opportunities for basketball to go in leaps and bounds. . . .

The history that I was taught . . . was that once the Melbourne YMCA built the headquarters of the center itself, they had a three-quarter-sized basketball court. I'm not sure if there were any other courts around at that time, but from there in the [19]28s, they developed the basketball competition, and mainly, in those days, it was only senior personnel. It was men only, and I don't think the women came into it until probably the fifties sometime. But the basketball itself, . . . the YMCA invited other organizations to participate, and the senior competition was always played on a Monday night. . . .

My knowledge, particularly once I became involved with Melbourne headquarters, was that the senior competition of basketball with invitations to various other groups was on a Monday night. It was a very strong competition, even though it was in just—probably just over three-quarter-sized court. Then the Victorian Basketball Association would have their competition on a Wednesday night, and that was by far more powerful than the YMCA competition, eventually. . . . The beauty was that the skills of the game came here when Mormons, the Latvians, migrants, population was starting to come in, and these people, particularly from the European countries. . . . The interest in junior basketball at the phys[ical] ed[ucation] schools, high schools, tech schools really came in leaps and bounds. . . .

I think that they [the Mormon Yankees] had a very good impression, particularly—not so much with the senior teams, but with the spectators that were watching and the kids who brought parents, the parents who brought their children along. Particularly the boys in those days started to look and say, "This is a sport that we could play." The parents were interested a lot because technically it wasn't a physical competition, and that had a lot of influence as far as parents' concern. I think because the skills that they [the Mormon Yankees] brought at the game, and . . . I think it's true that because of their skills and because of the way that they represent themselves had a great impact, particularly on the younger generation.

RODNEY BURT

SPRINGVILLE, UTAH, USA
FEBRUARY 17, 2011

PRIOR TO MY mission call, I had played basketball in high school and junior varsity, mainly, but that was the bulk of my experience—of course and men's ball. But after that, it was just recreational while I was working and going to school. I received my call from the bishop in the first of September of 1954. Within three weeks, I had been interviewed by all of the important brethren and I was on my way to the mission home in Salt Lake. I got in as a waiver on the draft requirement, Selective Service, in the early days of the Korean War, and our ward was allowed one missionary, and that missionary had already received his call. And I came in from work one late Friday night, and my parents said, "The bishop wants to see you." So I went to see the bishop, and he says, "We've got an opening. I'd like you to go on a mission." And I wasn't planning on it because I knew the other elder had already received his call. Anyway, the paperwork started rolling, and I traveled to Lehi to visit with Thorpe B. Isaacson, who was a member of the Presiding Bishopric, and then within a week I had my call, and I was on my way to Australia in the first part of October, and it was a great experience. . . . I was called to the Australian Mission with no intent of participating in athletics. In fact, I wasn't even aware there was a basketball program being utilized in Australia, but I was thrilled to go. . . .

When I went to Australia, or when I went to Sydney, we went down to Melbourne for a Christmas conference, and I was assigned to Perth. Now, that's about as far away from Melbourne as you can get in Australia. I had heard that there were various missionaries playing sports with different teams in some leagues. There was a baseball player playing in Adelaide, a sister playing softball in Adelaide. Basketball players were playing with basketball teams, but [I] didn't think too much about it. Out in Perth you kind of become separated from the rest of the country. . . .

I was called to Melbourne in November of '55, and I was set apart as assistant to the [mission] president and began working with the mission presidency, and this is when the interest started to come up with respect to the having a basketball team to participate in competition, as the Olympics were coming to Melbourne that next fall. . . . When I came to Melbourne, I was under the distinct impression that basketball was not going to be a priority. In other words, we weren't going to press sports; we wanted the missionaries to do missionary work. And then I think Ken Watson approached President Bingham and asked him if they could have a team of Mormon Yankees to just give some experience and maybe even instruct the local people, athletes, with regards to basketball. And he said this—he said, "We'll make sure that you get publicity, and we will not force you to do anything that you don't want to do that's counter to what the missionaries are doing." . . . At this time Ken Watson, who was the executive secretary of the Victoria Basketball Association and who would later become the Olympic coach for the Australian Olympic team, came to President Bingham and asked him if the Church would be willing to sponsor a team in the local league in Victoria, and [Watson] stressed that they wouldn't ask the missionaries to interfere with their work but they just wanted their expertise. They would like help in coaching. They would like help in instruction. They just wanted to develop basketball in Victoria, and President Bingham came to me and said, "It looks like we're going to play basketball." So we stared organizing a team, and by April we had formed a team, calling ourselves the Mormon Yankees. . . .

I think President Bingham actually called Elder [DeLyle] Condie in and asked him if he would coach the team and if he would help develop a good team, and Elder Condie agreed, of course. . . .

Elder DeLyle Condie had been a star with the University of Utah basketball team. He was, I think, a starting center before he was called on his mission and a tremendous player, great talent, and he was the nucleus for the Mormon Yankees for that year. He was the coach. He was the one who patiently showed us how to play basketball, in effect. In other words, the Australians weren't the only ones learning how to play basketball. . . .

When I came to Melbourne, President Bingham felt like the missionaries were spending too much of their time involved in activities that weren't teaching the gospel, and it was distracting for an elder to play basketball and then go tracting, or it was distracting for an elder to have a companion to go play basketball. And it was getting to where there was quite a bit of time being taken from several missionaries to play sports and the returns are [not equal to] the benefits. It wasn't realized at the time, they didn't feel. So they felt like the missionaries would better serve their purpose to be missionaries rather than basketball player or baseball players or whatever. . . . In November [1955], I sat down with President Bingham, and he said, "We're going to have a basketball team, but we need to have certain parameters such that these elders aren't detracted [from] missionary work. So we'd like to set up a time to practice, maybe one day a week. We'd like to make sure that the games only go one or two days a week and that type of thing, and you are to work very closely with Elder Condie. Elder Condie will be the coach, and he might have an idea as to what players we can use and this type of thing." Well, we got together, Elder Condie and I, and we located missionaries with basketball experience, and the first time in my life I became a recruiter. We organized our missionaries such that we could get a fairly good team. Don Hull, who played for Utah State University, was a forward. Elder Condie was a starter for the University of Utah. Elder Kimball was a star with Provo High School. Elder Garn was a star in Sugar City, Idaho. We just gathered the talent wherever we could find it and got together a group of elders and just explained to them what our goal was. . . .

As we got into the league play, the media became very interested, particularly [in] stars like Elder DeLyle Condie and Elder Don Hull and players of that caliber. They hadn't seen that quality of play in Australia before, and the radio announcer for station 3 AW came to us, and he said, "I'm new to basketball." He says, "Will you help me out with the publicity for this basketball program?" And when we inquired of him, he said, "Well, I want you to write the news releases," and so we wrote . . . the news releases for the broadcast which came out on a weekly basis just prior to the games. It was very enjoyable how things just opened up and how we were able to work. As the season progressed, we only lost one game well into the season, and people were very impressed. . . .

We had as a member of the team . . . Kimball, and he had been writing, English, this type of thing, and he would write news releases for some of the newspapers whenever they requested it. We had, of course, the radio broadcast that we were interested in; we even had the team on the radio at one time to discuss what we were doing there as missionaries, what we were trying to accomplish. In indirect ways like that, we were able to get our message across. . . .

I remember early in 1956, a large building program was started in Australia, and it was going to be throughout the country. When President McKay came and Elder Romney came, they could see what very poor condition our meeting facilities were in. We were cleaning out beer halls on Saturday night or Sunday morning to have church, and very few chapels. . . . Well, in Australia we had an extreme amount of red tape, government regulations, and . . . we were getting more and more frustrated by the red tape. We just couldn't get started, and we went to our solicitor, our lawyer, and he said, "Well, that's just the way it is. It takes time." And when we asked him if there was any way that we could expedite it, he said, "I can't." He said, and I don't know why he said it, but he said, "I think you three could probably have an influence." So he gave us a name, and we went into Melbourne and met with this fellow. He was the director of planning, overseeing what went on in the cities, in Victoria, and we explained that we were from The Church of Jesus Christ of Latter-day Saints and that we were interested in building chapels, and we asked him what we could do to expedite it. And he said, "Nothing. There's just rules and regulations you've got to follow, and that's the way it's got to be, and it takes time." And then he stopped and he said, "Are you Mormons?" And we smiled and said, "Yes." And he says, "My son played on a team that your team beat last week, and my son thinks the world of the Mormon Yankees." And what he's told me. He says, "Your missionaries come out at their own expense—they come out with no expectations of rewards and spend two years teaching your message." And we said, "Yes." He said, "Come back next week. I think I can help you." And boy, things just started to open up, and we really got going with the Church building program in Victoria. I think a lot of it was because this fellow's son played against the Mormon Yankees. . . .

I would get weekly reports from the missionaries on their activities, and as they came in, invariably many of them would say, "The Mormon Yankees must have played this week. Someone saw your blurb in the newspaper, and they were very willing to talk." The Australian people liked Americans; they loved to be around them. They appreciated what they had done for them during the Second World War, and they loved Americans, but they didn't want anything to do with Mormons. When the Mormon Yankees started being successful, then when the connection was made, it broke down a lot of barriers, and the missionaries, I think, had a tremendous opportunity to teach the gospel because of it. . . .

President Bingham . . . instructed me—he said, "Now when the missionaries get off the ship, of course, we always interview each and every one of them with the idea of assigning them a field of labor." He said, "I want you to ask one more question, 'Are you a basketball player?'" And of course, if they had had experiences of basketball, we would ask Elder Condie to talk to this missionary. That way we tried to involve members with experience; it was fascinating. Something was interesting—I always smiled about those missionary interviews. When that question was asked, you'd get almost a dumbfounded look from the missionary. . . . I wasn't aware of any concerted effort on the part of Salt Lake to send missionaries with basketball experience, but I was amazed at the number that showed up on the docks and that were there to teach the gospel that had played basketball at some point in their lives. It was interesting to me how that came about and how the players were there when we needed them. . . .

I think that the Mormon Yankee program helped the members with a sense of identity. It helped the members develop something that was a goal to strive for. We were getting good publicity for the Church, and very seldom would the Church get a good publicity prior to this time. . . . Members of the Church were approached on the street, and [people] said, "Oh, those Mormon Yankees are doing great." . . . It impacted their lives from the standpoint that they could see something good that was giving a good perspective of Mormonism. . . .

I would like to say to the Australian people through my basketball experience, thank you for the experience. It was great to meet all the people we met, to see the various teams and participate with them. I don't know how many meals they served us after games or after tournaments, that type of thing, but they were very hospitable. We couldn't have been treated better. Even when we trounced one of their teams, the crowd didn't like it, but they came to us afterwards and were very friendly towards us. And I've always appreciated that because they were good sports; they appreciated ability. . . .

I think the legacy of the Mormon Yankees during that period opened up the country more to the teachings of the gospel. I think people became much more receptive because of the image that the Mormon Yankees projected, and I think it affected a lot the membership growth during those next few years. I understand there was a rapid growth of the church in Australia. But I think the Mormon Yankees were part of that, and I think they contributed by just being Mormon Yankees.

BISHOP H. DAVID BURTON

SALT LAKE CITY, UTAH, USA
SEPTEMBER 7, 2010

I THINK THAT most of the young men we had the opportunity of either competing against or assisting in one way or another felt there was something different about [the Mormon Yankees]. There wasn't the typical Yankee that they were used to. You know, this was only thirteen years after World War II. World War II was still very, very vivid in the minds of the Australians. It was a time when anybody from North America, and particularly from the United States, was appreciated because of what happened during World War II. Australia was on the verge of being overrun by the Japanese. Just a few landings in the northern part of Australia and a few miscellaneous shells lobbed into Sydney Harbor was really about the only thing that took place there, but it was the United States' military presence that was very important in that era. Along with the good, there was also the reputation that sometimes was not appropriate there, and some of the activities of some of the military were not pleasing to many of the population. So there was a little bit of a reputation to live down, in some ways. I think most people of other faiths that we associated with felt there was something different about this cadre of young men [and] young women who were serving their Father in Heaven in Australia. . . .

I hope that when the history of that period of time settles in that basketball will take its appropriate place as one of the many things that missionaries did while they were there to build the Church. It wasn't the thing; it wasn't the end of all ends, but it was certainly an integral part of giving good publicity: faithful young men who were devoting their lives to the work of the Lord to introduce the gospel to the people in Australia. I hope that will be a part of the legacy, plus the fact that each, that I'm aware of, have been successful since they served there; they've been good spokespersons for Australia. They have raised righteous families; they have been leaders in the Church and gone on to give great service. . . .

A lot of these [Australian members] were second and third generations, but in some cases they were almost closet members of the Church. They didn't have any reason to go out and say, "Yes, I'm a Mormon." But with a little bit of success in the athletic endeavor, then some of these people were a lot more inclined to—I will say be full of pride—but at least have an opportunity for them to have a conversation, a positive conversation, and remind people what was taking place and who was a part of that and that they were a part of that organization. They felt an organizational pride and organizational enthusiasm, so it helped them that way, as well as introducing people to the Church. . . .

It was a time when mission presidents were still very cognizant that converts to the Church were not to be made just because they played basketball or because they saw the team play, but that they had a full quotient of lessons. They [went] through all of the discussions, they attended their meetings, they demonstrated their worthiness, and all of that went into the formula for success in that part of the world. It wasn't just a fling; it wasn't just a use of a gimmick. It was genuinely used to bring good publicity to the Church and introduce individuals to the gospel of Jesus Christ.

RICHARD D. CHRISTENSEN

SALT LAKE CITY, UTAH, USA
FEBRUARY 17, 2011

I WAS ALWAYS interested in basketball—had a great hoop out in the backyard, had great friends that played. I got cut from high school basketball [team]; all of my friends [were] much taller and were great athletes. I watched them from the band platform. However, I did play a lot of Church basketball. In fact, my senior year in high school, we took second place in the all-region tournament in Salt Lake City. We had a good little ward team, and we went a long way. . . .

[I] hadn't ever thought of basketball as a missionary, and when I got there, I realized that basketball was not a sport in Australia until just those recent years. In fact, when we did play our games, we didn't ever have a shower to go to: it was Johnson's Baby Powder that we could put on us before we finally left the game. But no, I had no plans that we would be playing basketball while we were on our missions. . . .

As the basketball team started to be considered, it had a lot to do with the teams in the south, around the Olympics in Melbourne, Australia, in 1956. And it turned out that their teams were playing the Chinese and other teams, and so we were given permission to go ahead and go to a basketball setting. It was really interesting. Our mission was a hat mission; we wore hats all the time, and so we got a gold and green uniform with high socks. . . . And when we would then got permission to play and the leagues were set up and the team members from the missionaries were selected, we went on our different route of playing the many teams throughout the northern-eastern Australian area. We would warm up in our long socks and wearing our hats. It got us a lot of notice, so that we were out on the streets and meeting people in the parks, a lot of them had heard from us . . . through the Mormon Yankee basketball team. . . .

We didn't have a car; there was only one car in the mission, and that was the mission president's down in Sydney. But a great train system, the old choo-choo, plenty of black smoke. To keep our shirts white, we had to wear handkerchiefs around our collars to keep them from being ruined when we went through a tunnel and the black locomotive smoke came into the windows. We traveled together and, you know, ate together and slept together. We stayed at members' homes. But a lot of our playing was in the major cities of Brisbane and Sydney. . . . It helped us be known because not only do we play, and they came and watched us, but there are newspaper articles and radio experiences that allowed people to say, "Oh yes, we have heard of you," or, "We saw you," and it made a difference when we went to the door. We did all tracting in those years. . . .

We did have halftime presentations, and we did interviews. Having had radio experience and television experience at the University of Utah, I was a player on the team unless we could get permission from a local radio station to broadcast the game over their frequency. That became my opportunity because I had been trained in it. What they wanted to hear was a play-by-play description of a Yankee voice doing Australian commercials. The main commercial that I did time after time was advertising the Hillman Minx automobile, the overhead cam, all kinds of things. But then when the play of the game took place, then I was able to give the play-by-play just like you would hear today. This allowed me, during timeouts and other times, to interview players, and, at the end of the show, to be interviewed and to talk about what we were doing there and . . . why we loved basketball and why weren't we at home either going to school or getting married, who paid our way. It allowed us to have all of those experiences to describe to people. . . .

Well, we planned ahead. We had our schedules and our areas that we were going to be tracting and our cottage meetings all on a schedule, and then we'd block out the time necessary for the basketball travel and the game. I can tell you that none of it was wasted. We didn't have any freebies; there weren't movies on the side and extra luncheon engagements. We went right to our responsibility, as I remember it, and concluded it, and then hurried back to our areas. . . .

I would hope that would be the legacy, that the preaching of the gospel expanded. When we were first there, it was all one mission, the whole nation, and now it's, what, eight or ten missions. I would hope that those Mormon Yankee teams opened the doors and made people realize that we weren't just a small little religion without a real doctrine but that we were a dedicated group of young men and older couples that wanted to accomplish something by bringing them into the fold of knowledge and testimony.

DELYLE H. CONDIE

SALT LAKE CITY, UTAH, USA
JULY 7, 2010

IN MY LAST visit with Coach Gardner, in his office, he seemed kind of bent on changing my mind [about my decision to serve a mission]. He pulled up some films, their University of Utah's basketball trip to Hawaii, which they'd taken two years before, so my sophomore year. When I was playing on the varsity, we didn't have that trip, but the year before they did it, and they usually did it every second year. Brought those films out and put them on screen, and before he said anything, and when they were finished, he said, "You're going to miss this, because we're going next year to Hawaii again. This sort of thing you're missing." And I said, "Coach, I've really decided it's the thing to do. It's the right time in my life; I want to go, and I am going to go on a mission." In a nice way—he wasn't threatening at all—but he said, "If you go on your mission, I don't think you'll ever play again." And I said, "Well, I still want to go." So we get over to Australia by ship, first night or second night we're there, Elder Johnson and Elder Christensen were playing on a recreation team, just as members of the team. They had been playing there even before President Bingham replaced whoever he replaced as mission president. They invited my companion and I, Elder Benson and myself, to go with them. On the way in, as they picked us up from the train station, they talked about basketball. They both had played at the U [University of Utah], so we talked about various things. Basketball was one of them. At any rate, they invite us to go, we went, and they played for the championship that night, their team did. And when we came back after the game was over, President Bingham was of course interested in how they'd done and disappointed a little bit, I'm sure, that they'd lost, but called us into his room, his office there, and talked with us for a while. And one of the comments he made was, "I hope you both know, all know, that this will be the last basketball we play. We didn't come here on our missions to play basketball." I felt fine about that. I hadn't expected to play basketball; it wasn't the reason I went on a mission. It was only a few months later—that was September 1, I believe, when I arrived in Australia. By Christmastime, I was now laboring in Tasmania, and all of the missionaries around the mission field were brought into, in those days, into Melbourne, and we went down to a YMCA camp for a week, ten days, two weeks—it was quite a period of time during the Christmas holidays. The general feeling was that during Christmastime, nothing gets accomplished missionary-work-wise because everyone's celebrating. Anyway, we had a lot of fun there, pardon me, and played sports, did all kinds of things. Of later time, I was called back into Melbourne. When I got back there, I was asked to pick out missionaries who would be part of a team of missionaries who would be willing to participate in this recreation league that had been going on for years in Melbourne. I was surprised, of course, having heard and remembered what he [President Bingham] had said, but his comment was to me that the Brethren had either suggested or approved whatever the comment was. It was clear to me that this had been cleared by the First Presidency and we were to have a basketball team and participate in it. . . .

I often wondered why we were playing, why there had been a change in a very, very definite opinion of missionaries not being there to play basketball expressed by Pres. Bingham. I'd always wondered about it. Well, my wife and I just a few years ago were able to serve in a form of a mission, doing legal work with the Church, the General Counsel's office, in Sydney. Had the opportunity, given permission, to go down to Melbourne and to visit with Lindsay Gaze. Lindsay Gaze had been the coach of the Australian Olympic team and was so for four Olympics, which was really an unbelievable thing for someone to be honored that way. . . . He said Ken Watson, . . . the head of the Olympic basketball team, . . . had gone to President Bingham early on and suggested that the Olympic Games were on the schedule and were coming up; they were forming, of course, selecting their Olympic players; and that they would appreciate the opportunity to have some competition, some players who maybe had some talent and some experience, like the Yankees did. There were Mormon kids had played over the years on some of the recreation league teams, but at any rate, he told Pres. Bingham that it would be a great proselyting tool for the Church, a benefit to the Church, and that he saw that it would be a great benefit to them when they were getting ready for the Olympic Games. . . . Pres. Bingham called me back into the office and told me about this and said, "They've asked us to put together"—this is after the team had played in the recreation league—"asked us to play the Olympic teams in the exhibition games," and we did that. I think we played them five times over a period of a couple of months. We always had good crowds out and always played well, fortunately. We were able to win each game, which was not important then, of course. I think they enjoyed the competition. On occasion they'd ask us to tell them a little bit about how we trained and how we practiced and those sorts of things, which we were able to pass on to them. . . . It was a great experience for us and [a] good thing for the Church. . . .

I have thought over the years, and looking back on this whole experience, that I was led to make the decisions that I made, to get on a mission, for a reason. I mean, all of us have reasons for doing the things we do in our lives. Fortunately, I was able to go to Australia and to participate in this particular event, or events, and do some good that otherwise may not have been done, at least to the scale or the extent it was done. I don't know whether Pres. [David O.] McKay had any of this in mind when he went over to Australia. I think, my impression is that when he went to Australia, he saw great opportunity for the building of the kingdom in Australia. The fact that the stakes were being formed shortly after this period of time, that the temples eventually followed that, during the period of time that we were serving, that is our group of missionaries. Building plans were being made by . . . Brother Mendenhall. He was there in Australia; he was looking for sites to build chapels. I think there was a feeling—I don't have any factual basis for this—but a feeling that the Brethren thought that there were going to be great things happening in that part of the world. I think the

Mormon Yankee basketball team and the experience then and after we were gone by those other missionaries who played and participated was just part of building of the kingdom, and to us, it was a very important part, very enjoyable part, a very satisfying part, but just part of the greater picture. . . .

What the people in Australia knew about Mormons were two things. They knew about polygamy. They knew about the Mormon Tabernacle Choir. The Mormon Tabernacle Choir was a great proselyting tool for us. I even had a person, when my companion and I knocked on a door, then we asked at the doorstep the church they belonged to. When they said, "We have our church," and we said, "Well, what church is that? I belong to the Tabernacle Choir church." There were broadcasts in Australia during this period of time of the Mormon Tabernacle Choir. People listened to those, and they knew about it, and it was a great positive thing for the Church. This was another positive thing I firmly believe that the Church [used] as it developed. . . .

While we were playing in the recreation league, and of course, it was magnified even greater as we had finished that league and started playing with some of the Olympic teams and with the Australian Olympic team for a number of games. We found articles in the newspapers every time. Australians are sports crazy. There would be an article about the games the day after. The games were played on a Wednesday night, and they would report who won, and they would report who scored the points. You know, anything like you would see in a regular sports article. They'd sometimes have little bits and pieces on people, particularly the Americans. If they played college ball, or if they came from a place that was unusual, or something like that, they would put little tidbits in. We found people who knew about the Mormon Yankees, either from the newspapers or from friends or someone who had gone to the games. The arena where we played the regular league games was not a big place. It was like what I would classify here as maybe a US Army armory or something, you know, with a big hall, and they'd made a basketball court out of it. That's the sort of place we played most of the times. We would have two hundred to three hundred people in attendance, and a lot of those were members of the Church. They loved to come and see us play, but publicity was good. We found people who had read about us in the newspaper as we knocked on doors. As we got into—the Olympic Games got closer and we were playing the Australian Olympic team, we found that even more people knew about the Mormon Yankees, and they became friendlier to us as we approached them. They didn't always let us into their homes, but at least they were kind to us and spoke well of us and were friendly, you know. They seemed to enjoy it and appreciate what we were doing. . . . Basketball at the time was not a big sport, but it was coming into its own; people were getting interested in it, but anything that dealt with sports was interesting, and they loved, and they appreciated. They admired, they almost worshipped people who are athletes, good athletes. . . .

The only people that I can remember who really asked me about basketball was the Russian [Olympic basketball] group. They wanted to know what conditioning we used, what conditioning methods, and it was almost embarrassing to say, "It's very simple: we live the Word of Wisdom." We explained what that was through an interpreter, and they all kind of looked. I don't think they were surprised that we didn't drink alcohol or smoke, because they'd seen us, but practice once a week. They would have been practicing every day. . . .

In choosing the teams we played in this buildup to the Olympic Games, we were asked through Ken Watson what teams we'd like to play. A number of them wanted to play us because they didn't have anyone else to play. The rules at the time with the Olympics were that teams could not play each other. So we were one team that they could play without offending any rules. . . . I was given the choice of teams that we would play, and they gave us the names of the ones who wanted to do that. We played Chile—we played in that arena; we played France; we played the Philippines. Prior to those, that group of games, we played at various places around the Australian Olympic team. We played them five times. . . . It was made aware that the team representing China, which was really at that time from the island of Formosa, they came in as the Chinese representative because the Games didn't recognize China, Communist China, as being the real country, the real government in charge. We became aware that they [the Nationalist Chinese team] would like to play us, but the games were already over. They were sticking around, staying to watch some of the other Olympic sports, and someone put it together. . . .

During the time that, in between, I guess, the league games and the Olympic Games, we were supposed to—we were scheduled to play the Olympic Team in Bendigo, I believe it was, which is a fairly decent-sized city just north of Melbourne. We went as a team to it [and] became aware when we got there that for some reason, the game had been cancelled. There was not an arena, a basketball arena, in Bendigo that we knew of, and it was scheduled to be played in the prison yard of the state penitentiary. We showed up there, became aware there was not going to be a game; we're already there. Somebody from the penitentiary office said, "Hey, we've got a team. Why don't you play us?" So we said, "We're here. All right." So we played the prison team. And there are rows of seats; this is an outdoor concrete court with baskets and a row or two of chairs on one side and a row or two of chairs on the other. We started as we always did in Australia, and it wasn't our decision. They always played "Sweet Georgia Brown," which was the theme song for the Harlem Globetrotters. Every time we played in a recreation league, that's what the warm-ups were about. It was amazing. They had it there, and so we're going in, and you know, you feel a little music, and so you're kind of in sync with the music when you go in and you put your layups and so forth; there were a couple of us who could dunk the ball. One was Paul Grant, Elder Grant, and I could. And so, I don't know how it happened, but as we're warming up, there are guys on this side, yelling over, "Hey, Peter," or "Ian," or whatever a guy's name was, Yanks, and the guy would say, "I'll take it," or "I'll give you ten points," or whatever. They were betting who was going to win the game. Almost all of them were betting on us, but the point spread would change, and so one of us goes in and stuffs the ball. This guy says, "Hey, Peter, the odds went up." Instead of giving him ten points, they might say it was now fifteen points. Then the other one goes right in, the next one, and dunks it, and the guy yells over, "Hey, Peter, Yanks twenty points." I mean, that was the funniness of it, is that they were betting on us, and here we are, missionaries, and because we could dunk, the odds went up, of course. . . . The thing that was nice about it, they treated us so well, with so much respect. As you come out of the game and sit down, the guy on maybe the second row would take off his parka, jacket, whatever it was, because it was cold, and come up and put it on you. It was that kind of stuff. There had to be some good there, good public relations in terms of these people. . . .

These missionaries who were on our basketball team were some of the finest missionaries in our mission. I had the opportunity to serve in a couple of the states as a supervising elder, so I knew what was going on with them in terms of those who got into the homes and those who were baptizing and those who were passing out copies of the Book of Mormon, because we kept those sorts of records. They were always very high on our materials, our reports. Five or six of them became supervising elders. . . . As I say, the impact on us, playing basketball, made me a better missionary. It, I believe, made them better missionaries because you had a diversion from the drudgery of knocking on doors, which is how we proselyted in those days. And so you got out of that drudgery on a Wednesday night when you played and on a Saturday morning when you took part of your P-day [preparation day] to practice. It was a healthy thing, and I believe that it was much good done for the missionaries involved, and I'm satisfied to know that people of Australia, in general, have come to appreciate Mormons in a different light partly because of that.

MARIE CRAY

MELBOURNE, VICTORIA, AUSTRALIA
DECEMBER 14, 2009

WHEN I WAS young, I was fortunate enough to attend religious schools. When I was fourteen, I was still at school—well, maybe thirteen when we first met the missionaries, yes. It was a very conservative Presbyterian girl school. Religious instruction was a weekly thing. It really meant that in those days. We studied the Bible, and I love doing that, and I had thought that I might like to be a nun for a while, but the trouble was that I just couldn't come to terms with the Godhead, the Nicene Creed, and that sort of thing. So that troubled me. One day when I went home from school, my mother said that two missionaries had knocked on the door and while she wasn't really interested, they had been very kind to her. She had my grandmother living with us, who was having a very difficult time, and she invited the missionaries to come back, which they did. So then my mother said, "Well, you're interested in religion. You should meet them," but I knew that they wouldn't have anything to say that would interest me. Presbyterians are very conservative, and what would Americans know about religion? Eventually we came to the stage where I did meet them when I came home, and I particularly asked them about the doctrine and about the Nicene Creed and their views on that, and when they explained their own church's doctrine, I think I knew straightaway that that was right. In those days, we were given quite a few months to go to church and to study and to really understand what it would entail to become a member of The Church of Jesus Christ of Latter-day Saints. So I was baptized in August 1951. . . .

I don't remember packed stadiums watching the games. I don't recall that there were a lot of spectators at all, really, except the few Church members are the only ones we're involved with, and because the Church was so small at the time, just a little group in East Melbourne, the missionaries were part of the Church family, more or less. We were more involved with them then and perhaps than we are now because it was so tiny. So we were involved in just barracking for them and making sure that we knew they wouldn't play foul, of course, and we didn't want the other side to as well, so there was a lot of fussing if we felt that the others weren't playing fairly. But I don't remember a lot of spectators. . . .

Basketball wasn't a very big sport in Melbourne at that time. In fact, I don't think I'd heard of it before the missionaries started to play, because the Australian football was the sport you heard most about, and that was a man's game, whereas basketball seemed to be more of a sissy game, and so it didn't engender the same enthusiasm for the sport. And I don't think it got a lot of coverage in the press either, but I'm not sure about that because I didn't even follow Australian-rules [football] very well. But I know that real men played football out in the elements, rain, hail, or shine, sliding around in the mud, running up and down on the grassy ovals, whereas for the missionaries inside, it was a little more refined and civilized inside, away from the cold and the rain, played it on nice, polished boards, not too far to run either way. You couldn't get into too much trouble because everybody's eyes were upon you. You were in such a little, focused group. . . .

I think by their demeanor in playing, but also in their faces, you could see that these were really good-living boys, young men, and naturally I felt that it was the right thing to do to join the Church. . . . When people took the opportunity to get to know them and to see what their sporting prowess was like—not just their skill, but their ability to play the game without resorting to fouls all the time, anything like that at all—I think all that helped to open doors for people. . . . I think that's what made us so proud of them, really. . . . Most of the stories heard about Mormons in those times were about all their wives, and they're a strange sect, and, of course, lies about things that they would do and used to do and why they were here, but any close contact with them converted people straightaway—if not to the Church, to the knowledge that they were good-living people.

LORNA CULLIS

MELBOURNE, VICTORIA, AUSTRALIA
DECEMBER 10, 2009

EVEN THOUGH IN Australia basketball was nothing, my brother-in-law, Ron Cutts, played basketball with the YMCA for years. And as the basketball stadium was built, and Lindsay Gaze's parents were the administrators of the stadium complex—Lindsay was a younger man and very interested in basketball, and so of course he and Ron got to be close friends and did a lot for basketball and establishing the basketball that we have in Australia now, which is [a] fairly quite healthy sport. We have quite a number of basketball competitions throughout the whole country. But before the war, before the Olympic Games, it was absolutely not even thought of. No kid ever wanted to learn to play basketball, or very, very, very few. . . .

When the Olympic Games came to Melbourne, it was such an exciting time for Melbournians and Australians collectively, and then when we had this magnificent Mormon Yankee team formed, who was sent out here to specifically play, and they were big, strong, healthy fellows. . . . We were lucky enough to go to a few of the games, but my husband, Bert, in particular. But I remember going to the Russian–Mormon Yankee game, which was so exciting because these Russian boys—and one in particular was just a giant. He was a goliath of a boy, but he . . . wasn't a really vivid athlete. And he was standing flatfoot near the goal area all the time, and he would just stop them every time they would come up, and so our boys would try and think of strategies of how to get past the block of the concrete man who was just standing there. And they did; they were smart enough to work it out, and it was just such an exciting thing. . . . It was such an exciting day to see them there, our heroes playing these giants. . . . I can remember Mark [Elder Frodsham] being so hyped up with excitement, . . . so hyped up that he could hardly talk. He was so excited, and the adrenaline was just absolutely flowing. . . . I can't explain the sort of inner joy that was coming out of the man and the team in general. . . . They were very good-looking young men, and they were beautiful, and they were exciting. They were young. They were single. And girls were ready to flock after them very gladly. . . .

I think they had an impact on the . . . sporting ethic. I think that they had an effect on how the younger people viewed sport. Sport is a good thing, not as such a competition, "I'm going to get you" thing. You know. They were such clean-cut and good and such a good example that it did have an effect on the youth. . . .

For me, the legacy of the Mormon Yankees is tremendously important because not only did it change the face of basketball in Melbourne, but it changed the course of my personal life because of Mark [Elder Frodsham] having such an effect on my husband, who was not a member of the Church and had no intention of becoming a member of the Church. And because of Mark's goodness and all of the things that he was to us, he had such an effect on Bert that it has changed not only the face of basketball; it has changed my whole life. . . . We just loved it when they were here. It was an exciting time, a wonderful time, and a hugely growing time for the people in the Church. The Church in Australia became a different situation entirely, because it suddenly stopped being this little few people, and it started to grow. . . .

I do think that having the Mormon Yankees play here had an effect on a lot of people who were interested in sport, because it allowed people to be more accepting of the Mormon people as a whole, and it allowed people to see that we weren't odd or different, that we were just ordinary good folk. And it made it more accepting to listen to the missionary message than it may have been before that happened, because when they were here in this area, those first missionaries in this area, I opened the door to them and said, "Come in."

GEORGE DANCIS

ADELAIDE, SOUTH AUSTRALIA, AUSTRALIA
JUNE 17, 2010

I CAME IN contact with basketball after the war, in 1946; [we] used to have, in the German camp, a little service fort field for the army. Two baskets; we didn't have any balls. . . . We went to high school, and I played in a high school team, and then I came out to Australia in '49. In those days, [you] went to school in the afternoon, and the rest of the day was yours. And since you lived in the camp, you didn't have to go to any drill holes. . . .

We would have preferred to go to the States, but since our family was Mother, me, and Mike, they didn't take us because Mike was underage. I was just seventeen, you know. I was declared a single man, so my mother was looking after Mike, and that goes a bit on the risky deal. The only place that took us [Latvians] was Australia. I suppose maybe we could have gone to Venezuela or someplace else. . . .

There was a difference, sure, because you came from the other side of the world, and [it was a] different setup all together. Australia only had seven million people, and you know, it didn't have the quality that Europe had, so I think these displaced persons put a bit of fresh air in the Australian sense and vice versa. . . . We sort of looked around and found out how many of our Latvian players [were] ready for playing basketball, and then we . . . established our own team, and we had a place in the top league. . . .

It was pretty rough; the floors were concrete, and some people did sort of tackles and whatnot. But we had a few injuries, but not many—we just got up and went on again. . . . [Loren C.] Dunn was a fairly big player; [we] had a bit of a contest under the basket and so forth. . . . The Mormons were playing fair and square, but I mean, in those days, the referees were very tough, so you couldn't do any pushing and shoving, like things happen today, you know; you were sent off the court. All you had to do [was] some misnomer, and you were out on a limb, you know. . . .

We didn't discuss much religion. . . . I mean, we were Lutheran, and we never had inclination to turn into Mormons, but nevertheless, we had a couple of Latvian[s] just that were in the Mormon Church. . . . I can't remember anybody asking me to convert to the Mormon [faith]. Well, we had contact, but we didn't have that much contact; mostly we had each a basketball, and we discussed—if we met on the street, we were talking about basketball. . . . I think that the Mormons coming in the competition, that helped everybody: everybody all took notice.

MIKE DANCIS

ADELAIDE, SOUTH AUSTRALIA, AUSTRALIA
JUNE 17, 2010

THERE ARE SOME three thousand Latvians who came to Adelaide [in the mid-twentieth century] and that formed quite a strong community, and we stuck together because of language barriers and other things with people here in Adelaide, and basketball was one of the things that people really enjoyed on Thursday nights. Across from the church, there was Our Boys Institute, a gym. On the first floor it had a roller-skating rink, concrete floor, . . . and . . . there was a running track, and that was filled with Latvians and Lithuanians, Estonians. And they came every Thursday to watch the game, so it was packed every Thursday night, and that sort of cemented the community with the basketball. That's where most of those people were exposed to the Mormon basketball, and they certainly enjoyed that.

PERCIVAL WILLIAM FREDERICK DAVIS

MELBOURNE, VICTORIA, AUSTRALIA
DECEMBER 11, 2009

IN 1951, I was living at South Crescent, Northcote, Victoria, and there was a knock on the door, and when I opened the door, there were two Latter-day Saint missionaries there. One of them was Elder Bishop, and he started telling me about the gospel. I was in a particular hurry at that time because I had to visit a cousin of mine in the hospital and I barely had half an hour to travel into Melbourne, so as Elder Bishop was talking to me, I was thinking about the fact that I had this engagement. Anyhow, he had to stop for breath eventually, and I said to him, "Sounds interesting, come back next week." And that's how it all started. . . . I was baptized almost a year after that. In the meantime, I attended church every week. . . .

Basketball was played in most church groups with amateurs, of course. As a competition, it wasn't universally known or accepted. Very few people attended basketball games. In the 1950s, leading up the Olympics, it received a lot of publicity. I think that's when Australian basketball really took off. . . .

. . . I remember when the name was given to the basketball team. We already had a basketball team then, and it was the Church LDS basketball team, but the name Mormon Yankees was given to them during

President Bingham's time. . . . I remember going to one of the pre-Olympic games, and it was against France. The Olympic committee in Melbourne had built a special stadium for basketball that held about five thousand people. It wasn't a huge building, but it was a good building. . . . And on that particular occasion, the building was filled with people. It was literally packed. The Mormon Yankees played a game against France which was a spectacular game, very interesting, very close, and we won by two points. And there was just pandemonium in the building; everyone cheered because the Mormon Yankees had won. And those who were cheering weren't all Church members by any means because the Church was very sparse at that time. A lot of them were not members of the Church. . . . The most vivid memory that I have of that game was the final few seconds when the Mormon Yankees—one of the Mormon Yankees hit the basket, and we won by two points, and that's when pandemonium broke out. Everyone cheered; it was an exciting [moment]. I was very proud, wonderfully proud, because I knew these young missionaries, of course, and here they were beating the French team. . . .

I could mention the article I read in the newspaper about Elder Condie. We had a newspaper at that time called the *Sporting Globe*, and it was full of sporting talk: football, cricket, whatever was being played, and they had a half page in one edition of it confined solely to Elder Condie, about his life, what he was doing out here, and different details about him, and I thought that was a great possibility for people to read and also to become interested in the Church. . . .

The Mormon Yankees played against the Russian team, and the Russian team were runners-up in the Olympics that year, and the game was played in an army military hall in East Melbourne. There weren't many people there. The Russian team wanted to win, and they were very rough, rough and ready, and they weren't afraid to knock the boys around. Russia won by about nine or ten points; there wasn't much in it, really. It was a close game. As I say, Russia were runners-up in the Olympics; it's a wonderful, wonderful record. . . . I do remember Russia's determination to win—at all costs, really—and the way that the boys responded to it, played very fairly, just gentlemen. . . . I was proud of the way that the Mormon Yankees conducted themselves under their circumstances, because they could have easily been provoked by the opposition. I thought they were examples to anyone who was there. . . .

I think that possibly President Bingham had the full consent about the missionary program [more] than the basketball program, and I surmise that it was some pressure from some of the Victorian basketball players [for] the Mormon Yankees [to play], and [the Victorian players] learned a lot from [the Mormon Yankees]. So I think there was some pressure from that angle to President Bingham to allow the Mormon Yankees to continue on. And it was such a big decision that I think that President Bingham would have conferred with the First Presidency in Salt Lake City and received permission for them to continue. I think that's what happened, really. . . .

I'm sure that [the Mormon Yankees] helped the basketball game in Australia to a tremendous degree, and I have a personal testimony of that from Lindsay Gaze, who has been the manager of the Australian basketball team for a number of Olympics. And I had a discussion with him just a few years ago, and we spoke about the Mormon Yankees, and I said, "What do you think about the Mormon Yankees, Lindsay?" He said, "Before they came here, we were just basketball players. We would get the ball and try to hit the basket. When they came, they taught us the science of the game." He said, "DeLyle Condie was a great communicator," and he also mentioned an Elder Skousen, and he said, "He was one of the greatest basketball players I've met." He said, "Victorian basketball particularly owes a lot to the Mormon Yankees."

SHERM DAY

DAWSONVILLE, GEORGIA, USA
FEBRUARY 15, 2011

I DON'T HAVE a lot of business experience per se. I finished two years at BYU before I left for my mission, and I was a math major and chemistry minor, but I met some people who did [have business experience], like Bob Pedersen. And so when we started thinking about taking the Mormon Yankees on tours, of course there's financial considerations, and so I knew we had to raise some money. So I went to my good friend and sometime companion Bob and said, "We need to raise some money if we're going to do this tour for the Mormon Yankees and go to all these sites," and Bob said, "I can do it." He'd been a pots and pans salesman, so he didn't know that you [could] say no. He was very optimistic; he said, "We'll do it." So we set some goals. I read in my journal just yesterday that we asked . . . [a] company for three pairs of shoes for each player; we asked another company for basketballs, four new basketballs; and the big one was Bob asked Volkswagen to provide us a [VW] Kombi van that we could drive around; and also, they came in and said, "We'll not only provide you the Kombi van; we'll provide the publicity in each town. As you come, we'll advertise it in the papers." So that was—so really I'd have to say that my stroke of luck was finding good people to help who knew how to do that. . . .

This all started with a personal priesthood interview with President

Zelph Erekson, who was the mission president. He called me in and said he would like me to be in charge of the Mormon Yankees in Sydney for the year '59. I was extremely flattered, and I knew all the fellows that had played, and it was a great experience. And I said to him at that time, "President Erekson, are you willing to explore taking this Mormon Yankee thing to even greater heights, to assist us in proselyting?" And he said, "Absolutely. What do you have in mind?" And I said, "I think we ought to go to a couple of cities that surround here where we've got missionaries, or where we want to put missionaries, and we ought to have the Mormon Yankees play their town team and leave these missionaries, or introduce these missionaries, and I think we can generate a lot of goodwill off of the goodwill that the Mormon Yankees have." And he said, "Elder Day, that's a pretty bold plan. How many cities do you think we should go to?" And I said, "Two," and it later turned out to be far more than that, but that's as big as I could think of at that time. He said, "Flesh it out. I'm going to be released as mission president; a new mission president will be coming in a couple of months, and we can present the idea and see how it goes." So that was the genesis. That happened; the new mission president liked the idea. By that time we had sponsors lined up, and it was basically a go, and we started notifying towns that we were available, and one thing led to another, and pretty soon we were riding around Australia. . . .

As we visited these towns—and we wrote letters to the federations and asked them if they would like us to visit. Now we actually were on the shoulders of the goodwill of all the Mormon teams that played in Australia. The Mormons were known for basketball, either these two people on a local team or this team—there must have been thirty or forty Mormon Yankee teams in Australia. We happened to be the Sydney team—it was a big city and maybe the best-known of all the Mormon Yankee teams—and so as we rode to these people, they were glad to have us. In terms of leaving the missionaries, we made sure they were introduced at halftime. As we gave each of the opposing players a Book of Mormon and they gave us a souvenir, usually a tea strainer or a spoon of some kind, we would introduce our entertainer, Roger Bown, [who] would say, "And now we've got a big treat for you. Come on out, Elder Gardner and Elder Smith. These two gentlemen are going to stay, and they're going to live for the next several months in Forbes, and they're going to be walking around; stop and say hello to them when you see them." . . .

We found along the way that, as we blended in with the culture of the community, that sometimes we were put on the spot a little bit and up against the principles of the Word of Wisdom. For instance, it was very common to be invited out for drinks after, and so this was an occasion to explain to people that we don't drink alcoholic beverages, but we'd love to meet them and enjoy the association, and if they wanted pictures or autographs or something like that—and so it didn't become an issue because people were learning about us, and they respected us for it. One of the more humorous things happened in two locations where the community invited us and had a dance on behalf of the Mormon Yankees. One time after discussing this, all of the team was back at the hotel, and I went back to the hotel and said, "The community is having a dance in our honor, and I think we should not disappoint them or embarrass them. And so I told them we'll dance, and I've already picked out ten young ladies; each of you will be responsible for one of them tonight." I wished I could capture the look on their face[s]. . . . So needless to say, we didn't dance, but we went and watched. . . .

It's interesting the schedule we followed. We would usually drive into a town around two o'clock in the afternoon, and we would drop by the Volkswagen dealer because they were our sponsor, and they would provide us with some refreshments and things like that. And then we were scheduled to go to the local schools, and we'd do clinics for the schoolboys and girls. And women's basketball was more developed in Australia than it was in the United States at that time, so we had a lot of young ladies who attended our clinics. . . .

Australians are very generous people, and they are very fun-loving people, and most of all, they love sports and athletics. And they play it and they watch it, and they are fierce, fierce competitors. The game of basketball in Australia when we were there was much rougher than the game here, and many people would foul out of the games, each and every game, including myself several times. I very seldom would foul out in other contexts. We would be real rivals with some of these teams, particularly the fellows who played on their Olympic team and the state-wide team, people like Bruce Flick: a fierce competitor, not a big guy but a well-built guy, but he put you in the third row if you were going in for a lay-in. He wouldn't want to hurt you, and if he did he'd feel terrible about it, but you weren't going to score easily on him. But after the game, after the fierce competition—and I use Bruce as an example because we played them many times—we usually ended up playing them in tournaments. At the end of the tournament—and I don't know how many times in my two years that I competed against Bruce, but it would be several—but after the game, you were the best of friends. Best of friends. Couldn't do enough for you. . . .

You know, as I think back on was this all worth it, the basketball and everything, there is no doubt in my mind that it was worth it because it gave the members there a sense of pride. . . . When we would go on a trip, we would receive several telegrams from members telling us, "Good luck on your trip. You're bringing such a delight to the people here, and the people are proud to be associated and to know they have these young men and to be able to point to their neighbors and say, 'You know these Mormon Yankees that are coming to our town? They're from our church, and they'll be coming to church next Sunday with us,'" because we did go to the church locally. . . . Basketball was Mormon Yankees, and basketball was associated with clean-cut young men who were serving their church unselfishly for two years, and there was a great deal of pride in that by the local people. . . .

The Mormon Yankees were really a band of brothers. And the Mormon Yankees changed from time to time—there were different people on the team at different times, . . . but we all had the same goal. And we basically all had played some basketball before, and we wanted to perform at a high level, but there's absolutely no question that the goal of performing at a high level was to advance the Church and to advance the teachings of the Church. And to advance the promotion of basketball was a secondary goal, and making everybody feel good, members of our Church feel good about the Church, was a secondary goal. We have lifelong friendships on our team, keep track of each other. . . . The legacy of the Mormon Yankees is basically fighting prejudice, promoting the gospel, promoting pride in the gospel, promoting pride in our standards, taking a group of people—elders and sisters, young members in a country that only had a few members of the Church—and making something that everybody recognized was good—not everybody, but most people recognized was good—and they said, "Hey, let's take a look at that. What is this that these people are? What makes them this way?" And I was just very proud to be a part of that. But it's the whole mission, not just the Mormon Yankees.

HEATHER DODD

BRISBANE, QUEENSLAND, AUSTRALIA
JUNE 25, 2010

IN JULY OF 1954, I'd just recently come home from high school, and I was helping my mother in the kitchen prepare the evening meal, and there was a knock at the front door, and Mum said, "Oh, you better grab that." So I went to the front door, and there standing on the doorstep were two young men in suits and hats, and they asked to speak to the lady of the house. So I went and got my mother, and she invited them in. And we had a little chat, and they told us that they were missionaries from The Church of Jesus Christ of Latter-day Saints, and could they come back when my father was home? So my mother said yes, and they made an appointment to come back the following night and meet with the family. So we had regular lessons with them and started investigating, attending the meetings at [the] Gibbons Street chapel, and eventually were baptized, back in 1955. . . .

We went through several sets of missionaries in these seven months that we investigated before we were finally baptized in March of '55, and the two missionaries that baptized my family—which was my mother, father, my sister, and myself—were Elder Butler and Elder Whitesol. And Elder Whitesol actually played on the Mormon Yankees team. He was a tour guy—or tour for those days, not tour man now—but he was one of the top players and played on the Queensland team back in 1955, when some of the missionaries were selected in the state team for the Australian championships. . . .

At the time I joined the Church, I was a netball player, and in 1955 I was selected in the Queensland team for netball. As the missionaries, the Mormon Yankees, were playing, we used to go to all their games, and I got interested in basketball. And the missionaries started teaching us to play basketball, and we actually formed a Brisbane Mormon Aussies girls' team that played in a local competition, so the missionaries sort of helped the female basketball get along as well. . . . As a result of learning to play with the Mormon Yankees, I went on and represented Queensland in basketball as well, and basketball has been part of my life up until now. I've been involved as a player, a referee, and a score table person on the national league, and I've also been a basketball administrator, and I was president of the Referees' Association for a number of years. So thanks to the Mormon Yankees, I guess, I've had a great career and a great life in basketball. . . .

Most of the games we attended of the Mormon Yankees were [at] David's Parkway Stand, which was on the riverbank, and in winter it was very cold there. It was all outdoor on . . . bitumen courts. And just one tiny little chain shed, and that was all the facilities they had. And that was where we girls, the Mormon Aussies, played as well. And it was pretty rough if you happened to fall. . . . It took some skin off, that's for sure. But another place they played was the indoor center at the YMCA in the city. And that was an interesting court because the sideline was only about six inches from the walls, and so to stand outside to throw the ball in, they sort of had to stand sideways because their feet were too big and they'd go over the line. And we used to watch the game from the balcony up above. So that was an interesting thing. Another place they played was the Naval courts, down in the domain where Queensland University of Technology is now, and, well, that was indoor. I'm pretty sure it had a concrete floor, so they didn't have the sprung floors like they do in stadiums today. . . .

The Mormon Yankees were pretty popular with the people because of their ball skills. They really improved the standard of play amongst the Brisbane teams, and I think they were recognized for their skill and also for their sportsmanship, and no bad language, of course, and very clean-cut players. . . .

The Mormon Yankees were very fortunate in that because they

were such good players, they got a fair bit of press in the sporting part of the *Brisbane Telegraph* and lots of headlines like "Nine Mormons in Title," "Yankees Beat the Live Wires," "Mormons Are Too Tall and Too Quick," and things like that, so that when they knock on doors, I'm sure that people have seen the papers and have said, "Oh, are you one of the Mormon Yankees?" So it was an opening for the missionaries so that they could talk about the gospel because of their basketball knowledge and because they were known as the Mormon Yankees. . . . I think the Mormon Yankees was a good opportunity for the community to get to know the missionaries as normal people and not just associate the Church with polygamy and so forth. . . . The articles . . . in the *Brisbane Telegraph* would certainly let the people know . . . the missionaries. . . . Looking back, the Mormon Yankees really moved basketball ahead in Brisbane. They put the Church to the forefront through their games and through their behavior because they were so well mannered and had such good sportsmanship. They were able to bring the Church to more people. . . .

The Mormon Yankees were a great example to the community, the basketball community in particular, by the way they displayed themselves, by their good sportsmanship, and their skills and being willing to teach others and being friendly about it. And I'm sure that even though many of the people that were familiar with the Mormon Yankees didn't join the Church, but it would give them a good impression of the Church and what they're about. And it's obviously a lasting legacy because there's still people today who talk about the different elders that played in the local competition, and I've got many friends in the basketball community that . . . asked me, "Do you ever hear anything about Elder So-and-So?" And so they do remember them with great friendship and great respect. . . . Having the Mormon Yankees play as they did for a couple of years here in Brisbane, such in high profile, and the media coverage that they had has been great for the Church. And bringing the gospel out to the public as just normal people, and it would be great if we could have something again like that because it really proved very successful back then. . . . As you're probably aware, sport to most Australians is almost a religion. They really take it up, and I think they're known as one of the countries most known around the world for their sport, and the Mormon Yankees were able to promote sport and also promote a religion at the same time so that it was able to probably appeal more to the Australians' community because they were able to combine the two. . . .

I do have the Mormon Yankees to thank for the impact they've made on my life, both religiously and also with my love for the sport of basketball, which has been part of my life, a big part of my life since I was fifteen years old. And I'm so grateful for their influence and them teaching me how to play.

JESSIE L. EMBRY

PROVO, UTAH, USA
SEPTEMBER 10, 2010

NOTE: *Jessie Embry is the associate director of the Charles Redd Center for Western Studies at Brigham Young University.*

IT'S INTERESTING THAT sports started out—basketball started out as part of a YMCA. It was kind of, had some spiritual connections, and right about the time basketball started [in] the 1890s, the Mormon Church started playing basketball. And they played usually just among themselves, but in the 1920s in Salt Lake, they thought they would start a tournament, and that grew to an all-Church tournament. The term that they used in the Church at that time was *spiritualized recreation*. . . .

Adolf Hitler, I think, was extremely excited that the Olympics were coming to Germany [in 1936], and he wanted to showcase how great the race was, and he wanted to show, "Wow, look how special we are." . . . [He] really wanted Germany to do well in basketball, a game that they really were not that familiar with. He looked at the Mormon elders who were preaching in the country, who he'd been aware of, and he said, "They know about basketball." So he asked the elders to help train the German basketball team, and they also asked the missionaries to help in the officiating of the game. . . .

Basketball particularly is a game that was formed by the YMCA as a Christian movement. It was a way to get those young men off the streets and into church. A phrase that had been coined by some historians is *muscular Christianity*, so that you're creating big muscles but also creating Christianity at the same time. Basketball is part of that movement; the founding of basketball is part of that movement, and the Church picked up on it and started being more involved in having sports as a way to keep people involved in church and also be able to maybe attract some new members as well. . . .

There has always been this sense that sports is almost a religion, and maybe it comes back from the starting of basketball where the YMCA started it. There is some connection between sports and religion. The way that—when I was doing my research, I picked particular countries, and I picked countries that I knew had a lot of sports going on. I think that the reason why those sports were going on in terms of missionaries doing sports is because there was a passion. It wasn't just that the missionaries liked sports. The country liked sports, and the country liked new sports, so I think that basketball became a big area in South America, in Finland, in Germany, in Australia and New Zealand because the people wanted to learn a new sport, and they didn't know that sport very well. Their Olympic teams would later become very good, but at that time, the Mormon missionaries were much better at the sport, so that was a way to encourage them. . . .

As I did my research and read diaries and read missionaries' accounts and oral histories about how they saw what the sports did, they said that as they played sports, as they participated on whatever level they played, whether it was at a carnival or in a league, that people recognized them, and that before that they had either not gotten into doors at all or people would say, "Isn't that the church that practices polygamy?" But once they started playing sports, they could go to a door, and they would say, "Oh yes, I read about your basketball team in the newspaper. Yes, let's talk about that." Even, in some cases, in a locker room afterwards, they would have a chance to talk to people. Some of the games I read about, they would play a game, and then they would show a filmstrip on national parks in Utah so that they could do a little bit of gospel discussion, but mainly it was to say, "Look, we are regular people. We sweat just like you do; we play just like you do," and there's some advantages of it. . . . The connection always with the

Church first is polygamy, and sports helped give [people] something else to think of first. . . .

The goal of basketball in most countries was not baptisms but public relations. I think it really served a good purpose. It gave people an opportunity to see that Mormons were regular people, that they enjoyed playing sports, and in these countries where sports really thrived, the people enjoyed playing sports. I think that that was a way of bringing people into the recognition of the Church. There were people baptized from that; there were people baptized from the old Church tournaments. It wasn't necessarily a huge number of baptisms, but it did a great deal of public relations. I think, though, that the idea to stop putting such a big focus on sports is the Church made a shift and wanted to go back to more spiritual kinds of focus. . . .

The legacy of sports in the LDS Church is that it was extremely important in the mid-twentieth century. Now, we've been talking mainly about sports, but we can take that spiritualized recreation [as] including all of the Mutual Improvement Association activities that took place. They were a way to keep young people in the Church and to attract people into the Church and to be a good public relations. Sports were a really important part. . . .

I think with the founding of basketball and the YMCA taking up basketball and then volleyball and other sports, that religion and sports became netted together and that muscular Christianity [and] spiritualized recreation are pretty much exactly the same thing. The LDS Church was adapting what it was seeing going on. And a lot of other different churches—and that other churches continued to see sports as an important way of providing activities for their youth.

ARTHUR EMERY

ADELAIDE, SOUTH AUSTRALIA, AUSTRALIA
JUNE 18, 2010

THE TEAM WAS actually a way of proselyting the gospel, and they moved from state to state, the American missionaries, because they were full-time missionaries, but they chose me for some reason to be a member of their team, probably because I was the captain-coach of the local LDS team. We played in the local competition. And I was number seven in the Mormon Yankee team, but then when they had been here, and we won the competition that we were in, and then the missionaries had to move on, and then that left me going back to the local team after that experience. . . . I was baptized along with my mother and brother and sister at the Adelaide chapel because there was only one branch of the Church here in South Australia at that time, and that was the Adelaide Branch. . . .

[Elder Loren C. Dunn] was a nice, very tall, of course, like all American basketballers are, a very compassionate man, and I liked him very much. . . . He was a wonderful man and a great example to the team. I remember we always had a word of prayer before the actual game—of course we were on the floor before we actually started playing—we'd always have a word of prayer. . . .

Speaking for myself, playing with the Mormon Yankees, that's the first time I had been taught and been part of different plays because usually when we played basketball, you did what you could with the ball. [There was] no thought of the forwards weaving here, there, and everywhere, the defense people coming up to wherever to retrieve a rebound, and that sort of thing, so that would have been one of the big features for me, was learning how to set up a play and abide by that. . . .

I was working during the day and used to go to the game in the evening because it became a part of Mutual Improvement Association activity within the branch. On a Tuesday night, we used to have the MIA for both young men and young women, by way of lessons, but then on a Thursday night, that's when we used to meet and play the basketball game as part of the MIA program.

RAY FEENEY

CAMPBELLTOWN, NEW SOUTH WALES, AUSTRALIA
JUNE 26, 2010

THE MORMON INFLUENCE wasn't very big in Australia back then. I only knew them through basketball. Basketball didn't start in Sidney up until 1938, so it was a very, very young sport, and what I found was that the American Mormons added a lot of skills that we were not aware of, I imagine, back in those days. We learned by playing against some players of very high standard, and we learned skills that we were only learning as a very young sport. So I think they brought skills of probably organized basketball more than anything. I think in Australia, we were only learning the game, and it wasn't a very popular game in Australia because we've got our own sports like rugby league and that sort of thing. So basketball was very new, and I think we learned how to play the game in a structured manner, and people liked the Mormons. . . .

I recall in 1955, around about that time, that [to] the Boys Club, the Mormons used to bring along a guy that I can remember his name as Mr. Bow Wow [Ronald L. Bouck]. [He] was only a short fellow, and he would wear a white track suit and entertain the crowd and cheer on the players, doing flip-flops up and down the court. We had never seen this sort of thing in Sydney, and it really got the crowd going. . . .

The Mormon Tabernacle Choir turned up one afternoon that I

recall, or one night after a game. And I can't say that it was the full Mormon Tabernacle Choir because I know that would be a very, very big deal, but probably twenty to thirty people, and they entertained the crowd after the game, and it was a custom then that the Mormon players and the supporters used to mingle with the crowd and talk to the people at the game and, I guess, try and sort of befriend people in that way, and, yes, and that was quite entertaining. They were a very good group. . . .

The Mormons, although they were missionaries and they were trying to gain converts through basketball, they were never pushy; they didn't push themselves onto the people. But everybody that came in contact with them—and I actually found my sister before this interview, and she used to score for our team, and asked her recollections. And the word that she said was, "All I can remember is they were very nice people, very nice." So, you know, they mixed with the crowd or mixed with the teams after the game and socialized in that way. . . .

The 1955 Australasian championships were held in the . . . Boys Club that year. . . . The championships would go around the country and be played in a different state every year, but in 1955 they were held in New South Wales. . . . I was lucky enough to see every one of those games. I was only eleven, ten or eleven, and it must have been school holiday time because I was courtside at every game, and I can remember—one of the people that sticks in my mind was Elder Bushnell. He was a fairly tall, solidly built man, very thickset man, and he was blonde. I can remember that. He was a very, very good player. . . . In that 1955 state championships, Australian championships, Elder Dunn, Elder [North], and Elder Smith played for New South Wales. They are not actually mentioned in the official team list of New South Wales team for some reason—maybe they weren't allowed to have their names mentioned, I don't know—that they were in that team, as was Elder Bushman in the Queensland team. . . .

I think the Mormons, as far as basketball is concerned, had a very lasting effect on Sydney basketball, and not only Sydney basketball but basketball in all of the states, in all of the other major cities. I think that they raised the standard because as you probably know, being a sportsman, that when you play against better players, you become better yourself. You lower your standard if you play against substandard players. So they lifted off the game; there's no doubt about that. They also lifted it as far as spectators were concerned because we, our team, my team that I played for, and the team that . . . Bruce [Flick] too played for were the top teams in Sydney, and the stadium would be packed out when new teams played the Mormons. It was just a spectacular time in basketball, you know; that period from 1950 to 1960 was a very spectacular time as far as basketball is concerned and the growth of basketball in Sydney.

CHARLES BRUCE FLICK

SYDNEY, NEW SOUTH WALES, AUSTRALIA
JUNE 26, 2010

WE WERE CONSCIOUS of the fact that the Mormon religion was there, but [we] didn't know very much about the Mormons in Australia. . . . Those days, of course, when we first started playing the basketball, you know, you always sort of coming up by under eighteen or something and very humble background, and so we didn't get exposed too much to religious situations. We were aware of it, and we'd done some reading of it, and the location in Salt Lake City. But virtually no understanding of it at all. . . . It was really the sport that introduced the subject to us, to pay more attention to it. It was something that impressed us from the beginning, the type of people that were there. . . .

The introduction of Mormons into the basketball arena in Australia wasn't right valued to the development of the game in Australia, and once that's happening, of course you then have the byproduct of it, but you get to know the people. And from my own experience and from most of the mates that I played with at the time, we all had high respect for the type of people that were the missionaries. . . . My memory of our games against the Mormons was it was going to be a tough game, a good game, and finish with respect for one another. . . .

Up until the Mormons were actually active in their game in Australia, we didn't use the jump shot. And any of these guys would go up over us and throw baskets, and that was the technique, and personally it was something that I fell onto very quickly because it was the development of my game, which hadn't been offered to me from anything likely. And learning when you're on a defensive situation with a very good point guard and he's got a jump shot, it has a very, very definite effect upon how you're going to guard that person. . . .

Nineteen fifty-five really was a turning point, as I saw it. For the first time in Australian basketball history, Mormon missionary members were actually members of a state team; the New South Wales state team had three members, Elder Loren Dunn, Elder Sherman Day, and Elder North. And so that was a breakthrough, and it was the only time it had ever happened because I'm not sure whether it was the rules or the politics or whatever else it was, done. It didn't happen again. . . .

The fact that we had developed a relationship with people on a common ground, being sport and basketball, it engendered a respect factor between ourselves, so that when in later times the Mormon missionaries used to knock on our doors to talk to us about their religion, the door was always open. So I think the word "respect" is what engenders all of that is—from sport, that respect for the people. I'm not a great delegate on religion in itself; we're believers, but we're not practitioners. And what they actually taught us was there are good, quality people in any walk of life. And we learned that about the Mormons, just through that relationship. . . . When you have a relationship with anyone, if you don't develop respect for the people you're dealing with, it goes nowhere. The door is always open because every exposure we had to a Mormon missionary was always one of respect. And that was a two-way street. . . .

With the Mormon Church, if they invited me to that conference in 1961, I would have tried very definitely to convince them not to discontinue, because it was, certainly to young Australians, I think it was a very valuable experience because we are a rather isolated part of the world, and getting access to other parts of the world is how we learn. Pity I didn't get an invitation to that conference; I might have been able to sway it. . . .

My memory of the Mormon basketball team in Melbourne just prior to the game was that they were a quality-enough team to be involved in doing international, unofficial games. DeLyle Condie is the only name that I can recall of that team because they were located in

Melbourne. We knew pretty much all of the Sydney people, but Melbourne we didn't know all that much about. But the quality of him as a player—and the Mormon mission team beat our Australian team at that time, and I think the main reason for that was DeLyle Condie's skills. . . . I think the Mormon mission team was also used in some other unofficial pre-Olympic trials in other international teams, and they walloped a couple of them as well. . . .

Our exposure to the Mormon mission players at that point in time really was coming to the game, at the game, dressing room thereafter, and then moving away again, so [we] didn't get to know them specifically as individuals quite so much. Other than that, the way they went about doing what they did was introducing another international aspect to life. And it just commanded respect, the way they did. . . . We knew they had, as missionaries for a religious organization, obviously they had to conduct themselves with all of the expectations that they would be promoting an image, but as individuals they were just young fellows like ourselves, really, but life was still there as a challenge, and the respect that, if someone was to give two years of their life to promote their religion in another part of the world, was always one that just had me saying, "Gosh, that is one heck of a sacrifice," in my view. So that developed respect as well. . . .

Twenty years after we stopped playing, I was in a hospital having a hip replaced because basketball had knocked a few joints around, and I had a visitor in hospital, and Loren Dunn actually came. Twenty years after we quit [playing basketball], it was just something that . . . I would like to sit and have a cup of coffee with Sherman Day sometime. And he accorded me a wonderful compliment. He made a statement and wrote an article in one of our magazines here, that he thought I personally would rate quite well in the varsity basketball in the United States. Across the Pacific from here that was just out of touch, and he made this sort of comment. . . .

Just prior to actually becoming exposed to the Mormon Yankees, I had been called up to the National Service in the war of Australian Air Force. In that point in time, you have to allocate six months of your life. Now I was on a student intake, and we did it in two breaks and three months over Christmas periods, when the colleges we were attending to do our vocation. In between we'd get our two-, three-months period, but at that point in time, the Korean War was on. If you put your hand up to go in the Air Force, you . . . would be drafted overseas to Korea. It didn't happen, but the point is what struck me at that point in time was six months for military service. I then looked at the Mormons, who put two years in another part of the world. That, to me, is a commitment to a cause. Respect is everywhere.

INGA FREIDENFELDS

ADELAIDE, SOUTH AUSTRALIA, AUSTRALIA
JUNE 18, 2010

I THINK, AND it really delighted the Latvian community more than probably myself in that particular instance, because to be captain of the Olympic team, I get to get naturalized, as most of the other immigrants did to be able to play in the national side. And to me, they were split emotions, really, because although I do come from Latvia, I did leave Latvia when I was ten years of age. I already lived just as long here in this country, so it was in my mind: Australia was the country that I had been brought to, I had elected, and I remember [to] do as best as I can. . . . The Mormon Yankees team was better than [the] Australia [Olympic team] . . . at the time. . . .

The Mormon Yankees were very good sports; they were very, very polite most of the time, and they weren't out to hurt anybody by any means. You know, sometimes when you play against a bigger player, you're going to get hurt because . . . that player just happens to be bigger. But I have never ever witnessed any of the Mormon Yankees, the players, going out there with malice in their thoughts. . . .

We hadn't heard of Mormon religion or of Mormons or such, I mean, from Europe. Maybe they were there, maybe not. . . . This is where we first heard of them, and of course there were always the missionaries busy knocking on doors, always clean, neatly vested, even in this weather, walking around in pairs. . . .

What I remember about Elder [Loren C.] Dunn was that he was a big man, and he was quite skillful in the game that he was playing. While in Adelaide, I think he was also coach for the Mormons. . . . It was interesting to watch the Mormons taking notes—they were—at the key players that they wanted to play next. They were actually scouting to see whatever opposition they were going to have. I believe that that probably was Elder Dunn's doing, to try and set up the right players or whatever he wanted. . . .

George [Dancis] being a big man as well, and he couldn't be shifted—like you couldn't push him or shove him in any way or form—but then Elder Dunn left him for dead as far as basic skills are concerned. Also, George used to do heavy cement work all day, every day, and that made him quite stiff, if you can imagine traveling concrete on quick paths over river, and then he would come and play basketball. . . .

What I remember about Elder [Paul] Grant was the game. He was a big man, and when he came to Adelaide, he was probably the mainstay of the Mormon Yankees side here in Adelaide, to the extent that he actually was picked as a member of the state team for [the] 1957 Australian championships, and we had a really good time training and playing together. . . .

I think in total, over the years that we were associated with the Mormon Yankees, I've got nothing but respect for the way they played, for the way they behaved, for the way they carried themselves. And it was a pity that there weren't more coming out of the higher caliber. That might have perhaps given our country a shot in the arm much earlier. As I said, after the Mormon Yankees came, the Hungarian team came later, and all of that aided the quality of the basketball in this country.

LOLITA FREIDENFELDS

ADELAIDE, SOUTH AUSTRALIA, AUSTRALIA
JUNE 18, 2010

PROBABLY 1952–53, AND we had two Latvian teams, and I was sort of a little bit keen on this Inga Freidenfelds, and I used to go to the OBI [Our Boys Institute], which is in Adelaide city. . . . When we came to Australia, we had no language—like, the English language—so of course all the Latvians stuck together, and we had the youth group where we played basketball, volleyball. . . .

We heard about them, the Mormons arriving, or I guess everybody in Australia, because we didn't know very much about the Mormon religion or anything until they came. Of course, they were an exciting new side to play, not just some run-of-the-mill. . . . It was all very exciting. They were all good-looking guys; I mean, I'm sure there were lots of girls falling over each other to say hello to them. . . .

We come from a long line of drinkers, . . . and every time there was a party after basketball and that, they had to refrain from having drinks or even Coke, which to us . . . "They can't even drink Coke or coffee or something." So a lot of times we did get stuck into them, and . . . used to razz them and have a go at them, if you like, about all this. . . . It was all in good fun, and they didn't take offense. No offense was meant. It was just a good time together. . . . They were very good sports. . . .

Elder Paul Grant came to Melbourne when I went with the boys. I think I was the only girl going over there with the boys, and again, you know, there was the basketball and the party after and all this camaraderie, if you like, and it was a really good time. . . . They [the Mormon Yankees] were very nice, polite, and you know, maybe the Aussies aren't that polite, but they were gentlemen, and they were very good-looking. I think everybody was really happy that they came. . . . Elder Grant, when we were in Melbourne and we were carrying on there—I don't know what we were saying, but he said [to Inga Freidenfelds], "Well, you better marry her," because we would like to get married in 1959. He said, "If you don't marry her, I'll come back, and I'll marry her myself." . . .

If Paul Grant and everybody else in the Mormon Yankees would see this film, I would hope that they remember me and the good times we had together, [I] was very happy that they came out here and that we met them. We probably wouldn't know each other if we passed each other in the street, but yes, it was great meeting you guys. . . .

I think the Mormon Yankees coming to Australia and playing here put the Mormons on the map, if you like, because I'm sure the Australians didn't know who Mormons were either. Nobody knew here, . . . but I'm sure that people were interested . . . to find out, and they did go out from home to home and talk to people, so of course it made a lot of difference, I think, in Australia.

MARK J. FRODSHAM

SALT LAKE CITY, UTAH, USA
JULY 9, 2010

I THINK THE Mormon Yankees were successful as a team because of the coherence we had with each other. The thing I can distinctly remember during and since is there was no competition between us. We all kind of knew our niche on the team, and we had respect for each other. If I had ever thought at that time . . . I'd be happy playing with [two] University of Utah . . . players—but we really did and really enjoyed it. And I think the people felt we were genuine. We weren't there to show, win championships or anything, and I think that was one of the reasons we were as successful off the floor as we were on the floor. . . .

A bunch of rough kids who hadn't had much experience in basketball, but the way I can describe them, . . . the kids were willing to learn, and they were all eyes and ears. They would flock, probably twenty of them, and then you try to take these kids and divide them into teams and referee and coach, and they have no idea what double dribble is; they have no idea on any of the thing. If they could drill on one end or the other—so we set up a plan for them. I set out chairs; they had to dribble around the chairs. Simple things that we learned in high school, they had no idea about. . . . This was all done on P-day [preparation day]. This was not done during regular tracting time, so that's interesting. This was on our own time. . . .

I feel the Mormon Yankees going through this and spending all the time and all the effort we made as missionaries and that was well worthwhile because of the PR between the Australian people, Americans, and Mormons. I think it made a bond between the Americans and the Mormons, and it's lasted through the years. The missionary program is only successful if the people will accept what we have and who we are. . . . People don't understand; they can see through you if you are baloney, believe me. They can see right through it. And they feel our sincerity. They felt our sincerity in there, and I had such respect for them. If they weren't interested in what I had to tell, they knew I was interested in them. And I wouldn't just brush it off. Maybe some people might think that's not good tracting policy, but I wanted to find out how many kids they have and where they lived and what they did for a living, and you just get a bond going rather than just stand at the door and try to push too much on them if they are not interested.

JAMES NYLE GARN

ST. GEORGE, UTAH, USA
APRIL 13, 2011

I'D PLAYED BASKETBALL all through high school and tried out for the team at Ricks College but was told that I could play maybe periodically with the varsity, but I'd be on the JV [junior varsity] team mostly. And the JV team in those days at Ricks College just played Church teams around the area, so I thought, "Well, I think I'll play Church ball." And so I played Church ball, and in those days—this was a time when there was an all-Church tournament, and so all the time for those three years while I was there, we went to the all-Church tournament and played in that tournament and either got second or third place in the all-Church tournament for the three years that we were there. . . .

I really hadn't known much about Australia, but I started to study a little bit about Australia when I received that call. And I was just very excited, not knowing exactly what the situation would be, whether I would have to learn a new language or what or exactly what my situation as a missionary would be, and found out that when I went to Australia, they said that I wouldn't have to learn a new language, but [I] found out that I really pretty much had to understand their slang words, the "two right mates" and all those. . . .

I was there in 1956, and that was the time that the Olympics were in Melbourne, the Summer Olympics. And I'm not exactly sure how it all came about, but we ended up having a missionary team, of course designated as the Mormon Yankees, and we were invited to play in a tournament that was organized. And I think one of the reasons for the tournament was for the Australian Olympic committee to select an Australian basketball team to represent them in the Olympics. That was in Melbourne at the time, in 1956, so we joined that tournament and played lots of Australian teams and really won the tournament. So they were kind of excited; we were excited about that. . . .

Following the Olympic Games and the basketball part of the Olympic Games, we were invited to go with the Chinese Olympic team, which was actually from Formosa, and to go down to Tassie—down to Tasmania—and play them there. And I don't recall how many games we played, but we played exhibition games, and I think they beat us a couple of times; we beat them three or four times, but it was a great experience. With them we made good friends, with the Chinese Olympic team. . . . We traveled together. The Australian government flew us to Tassie and around, so we were right together. In fact, one of the Chinese Olympic players, whose name was James, James Chang, sat by me in the plane, and my first name is James, and we had a very good relationship, and I corresponded with [him] following the Olympics for a couple of years, and he became a doctor back in Formosa. . . .

We played the Russian team twice, and they beat us; they beat us twice. They beat us—as I recall, they beat us [by] eight points once and fourteen points another time; they were a good team. They had one fellow who was, I think, [seven feet two inches], and in those days that was an extremely tall individual. And to shake hands with him, I couldn't just put my hand around his hand—he was huge. And I think he wasn't a great basketball player, but he was there for intimidation, I think. But that was a fun experience to play them. . . .

We were encouraged wherever we went to participate in community teams, and wherever I went, I had the opportunity to coach local community teams and participate that way. We continued—many of us found that we'd been moved to Adelaide after our experience in Melbourne—went to Adelaide. I then went down to Tasmania, and I played and coached local teams there along the east coast of Tasmania, and Devonport and Ulverstone and Burnie and those areas. . . .

Our success rate, as far missionary work is concerned, after the

Olympics—because we'd had that exposure—was good. Those of us who were on the team, on the Mormon Yankee basketball team, kind of changed our approach a little bit. Some of us, rather than say, "We're missionaries from The Church of Jesus Christ of Latter-day Saints. We have a message for you," we would sometimes approach it, "We're members of the Mormon Yankee basketball team, and we have a message for you," and that got us into some homes. The Australian people are very sports-minded people, and they appreciated that. They appreciated the opportunity to talk to Americans, especially who were sportsmen. . . . We did have quite a few people who became interested in the Church, I think, through the Mormon Yankee program, particularly young men who played against us. I think they could see there was a difference in us and others as far as the way we talked, the way we lived, the things we did. And yes, I'm not sure, but I know that there were at least three of the young men who participated against us that joined the Church, and beyond that I'm not exactly sure what happened.

LINDSAY GAZE

MELBOURNE, VICTORIA, AUSTRALIA
JUNE 15, 2009

NOTE: *Lindsay Gaze has participated in seven Olympic Games as both a basketball player and a coach. He was named Father of the Year for the state of Victoria in 1992, and his son, Andrew, won the same award in 2004.*

THE EXHIBITION GAMES that were played by the Mormon Yankees against visiting, the international teams, were very important for us because it helped promote the sport—it helped promote the Olympic Games—and as a basis of education for our players and coaches and seeing those teams play. The Mormon Yankees did very well in all of those games; they never played against the United States. . . . I can't remember exactly how many games that were played—there were four or five games, anyway, that were played against other teams. I think France, Uruguay, one or two of the Asian teams who played were [all] part of the exhibitions. . . .

There was a guard on their team, I think [it] was Kimball. . . . He must have been the itchiest player in the history of sport and basketball because as he would advance the ball down the floor, usually, occasionally, he'd be scratching his ear or be scratching his chest or which way. Of course, later [we] realized that these were calling the plays, the set plays. We find something of a bit of humor about the way that he was sort of scratching and itching in the way he called the plays. That was sort of quite revolutionary for us at the time. . . .

When you think of the development of basketball in Australia, here in Victoria and to some extent in New South Wales, [we] were influenced greatly by the American influence, by far the Mormons. But in South Australia they're influenced much more by the Europeans and particularly the Latvians, to some extent the Lithuanians and the Hungarians. Those prominent basketball players tend to settle more in Adelaide; they became more mobile and moved to other states later on, but they were the leaders in the field. Most of those had learned their basketball in the refugee camps during the war. Some migrated to Australia and were a major influence on basketball in Australia because we had no education from others. . . .

December 10, 2009

Ken Watson was the secretary of Basketball Victoria, Basketball Australia, . . . and the coach of the 1956 Olympic team, the first time Australia was represented at the Olympic Games. He's a mathematics teacher, outstanding mathematics teacher, so something of the order of a scientist when it comes to mathematics, and of course, he translated those attitudes to basketball. So he was very much a student of the game and would subscribe to coaching magazines from the United States, meet anyone he could who knew anything about the game, particularly from the United States. . . . He developed a very good friendship with DeLyle Condie, who was the player-coach of the Mormon team in 1956, and the discussions that he had with President Bingham about getting the Mormon team to play, and then, of course, to promote the game through that medium. So there's a lot going on behind the scenes in the way in which we were trying to develop the sport, to improve our playing standards, and—which was a very, very difficult task in those days—to promote the sport, because there's very little media coverage. . . .

During 1956, the Mormons were playing in our state championships and playing very well, not surprisingly, because all of their players were prominent players from college basketball in the United States, and that was likely the head of our competition at that time. So what they did is that they provided great role models for our teams, not only in the playing of the game but in the conduct of the play—we'll call it the sportsmanship of play. Their willingness to share with their opposition was very important for us at the time because we had all grown up in the environment of Australian-rules football where you knock them down, tread on them, shorten your steps as you walk over them and that sort of attitude, you see? So now in the world of basketball, which was a noncontact game with high levels of sportsmanship expected, at the end of the game you gave three cheers to your opposition and showed that sort of sportsmanship. These were part of the culture and the way in which the game was played. So then at the end of the season, which not surprisingly the Mormons won that state championship season in 1956, Ken Watson was once again trying to promote the Olympic Games, get ready for the Olympic Games, and was able to get the support of the Mormon Yankees in setting up a series of exhibition matches against the visiting Olympic teams. They were very, very popular because it was somewhat less expensive to go and watch those games, which were played around the metropolitan area and the new Olympic venue and so on. . . .

The support for the Mormons was one of admiration because they were the best. Others tried to emulate them, but whenever they were playing against a team, then of course, their opponents of the team would ridicule them, would bash them, would try to put them off their game, which they never ever did, of course, because the composure of the American Mormon teams was always superior. Post-game, they would mingle with the crowd, make friends, and I've got to say that there are some members of the Mormon teams that I'm recalling who were more than popular, especially with the young females of the audience there. . . . So you know, it showed that they were like any other young fellows, young athletes competing, playing their sport, mingling and mixing with the community at large, and making friends, sometimes very, very good friends. . . .

There was never any overt proselytizing, and I never really inquired about that. I was never involved, and that sort of thing, and I've never heard any criticism or praise or just really never tried to assess that. It was just the way it was at the time. But the thing that affected me more in those times was their friendship, the way in which they were so easy to relate to, both in a sporting sense and just in a community sense and general circumstances, so it wasn't surprising for me that some of the female fans would relate pretty well to them as well. They were just good human beings, good social behavior, good connections, and I think proselytizing was confined to, let's call it their working hours, away from their sporting environment, so that then when they would go and meet people, they could talk on the same level. "We're playing basketball—we play at the show grounds," just by way of introduction and explain themselves as being much the same as anyone else. . . .

From my own personal view that the Mormons in Victoria, and Australia for that matter, from an observation, I respect them. I think that's because they depict the image of cleanness, of being genuine, in some cases maybe being a bit persistent, maybe a bit goody-goodyish, you know, but nevertheless for all those things, very well respected, not the ad-sell type of proselytizing that you associate with some other faiths that abound, that come and go, some of them. So I think in an enduring way, the image of the Mormons as I was first impressed back fifty years ago has never been tarnished. . . .

If I was to make a final statement about the Mormon Yankees and particularly their basketball team, it would be that I'm very disappointed that they're [not still] there. I can remember the decision that was made by whatever, the powers back at the headquarters, to say, "No, this will no longer be part of the policy to allow that." And I still remember meeting with the president here in Victoria [Bruce R. McConkie] trying to convince him that we should be the exception, that in the interest of their work, that there are still benefits for the Church to have their missionaries assembled here and participating and doing the things that have been done in the past. I still believe that strongly and would say that it is disappointing to me that that policy has been made because I think whatever they did in the, we'll call it the pioneering years in basketball, in Australia, can be just as influential and just as powerful and just as contributing today. But I haven't won that argument. So it's for others to take up the cause now and say, "Strategically, I think you could do better here."

June 21, 2010

Prior to the 1956 Olympic Games in Melbourne, basketball was almost unknown as a broad-based participant sport. . . . So in an era when there was very amateur and very basic local competition, where now we have very high, elite, international standard being played in

Australia. On the way, of course, there are many changes, stepping stones to improvement. And for us in Victoria, the improvement started with the influence of the Mormon Yankees teamed that played in our state championship, led by DeLyle Condie, so they had a terrific influence on the game by demonstrating how to play. But then Condie also helped in regard to teaching or explaining how to teach the game as well. So that was a very important contribution that was made at that time. . . .

In Australia, sport has been classified as a religion, but more importantly, it's just some sports. So here in Melbourne, the religion is Australian-rules football; in Sydney, the religion is rugby league football; soccer is just starting to make its interventions into those characteristics. But Melbourne, my city—it is classified as being the sports capital of the world. Not satisfied as a religion just for a sport, but pretty much all sports because whenever a major sporting event is promoted in Victoria. . . .

Basketball in the 1950s was virtually unknown until the media came out of the Harlem Globetrotters. So when that movie was shown, it created an awareness and a popularity, albeit that not many people knew about the game that much. So the 1956 Olympic Games was an awakening for the sport in Victoria and Australia, and many people wondered whether it was going to be popularized further or whether it would be like the advent of indoor bowling in Australia: created a lot of interest but quickly died out, and many people thought that basketball might be the same. It became very popular quite quickly. . . . The Harlem Globetrotters had an impact because their reputation of winning some phenomenal amount of games without a loss, enough of the people had a fascination and an interest about that. And then, when the Mormon Yankees were playing our state championship—Americans, not quite the same as the Harlem Globetrotters, but nevertheless Americans playing—they attracted people to the games, and that in turn popularized the sport. The way I view it, it was like providing the foundation of awareness of the sport and awareness of the abilities of those players that played. So when they were playing in our state championship and winning it—oh, but there was some close games—and then going on to win three Olympic exhibition matches, the people here came to understand they were watching something special. This wasn't just ordinary, this was something right up at the international level, and that inspired many of our young players to emulate them and say, "If they can do it, well, maybe I can as well." . . .

I think that the Mormons playing, and I think it was always a good strategy—a good strategy for us and the sport and the propagation of the sport, but I think it was a good strategy for the Church as well because it gave them access to people. They could express themselves and their faith and make friends. I can tell you without a doubt that the Mormon Yankee players were very, very popular with the female section of our community. They would talk, they were open and receptive of—I don't know if there were any conquests out of all of that—but there was no doubt that they were popular with the females, probably for different reasons than it was for the male players playing basketball, but all that is human. That is the way people respond. When our teams have traveled, our boys have been popular with students and faculty around the place as well. You get to meet them, you get to share your experiences, your attitudes, your beliefs, and make friends, and that is what they were doing here. So, clearly, the result was the proselytizing, the awareness; not surprising, but the Church expanded. So, the Mormon Church now lost their . . . bragging rights that I understand, from my observations will say from afar, that the Mormon Church in Victoria, anyway, might well be one of the few that is still expanding. Other churches talk about it, but I think the Mormons quietly are displaying that that is a growing church. . . .

Through the mid-fifties, when we were experiencing the migrant burn—the Latvians, Lithuanians, Estonians, and so on—and along with the advent of the American Mormons, there was a very interesting contrast, if you like, of lifestyles. Alcohol was pretty much fundamental, particularly with the Latvian community, the Latvian players, and so it was not uncommon for them after games or at a tournament or an event or functions or whatever to imbibe, what I would say, excessively. But from my observation, it was always spirited. Good fun, good spirit, the way that they interacted socially and never ever criticized that I know about. By contrast, the Mormons, they were at the other end of the spectrum, and in Australia, I think Australians have been known to favor a beer or two, and it becomes part of the social culture. And if you are like me and one who doesn't drink, well, you got to treat these guys with caution. I think there might have been a little bit of that with the Mormons as well because it was no drinking, no smoking, puritan-type behavior, and they really, us, it is not the way it might be. So once it was recognized as a contrast between the Europeans particularly and the American Mormons, I think there was respect all around. The Mormons were respected for what they did on the court and their standards, their ethics and their choice about their health outcomes.

Bob Skousen was noted by me and others as probably the best pure shooter that we saw, particularly in that era. When we look back and compare his era to the current era, you would say, "I think he would have done pretty well now as well." I still remember him beating us with a shot that he literally said, the moment before he released the ball, "I have never done this before." I know that because I was trying to defend him. One of my teammates were trying to defend him as well. We had him double-teamed in the corner with his back to the basket, and we were a point ahead. So he did a turnaround jump shot with his back to the basket from the corner . . . nothing but net. See, he had that phenomenal ability to make something out of nothing under all sorts of pressure, consisting with what it was at that time. So he was the best pure shooter. DeLyle Condie was the best player, I thought, because of his intellect, his ability to be the leader of the team, and his skill. So whatever was needed, he was out at the front, either himself or leading his team to that. Skousen was the best pure shooter. Gardner—I forgot his first name, might have been Bob Gardner—may have been the best competitor. He won a state final, in the last year of the Mormons playing in Victoria, literally with a broken arm. We thought we had a pretty good chance of beating them because we'd heard that he had a broken arm from the game before. He came out and played with the broken arm, shot free throws left-handed, and whilst he didn't have the same talent as the likes of Condie or Skousen, as a competitor he set a phenomenal example. And no fuss. It wasn't like he was out there trying to be the hero. He just demonstrated by his performance of what it meant to him as a competitor, and he was outstanding. Others like Paul Grant—was exceptionally tall for an old basketball[er] at that time, another good leader. . . . Kimball, I think it was, was the guard on Skousen's team. Terrific playmaker, organizer—did very well. There were some highlights there.

I never had a great deal to do, personally, with Bob Skousen while he was here other than playing against him and the few words that you might speak after a game; I think you'd have a chat and then move on.

So we never really had the opportunity to socialize, if you put it that way, or talk about different things. There might have been occasional comment about the, shall we say, the proselytizing objective. That didn't get too far. But that was about it. However, when we were visiting the United States on one of our tours, our club team was making a tour of the United States, and our schedule was BYU, Utah, Utah State, around that area. And Bob came to a game, and this was early in the series that we had, and so I suggested to him whether he might like to join us for the remainder of the tour. We think he would adjust to our methods very quickly, and we would adjust to him, and he would obviously give us a boost of our playing personal. His immediate response was very positive: "That sounds terrific and very lovely." Then the next morning we called up, and he was very apologetic and said, "I'm sorry, I can't go; we can't get off." And that's all he had with him, his wife, and I immediately said, "I thoroughly understand. There's no way that I'd be leaving that woman for three weeks on a tour, that's for sure." She was absolutely beautiful, and so we had a jack about that, of course, and that's the sort of fellow he was. Very friendly, had a good sense of humor, great athlete, good sportsman and ready to share in the joke that we might have had with him. All of that was genuine, from my point of view. . . .

DeLyle is still my role model. So when you think about when you're dealing with a person—and you might [be] dealing with some pretty angry opponents who are trying to make a name for themself and build a reputation for how we beat the Yanks—his ability to deal with those varying elements of competition in sport was outstanding. So you learn from that vicariously, if you like, or by using those examples and say, "Would I deal with that situation the same way?" Now, he's managed that very well, and I admire that. Bob Skousen's personality came out with his playing. There was excitement, there was fun, there was adventure, character, those sorts of things that you'd identify with him. Paul Grant was typically more conservative, very thorough, very efficient, very effective, and those measurements that I might have had with him, I think, have probably been reasonably accurate when they consider his career and how he's gone on with his family and those sorts of things and been associated with that. So the others—I remember when we talk about it with my teammates, but I struggle to remember all the names of those people at the time. Like I said, Kimball was a great guard.

Frodsham was blue collar, more a blue-collar type player, you know.

I think because of my involvement of sport over a very long period, it's not surprising that some people have asked me whether I would write my story, and I've contemplated trying to do a history of Australian sport, and I haven't been able to come to grips with that because I'm not too sure what theme to take. . . . If I get to do that, . . . there would be a very strong influence that the Mormons had on how we play, and considering our development on that, very, very important to recognize that. . . . We here in Victoria recognize . . . having more of an American style of play, and that can be attributed almost exclusive to the Mormons in the early stages and later with the influence of the American teachers. So looking back, that I think it's more than just the play and the structure of play; to me it's also the behavior of play. So when you think about conduct and playing with integrity, then I think the Mormons set that as the foundation as well. . . . When you are looking at role models and examples, what the Mormons did for us at that time was very significant.

PAUL G. GRANT

MORAN, WYOMING, USA
AUGUST 28, 2010

I JUST ALWAYS planned on going on a mission because my father had not, and from the time I was a little tyke, that was ingrained in me to do two things: go on a mission and graduate from college—two things he hadn't had the pleasure of doing. In those days, the college teams had a freshman team and the varsity [team]. You couldn't play varsity as a freshman. So I had graduated from high school, and I was invited to the U[niversity] of U[tah] to come up and play on the freshman team, which I did. Thereafter I was invited to join the varsity as a sophomore. My skills weren't that great—I have to be honest about it—but it paid for school. Then I announced to Jack Gardner, who was the coach, that I was going to go on a mission, and he'd already been through this with DeLyle [Condie]. So it wasn't anything new. We talked about it. He said, "It would be much better if you just played and then left after you finished playing." But I thought I'd go with it the way it was, and I did. So name went in, took forever to get a call. I don't know what was going on, and finally I was told to go to the old missionary training place on North State Street and did so, and then the boat didn't leave forever. So as a result, I didn't get to Australia until about the eighth of November [1956]; there was a lot of frustration. I was not aware of any Mormon Yankees at that time. President Romney set me apart, and he was an old-time missionary in Australia, and he said to me, with a twinkle in his eye, "Well, you've got a purpose in going down there." He knew a lot more than I did. And so I arrived, and that's when I discovered that there was a Mormon Yankees basketball team. . . .

The missionaries had a team, and they had been playing against the Australian National team. They'd practiced a lot together, and they'd help the Australian team. I didn't do any of that; I got there too late. But upon arriving, I think there was already a game with an Olympic team that had been arranged, so I was informed the evening after I arrived that we were going to play basketball in a couple of days. Obviously I wasn't upset by it—more than happy to take my assignment in that regard. . . . The mission president made it very plain to us that we had to be on our very best behavior and be nothing but fantastic examples. Melbourne at the time was wild about the Olympics, . . . so the fact that we were engaging and playing Olympic teams got a lot of publicity. Everything about the Olympics got a lot of publicity. . . .

The general format was that we would link up on a practice with these national teams, kind of had a clinic-like thing; DeLyle did that. We ran plays. We ran drills. We did different things to help these teams understand the better points of basketball. Four out of the five players had played in college, so it was a fairly skilled team. . . . There was DeLyle and myself from the U of U, and there was Mark Frodsham from BYU, and Don Hull had played at Utah State, and then Nyle [James Nyle] Garn had played junior college up at Ricks [College]. . . .

The members were very supportive; there weren't that many. I believe when I arrived in Australia there were 1200 members in the whole country, which is the size of the United States; that gives you a fairly good idea. There weren't that many, and it was hard to be a Mormon in Australia at the time. Just like now in so many other parts of the world, there wasn't a lot of activity, but those who were active were really strong, and they supported us in everything we did. . . .

Two days before the Olympics began . . . here, a bunch of Mormons were all over the country playing this basketball. It happened to be something that worked favorably for us and got the Australians kind of behind us. I think suddenly for the members, it was a confidence builder. I think they realized that they didn't have to walk around with their heads down. They could stand tall and be proud of being members of the Church. Like I say, it was not easy. There were all kinds of stories in the *Melbourne and Sydney Truth* about polygamy and Brigham Young and you name it. So the press was anti-Mormon. I think that helped with the press, that we were appearing with these Olympic teams. Then I think they saw the missionaries in a different light instead of these fellows out trying to get in their homes and steal their daughters, they thought. They saw that we were young twenty-somethings and we were normal and we competed. We did have to be awful careful about what we said, though. . . .

I think it definitely had an impact in how people viewed the young missionaries. A year after, when Mark Frodsham and I were companions together in Melbourne, people mentioned that they'd seen us on television. Obviously we're easy to recognize with our height, but nevertheless, they still remembered. I think the Australians that worked with us and interfaced with us had favorable impressions of us, and we hope we were gentlemen and kindly people that you'd want to be around; that was the purpose. Yes, I think it occurred because the Olympics were in '56; the Mormon Yankees played in Adelaide in '57. There was also a Mormon Yankees team in Melbourne, Sydney, and other places. In '58, the main team went back to Melbourne, and so it was an ongoing thing with basketball, and the Olympics ignited the interest of the Australians generally in basketball, so there was a good tie. The mission in Melbourne, about six years, seven years later, all of a sudden just blossomed, and that's when the growth of the Church really occurred in Australia was in that middle-day sixties to middle seventies, and from what I know of it now, they have almost a harder time getting converts now as before, but there were probably thirty to forty thousand people that joined the church in Australia over twenty years. Obviously it's not just the Mormon Yankees, but I think it made us a more kindly group. . . .

[During the Melbourne Olympic Games], the Chinese played in the first round, as every team did, and they lost out. And someone put this tour together. I can't tell you who asked the mission president if we could do it. He thought it was a good idea, and we went. Whoever put the tour on paid the expenses, and it was kind of interesting. You know, China at that time was a very strong Communist country, but they didn't treat their players like Russia did. We got along with the coaches and the political people with the Chinese very well. They were very friendly; most spoke English reasonably well. We stayed at the same hotels, although later we stayed with members to keep the cost down. It was a fine experience, and by the time it was over, we were all friends. Chatted about everything except the political circumstances, which we realized we shouldn't be talking about; that was not wise. . . .

The Russians were in extremely good condition; they could run forever. Of all the teams, they had the most skill levels, and they were disciplined—they had pretty good coaching. Our first get-together with them, as I recall, was in an armory. We kind of talked about plays, we demonstrated some things; we worked with them. We did scrimmage—there wasn't much to that. Then they wanted to play us a game, but there wasn't time to play then, so it was set up, and we played them at ten o'clock in the morning, one game. We were able to play with them very well until the fourth quarter, and then these Mormon kids that went out tracting every day [weren't] in that good of shape, and they eventually would win the game. They were close all the way, but they just were in too good of shape for us. They were a physical team. They were the ones who played the US team for the championship of the Olympics. The political people were there everywhere they went. There were as many "coaches" as there were players. The players would talk to us on the floor but never look at us. If we were lined up for a foul shot, they'd talk, but looking at the ground. If we got back and there was a pause, they'd say a few things, but never looking at us; they were very careful not to appear, and we were very careful not to create, any situation or circumstances, but they were regimented. . . .

Inga Freidenfelds [captain of the Australian Olympic basketball team]—Inga was a character. He was probably too good-looking for his own reasons, but he was one of the good players with the Latvians. He had a girlfriend, Lolita, beautiful girl, and I kept asking him why he didn't marry her. . . . I remember one time after I'd played for the South Australian team, there was a big party after the championship was over. We were sitting there, and I said to Inga, "When are you going to marry this girl?" He says, "Ohhhhh, when it comes, when it comes." He was two sheets to the wind anyway. I told him, "Look, if you don't get her married before I finish this mission, I'm coming back to marry her, and you're not going to have her." They all thought that was a hoot, so we were on that kind of good friendships. . . .

I played in Melbourne, Adelaide, and in Perth. In Perth, the competition wasn't very great, but there was a young man, sixteen years of age, who was [six feet eight inches]. I thought he had potential, so I invited him to come and practice with the Yankees, when we practiced at six o'clock on Saturday morning. I tried to work with him and help him move his feet and all of that sort of thing. We developed a nice friendship. I wasn't there that long, but lo and behold, what should happen? But my son Josh played at the University of Utah, and his son was at New Mexico, so it's a small world. That was always interesting to me. He was aware of who I was, and Josh and he talked over the band of a couple of years. That young man [Luke Longley] went on to play with the Chicago Bulls; he played with Michael Jordan. . . .

About the Mormon Yankees, I would say that I probably didn't appreciate what was going on while I was in the middle of it. But as I reflected and pondered it, I don't think there's any question that the Brethren were inspired, that the mission president was inspired in what he did in regards there, too. And I was proud of the missionaries. They did present an appearance of what the gospel is. It was hard at times because these referees they had, they were terrible. I mean, American referees are controversial, but they were horrible, and not to be able to say anything, to smile and not react, was a great blessing in control, self-control, for me. All in all, every young man ought to go on a mission, even though it's not going to be a basketball mission. I didn't know that. I guess that's what happened to me. But I was just happy to be there and do what I could do.

GAYLE HAMPSON

BRISBANE, QUEENSLAND, AUSTRALIA
JUNE 24, 2010

THE MORMON YANKEES bring to mind a loving memory of Harold Turley teaching our family the gospel. My mom and dad—my dad was a professional drummer at the time, and I was only nine years old, and so I guess we were very of the world. But these wonderful young men came here, us knowing that he had a career and had given up something to come and serve a mission; that was great. . . . When I first met Elder Turley, . . . he came into our home to teach the gospel to our family. The sister missionaries had taught us before that but [were] having trouble with my dad. And Harold Turley was the one that had the key to unlock his heart, and he accepted the gospel. . . .

The great memory [is] of . . . Harold Turley as being one of the Mormon Yankees, . . . a part of a basketball team, and us kids, children from other families that were converted. We would cement our feelings towards these missionaries and the message they brought to us. We would go and watch them play basketball, and they were good, really good. . . .

The people that watched these games loved the Mormon Yankees. I think they loved this spirit that had stretched the wholesome look of the way they played fair, and just loved the game. . . . I'm so excited to say that we've been able to stay in contact with Elder Turley and build a relationship that's ongoing with our family. We've visited with their family in Sandy, Utah; they have visited with us, here in Australia.

TED E. HAYNES

MAGRATH, ALBERTA, CANADA
APRIL 8, 2011

I WAS BORN in Taber, Alberta, and I was involved in quite a few different activities in the Taber area, and I had always wanted to go on a mission. . . . I eventually did get my call to go on a mission to Australia. I got the call in the early part of June, I think, of 1953, went to the mission home before the end of June in Salt Lake City. The ship that I was to go out on wasn't ready to sail, and so I came back to Taber and stayed there until the ship was ready to sail from Los Angeles in the first part of September of 1953, so I was home about two months before I left to go on a mission, and the rest is the voyage out across the ocean, twenty-one days to get to Sydney, Australia. . . .

I had no idea that I would be involved in sports, really, at all. I did take a pair of gym shoes that I knew that I would, you know, on a prep day be able to use. . . . I played quite a bit of baseball, and I took my baseball glove with me, and those were basically the two things as far as sports were concerned that I took. But I had no idea that I would be involved in the activities that I was involved with in, got involved in, in Australia. . . .

Elder Dunn worked with the mission president, and Elder Dunn had played four years for Brigham Young [University] and was a pretty good promoter and became a very effective missionary. And when they started sending out other players at the beginning of 1954, of course the mission president had their résumé, I'm sure, and he was able to get the ones that had played in college and at university and sent them over to Adelaide to formulate the team. Elder Dunn was assigned that responsibility as coach, and there was a few missionaries shifted around to make sure that the ones that were sent to Adelaide had played a fair amount of basketball, and from there they . . . [were] called the Mormon Yankees and given the opportunity, or they decided that we should play in the senior league, or in the premier league in Adelaide, and have as good a team as we could have. And we had to—Elder Dunn had to—shift a few of the players around to make sure that we had a team that was very competitive and could, in most instances, compete and win. It was important for us to not only compete, good sports, but you got better coverage, of course, if you won most of your games. . . .

The name of the team, the Mormon Yankees—most of the players, all except two, were Yankees, were Americans; and one player from Adelaide, who was a local member of the Church, of course was Australian. I was Canadian, but I think most of them felt that because of the way I talked—was quite similar to the Americans—that I fit the mold half decent, and not only that, when it boils right down to it, I am American. I have an American passport even now, and my father was born in the United States, and so according to the nationality of the Americans, they consider me today to be an American, and even though I thought I was a Canadian then, I would have been coined an American as well. But we did have two players, a Canadian and an Australian, and that fit quite well with the term *the Mormon Yankees*. There was no problem. . . .

We were always trying to find different ways to communicate with the people, and it was a little difficult just knocking on the doors, even though that was the way that the gospel was carried to the people at that particular time, was through the process of knocking on the doors and getting into as many homes that way as you could. But the people, of course, were to some degree reluctant for you knocking on their door and letting you in, so this was a program that could, we'll say, open the doors and let you go face-to-face with the people, and they were more inclined to let you in and to discuss the principles with them. . . .

In Adelaide, we played in their premier league for that season of 1954, and we were successful in winning the state senior men's basketball championship there and received a lot of publicity and good will from that. And we feel that the members benefitted, and also it opened doors for us, and we were able to meet quite a number of people through that particular method and also with giving different camps and playing in front of the crowds that we played in front of. The mission president at the end of the year, I think, maybe had decided that it would be worthwhile to start another program. This next year, in 1955, he assigned myself to Sydney, and there we were to formulate a basketball team and enter into the senior men's league in Sydney, and that was my chore as a missionary: to go to Sydney, to help organize and coach the team in Sydney, and to play in that league in Sydney. And we—the league was not as prominent as the one that we played in Adelaide, but it was still a benefit to some degree that the team received there. . . .

The team that played in Adelaide, we were all dispersed. Some couple remained in Adelaide; some were sent to Melbourne; I was the only one from that particular team sent to Sydney; a couple of them were sent to Brisbane in Queensland, so we were all dispersed. But by that time, there were any number of Americans that were pretty good basketball players that had been sent out to Australia, and so we had a number of college players, university players, sent to New South Wales, to Sydney, and that was my responsibility: to coach the team and to get them going in that particular area. . . .

There's no doubt that during our time there, our involvement with the other teams and with the other players and with the basketball associations—they were very complimentary to us with our participation. And playing the way that we did and doing what we could to help promote the basketball program, and we'll say that that was sort of the beginning of the real basketball program that began with even more participation later on in the next five or six years, and this was no doubt beneficial. And the basketball association and the players were very complimentary to us. There was no feeling of ill will that we were aware of that concerned the Mormon Yankee teams. They were very favorable towards it and appreciative of whatever we could do to help promote the sport and make it better known throughout the states in Australia. . . .

I think the basketball program that we got involved with initially in South Australia—I think during that time that we were there, I think the missionaries noticed that knocking on many of the doors, the people already knew about you when you knocked on the door, and they would in a lot of instances say, when you introduced yourselves as Mormons, they would return and say, "Oh yes, we've read about you and listened to some of the comments made on the radio." At that particular time, they didn't have TV in Australia, and so that part and recognition was brought in, and this no doubt spread to different areas, and it made it somewhat easier—and it was never easy, but it made it somewhat easier and more compatible when they could see you were people, that you were individuals that participated in activities with and against some of their own people. It made it easier to, no doubt, get in doors, and I believe that the growth of the Church probably started to increase significantly from the period of time of, say, the Mormon Yankees' involvement, first in 1954 in Adelaide and then through the following years—was very noticeable throughout the country, and many people became interested and joined the Church, we feel, from those activities. They didn't—we hope they didn't—join the Church just because of the athletic program of the Church or the basketball program, we hope. We know that most of them joined the Church because the Spirit testified to them that the Church was true, and many—there was certainly an increase in membership of the Church, new members of the Church coming in after that period of time. . . .

The program was not really a program to trick the people. The program of the basketball program, we feel, was a program that would let the people recognize that you were common people and people interested in them, and that that particular way, they would get interested and they would listen and [start] listening to the teachings and the message of the restoration of the gospel. . . . We just did our work there and hoped that there would be good things come from it, and we think that there were quite a few good things that came out of those activities. . . . It was a great pleasure for me to serve as a missionary in Australia from late 1953 to 1955 and meet any number of people and a lot of real good people. Certainly the opportunity of teaching the gospel and bearing one's testimony of the truthfulness of the gospel was a big part for me.

GEOFF HESKETT

MELBOURNE, VICTORIA, AUSTRALIA
DECEMBER 13, 2009

I WAS BORN in Coburg in Victoria on the third of August, 1929. . . . Probably like most children, I was a little bit of a nuisance around the house, and my mother said, "You're going into the YMCA." . . . And I went in there, and we used to have relays around the gymnasium and at the swimming pool, and all of a sudden a basketball was introduced to a group of boys who had never played basketball, didn't know anything about it. Slowly we sort of got the hang of it, and we thought, "This is not a bad sport." And from there it just sort of flourished. . . . There were only a few people playing [basketball], and it was mainly with church halls, and the YMCA was probably the center of that stage, and then it moved to the exhibition buildings where they played to Olympic games eventually, but that was where the main basketball was played. In the YMCA we had our own competition, and I would say at that stage, the YMCA when I started was the top team and the top venue for basketball, but it took a while to flourish from that place.

I think it was probably around about 1950 when I first met the Mormons, but this Graham Coulder, who eventually played in the YMCA team, he was—the way I recollect it was—he was a member of the Mormon team. Somehow we coerced him into playing in the YMCA team in . . . 1951, when we won the Victorian state title. The rest of the

Mormon boys would have started around about that time. . . . [DeLyle] Condie was one that was outstanding. He had a friend—whether they worked together I don't know, but in the basketball they worked together very nicely. We had sort of a mutual understanding with these guys. They were there—we knew eventually what they were there as missionaries. It was strange when the first was introduced: "Oh, this is Elder So-and-So," and I thought, "Oh yes, hello, Elder," and then the next one came up, and that was Elder [What's-His-Name]. [I thought,] "They're not all Elders," but they were. To us as Australians, it seemed strange that it wasn't Tom Condie or somebody like that, but our relationship with them was very nice. Inasmuch as the guys at the YMCA weren't, shall we say, the rough swearing type, these guys fitted in very well in that venue. You never heard them go [to] the umpire; they may have thought he made some bad decisions, which he did, but they didn't at any stage abuse him. And to play against them, you knew you weren't going to get hit behind the ear, and they were good sportsmen, and we appreciated the way they played the game. I think we learned a lot from them because they had come from the country where the game was invented and they had better skills than we did, and we obviously learned from them. It was a bit like [when] the Europeans came after the Second World War: they had a lot more experience in fundamentals that we just didn't have, and we learned a lot from them. So yes, the Mormons fitted in very well in the YMCA comps [competitions]. They didn't go into any other comps as far as I know. They didn't play as a team in the state titles, but the ones we met were quite friendly with [us], and it seemed to show up like they were appreciated our participation in the game with them. . . . I hadn't heard of the Mormons as a religion or the persons at all. At that stage, we hadn't seen them around the place; they hadn't been identified. We probably would have seen them, but we wouldn't have known them to be any different from any other people. . . .

The game was promoted in the YMCA, and we had, I think, two or three nights a week; there would be competitions, and there would be six or seven teams, which means that would take quite a few hours to get the teams through. But when the Mormons came, we obviously learned a lot more of the fundamentals that we didn't have. How to pass a ball properly, what do you do, what you don't do in basketball. . . .

We were overtrained at the time [of the Olympic exhibition games against the Mormons], and when we finished our scramble or practice match, whoever it was against, we would be then rushed out into the exhibition gardens to run around or go back to the village, have your lunch, put on another shirt, and come back and play somebody else in the afternoon. . . . I can picture Condie as a great basketball player and a person. He was a very affable sort of a gentleman, and I appreciated—well, he even assisted me with certain things: "Don't do certain things," which to me was very helpful, whereas a normal thing, if you're playing against somebody, you don't tell them [what not] to do or what to do. The only thing you tell them what to do is to get out of my road. But he would sort of say, "You would win better if had you done that," even though we might have been beating them at the time. No, my recollections of the Mormon Yankees is not at all vivid when we were playing before the Olympic Games. . . .

They were very keen on man-to-man defense, which to me is the only way to play, to enjoy it. But then, we have the Europeans come in, and they're on the zone defense, which sort of didn't appeal to us at all. But the Americans, one-on-one sort of thing; if a guy beat you, well, in that particular instance he's too good for you. And this is where Condie, to a certain degree, did help me. He'd say, "You're an attacker; you shouldn't be playing behind me," and I realized quite sensibly that I had to get in front of him all the time. Well, that keeps you on your toes, and you start thinking sort of thing, and then if you set up a screen, you sort of got to be aware what's going to happen when you set up a screen. Well, with the zone defense, you're only filling one sort of area on the court, say a couple of square meters. That's yours, you look after that; whereas the Mormons, they were very keen on this man-to-man, and I learned a lot from them from that attitude of the game, and I appreciated that, whereas the zone defense—it just didn't appeal to me because you could always blame the other guy, sort of: "Well, you weren't minding those guys," or, "That was in your sort of square, your area." . . .

In most cases when we played against the Mormons in the YMCA, I would be against DeLyle Condie, he being the center and I being the center on the team. So it was quite a great experience to play against a guy who had had international experience and playing top basketball in America, so I was a little bit humbled playing against him, but overall I thought I held my own, but I learned a lot from playing against and sort of with him. . . .

They generally had their own supporters with them, the Mormons. Probably from the Church, and they were quite vocal, and we didn't mind beating them. We didn't at any stage turn to the crowd and say, "Oh, you know, we're Australians," sort of thing or something like that, but they had the crowd, and they were vocal. But I think they appreciated that they had the opportunity to see their boys play basketball, and without that, they probably wouldn't have never seen a basketball. And we didn't mind them because we had our die-in-the-hard supporters also. . . .

Probably the greatest memory of playing against the Mormons at the YMCA was that they were exceptionally good sportsman, and not at any stage was there any abuse or, what do you call, tripping or unnecessary violence, and at the end of the game, they all went around and shook hands. You know, "Well, that was a good game. We had a lot of fun. I am sorry that you beat us." But we were sorry—of course, I mean, we weren't sorry that we beat them. They were great guys on and off the court. We had very little to do with them off the court because when they would finish the match, they had other things to do, and we generally stayed and watched the next match or whatever it may be. After our matches, we would probably go to the local milk bar and have a drink, while those guys would go and do whatever they had to do. But, no, it was very enjoyable. We never had any ill feeling against them. Well, every now and again they would beat us, and that's not very nice, but we had to put up with that, too. . . .

We were playing against them at the exhibition building, and a ball hit the ring, and DeLyle Condie—and this is how the guy came—and the three of us went for the ball. And sheer luck or otherwise, I got high and tipped it, and it went into the ring. "Gee, that was a good shot!" I can remember him saying that. I mean, that is sixty years ago sort of thing. The others guys said, "Oh, that is [a] lucky shot. Oh gee, you were lucky," But he said, "Oh, that was [a] good shot." . . .

I think the main thing is that the skills that they brought into the country when they played with us, even though they probably weren't anywhere near as good as the Australian guys because they had a different lifestyle, but they brought in experience, and we learned a lot of them. Now, as far as the Mormon missionary: well, obviously it wouldn't be any different from any other American team that we played when they came out here. We had the . . . air force, and they came here and we played a lot of basketball against them. But we had probably a little bit of strife against those guys because they had to win, whereas the Mormon missionaries, they were very happy to play and enjoy the game, and we learned a lot from playing against them.

GORDON HOLT

West Jordan, Utah, USA
July 6, 2010

BACK IN DECEMBER of 1960, we had a conference where all the missionaries attended that were in Australia, and they made transfers at the conference, and they released all of the supervising elders. And when they got through—there was like two hundred of us, so everybody was keeping track of where they were going—and my name hadn't been read, and I thought somehow they forgot me. Actually, there were eight of us whose names hadn't been read, so there was a little objection before they closed the meeting. I don't remember who said, "Well, you forgot me," or something; it wasn't me. [President Johnson, a counselor in the mission presidency,] said, "Oh, yes, we have some other transfers I haven't told you about," and he said, and then he named the eight of us. And two of them were going to Darwin, and two of us—Elder Gary Blacker and I—were going to Thursday Island, and the other four were going to two cities in New Guinea. . . . I was Gary Blacker's junior companion. . . .

After we were transferred to Thursday Island, we all had an adventure getting up into these new areas that had never been opened before, and it—my memory is that it took Gary and I the better part of two weeks. We went on a train part of the way, a plane part of the way, and a boat. On the airplane part of the trip, it was a cargo plane flying into the north part of Australia. It was an old DC-3, and they only had one pilot, and I don't even recall there being a door between the cargo and going up to the pilot's seat. And so anyway, I talked to him, told him I was a pilot, and so he allowed me to sit in the copilot's seat. On the trip up, we actually had some engine trouble and landed on a little dirt strip—there was nothing else there, [but] he knew about it—and it was four or five hours before we got the plane going again, and the strip was surrounded by anthills that were about six feet tall. I'd never seen those before. It was an interesting place. . . .

When we arrived on Thursday Island, we came over on a little boat from Horn Island, and they have a little dock there, and we got off, and it was a wooden dock, and people fish from it. And, thinking about the first couple nights, we stayed in a hotel that had a room, and then Gary and I were able to rent a papa house, and the houses were all up on stilts, not so different than northern Australia; lots of the houses were built that way. The island was about maybe three miles all around the circumference of it, and it had a hill in the center. . . .

One of the things that happened is that Gary Blacker had played basketball for a college team before he came on his mission, and Gary was a good ball player. He'd also played on the Mormon Yankees teams down in Queensland and New South Wales, so . . . his idea [was] to form these two teams, both girls and boys. And the girls were every bit as interested in learning and practicing and being involved in the team. It gave the kids something to do. The kids really didn't have a lot to do on Thursday Island; it was pretty primitive. . . .

As it developed, . . . some of the parents started to show up . . . to see what the kids were doing, and that's how we started to interest them in the Church. Gary ordered some uniforms for the kids, which really encouraged them to learn the game more. . . . Along the way, actually, when the teams went down, when they really showed what they could do, when they went to the [Cairns] tournament, I had just left [Thursday Island], and Elder Lundahl replaced me. And it was Elder Lundahl and Elder Gary Blacker that took them to the tournament where they did so well. . . .

I think the value of the [Mormon Yankee] basketball teams [in our mission] was that every time they go to a town, there'd be a big news article in the newspaper. There would be pictures, and there would be interviews about what the Mormon Church was all about. That's what we were trying to do, is spread the story about Mormonism and get people interested any way we could in investigating the Church and having a good feeling about the Church. I think the team did that. I think years later, people who are in their sixties will still remember those games because they were few and far between. They were a big event for the town.

OWEN HUGHAN

HORSHAM, VICTORIA, AUSTRALIA
JUNE 16, 2010

THE MORMON YANKEES were playing what they call Division 1. . . . My brother had took me down to see them play in Division 1, and that was the first time I heard some kind of introduction to the Mormon Yankees. . . . They used to come here [to Melbourne], and I always remember because they used to have hats; they wore hats, and they had those . . . coats, and they used to go around . . . in the crowd and start shaking their hands and things like that. It was so very unusual. I remember my brother saying, "Oh, they're really not very nice," and of course they could all play. . . .

I was a nonmember, but I knew where they were. I used to live in East Melbourne, which was very quietsome; that's where I actually did meet, so I had some idea where the head office was at the time. . . . I suppose of anything, I knew a little bit about polygamy and that issue, but that's about all I really knew. But somehow I was so attracted to them. . . . I sort of felt something, and I said to myself, "When will I go down to that church?" I was only very young at the time. . . .

I think you get a little bit public, this side of Australians; I think they're pretty conservative, I suppose. They sort of always stand back, and they didn't want to talk to them. I think sport is such a big thing in Australia that nearly everyone played some kind of sport, was tied up in it. The Mormon Yankees, being tied up with it, would have made the . . . barrier sitting in a different light than a religious light. . . .

We were introduced on the court, and the missionaries come across and shook our hands and presented us with the Book of Mormon as a presentation. . . . President Simonsen also gave a little bit of a speech about the book and what it actually represented at the time. . . . A lot of times, it would have been the first time any had some Book of Mormon and give it to them, and they'd be wondering: "What have we got here?" And I remember him saying, "You're spiritual." . . . We received the book at this game, and it was signed by the players we played against, and also it was presented by the mission president, and he did do an explanation of what the book was about and for.

DR. DONALD F. HULL

LOS ALTOS, CALIFORNIA, USA
APRIL 15, 2011

I HAD HEARD of the name Mormon Yankees, and somehow I'd known they played basketball, and I thought, "That's a good way to proselyte." Actually in Australia I played almost every week, somewhere; some were winter leagues, and it was a great proselyting tool, and there were people who were baptized after we left, and we got to know them and became really good friends. . . . In 2002 we went back and played in the World Games, and there were a couple of men [who] remembered Elder [DeLyle] Condie and Elder Hull from back in the heydays of '56, and it was kind of an ego boost for me to know that. In fact, when I came back and talked to DeLyle [Condie], I said, "Do you realize they remember us by name?" And his comment was, "Well, they ought to. We were really good." . . .

We . . . played on Wednesday nights and practiced Saturday mornings. We always tried to work really hard so that he [the mission president] wouldn't take the privilege away from us, and we wanted to make sure we had plenty of tracting hours. Anyway, he was a great mission president and very supportive that way. . . . It was a good experience—wonderful guys, Elder Garn, Elder Kimball, Elder . . . Frodsham, Paul Grant. They've just become wonderful friends through that experience. . . .

When they asked us if we would open the Olympic Stadium, I didn't realize how big a deal that was, having the IOC [International Olympic Committee] come and say, "Would you come and represent Australia and do that?" We were interviewed, DeLyle and I were interviewed on the radio, and so when we went tracting, people would say, "Oh yeah, Elder Hull, I heard you on the radio the other day." We signed autographs; we thought we were hot stuff, I guess, in those days. You know, young kids. But it did help, and it was a good proselyting tool. When I went out to—I was up in Whyalla and Port Augusta; they had summer leagues, and we would play in the summer leagues with them, my companion and I. We got to know a lot of people that way, through sports. Australia, great athletic country—I mean, what else? That's what they think. They sleep and dream that, and basketball wasn't a big deal in those days, but it was becoming a big deal, and I think that that period of time helped to boost it along. . . .

The first [Olympic exhibition] game against the Russians, they wouldn't let anybody in. In fact, they almost didn't let our mission president in, and he was the only one in the stand, if I remember right. We played against them with Russian referees. No contest; I don't know. I remember them beating us [by] thirty-four points. They'd knock you down, run over you, and they'd call a foul for blocking. So they said, "Well, we'll play you again. This time we'll open it up." DeLyle and I went over and said, "Well, we've got one request," and they said, "What is that?" And we said, "We would like international referees." Which was our way of saying, "Look, we want to even the [odds]," and they [had] beat us so badly, I think that they thought, "Well, we could still do it." So the next game we played, we had a Chinese and an Australian referee, and we almost beat them. We played them right head to head, right until the end. The stands were full. It was a fun game. . . . I remember the game against the French—played them twice, beat them once, and they contested that, even, but we did beat them. We played Chile and beat them, and they took third. The Philippines beat us the last night, when we played three nights in a row. We beat the French; Chile, I think; and then the Philippines beat us the last night. They just ran us ragged. They were good little players. . . . Anyway, great time.

FRED E. WOODS

ELDON J. HUNTSMAN

AMERICAN FORK, UTAH, USA
MAY 5, 2011

IT WAS INTERESTING for me . . . when we got the call to go to Australia. Back in that time in the mid-fifties when I got my mission call, the Church was in the mode of sending missionaries to their field of labor in the least expensive manner of travel to get there. So initially when I got my call, I assumed we'd just be flying to Australia, but that didn't happen. We went by boat, and it took us three weeks to get from San Francisco, where we got on the ship, to get to Australia. We stopped at many places along the way, and we had multiple missionaries who traveled with us. For instance, one of our first stops was in Vancouver, Canada. We went north instead of south, and we had some missionaries that got off there. We had missionaries that stopped in Hawaii, Fiji, Samoa, as well as New Zealand, before we finally got to Australia three weeks later. . . . We pulled into Sydney—actually left Auckland, New Zealand, came across the strait there, landed in Sydney, and we took an overnight train from Sydney to Melbourne. . . .

I didn't realize at the time that I was called to Australia that there would be a basketball connection. I had played freshman basketball at BYU. In fact, as I got to the mission field, there was another elder, Frodsham, who I had played with on the BYU freshman team, and I met him there; he was ahead of me by a few months. And it wasn't 'til later that I realized there were a lot of basketball players who were called to go to Australia. We had basketball players that played at the University of Utah; there was a couple of us from BYU; there were some that played; Elder Hull, who played at Utah State; Elder Reeb, who played at Arizona State. And it suddenly dawned on me: one of the reasons I probably was called to go to Australia was for the basketball program. . . .

When I first got to the mission field, one of the first things I did was had an interview with our mission president, which was Thomas Bingham at that time. And right towards the end of the interview, he said, "I understand you've played basketball some." I said, "Yes." And he said, "Well, we've got a game tonight. Could you play with our team tonight?" And I said, "Yes, of course." And so they furnished me with a uniform, and so my first exposure was the very first day I was in the mission field. And we played an exhibition game in Melbourne against a Victoria local team. And so that started my career with the Mormon Yankees. . . .

It became very evident that it was a missionary tool; it was a proselyting tool. Number one, the exposure in playing exhibition games against other teams and, in fact, there were times when we played exhibition games against ourselves. In other words, we would have an A and a B team, and the Mormon Yankees would play the Mormon Yankees and put on exhibition games. And during the game and after, and even before, while we were playing, other missionaries would be out in the audience passing out fliers and Church pamphlets and so forth with, of course, the names and addresses of our mission leaders and missionaries, so that if their people were interested in learning more about the Church, this was one way they did it. And wherever I went throughout my mission, we had several basketball teams; there was one in Melbourne, there was one in Tasmania, one in Adelaide, there was one in Perth, and wherever we had those teams organized, they were used basically as a proselyting tool. . . .

At that time, basketball was in its infancy in Australia, really. So they didn't have any large venues to hold these exhibition games. They were usually either at a school, or some communities had recreation centers and so forth. So the fan base was not overwhelming. There might be as many as a few hundred, but there were never big audiences other than the Melbourne area when we were playing against some of the Olympic teams; those were better attended, and there were bigger audiences. . . .

Australian people as a whole are very, very interested in athletics. They're a very athletic people, although basketball was probably not one of the big-time sports in Australia. They had Aussie football, which is a huge sport down there; soccer was huge; they played cricket and all kinds of other sports. But they're a very gifted, athletic people. One of their prominent sports was tennis. We have a lot of tennis champions that come from Australia back in my day. Rod Laver, for instance, who was the champion of several tournaments, was from Australia. John Nukem was another very prominent tennis player. So they were a very gifted athletic people, and once they grasped a sport and embraced it, they were very enthusiastic about sport. . . .

I think the basketball exposure did a lot to open doors for the missionaries as we were tracting. The Australian people as a whole loved the Americans. And if they picked up on your American accent, the doors opened simply because they liked the American people. They liked our culture, and basketball did a lot to open doors, but the Australian people were very open and friendly as a general rule. . . . There were several occasions when we—actually just out proselyting, knocking on doors, doing our normal tracting, where the door opens simply because they recognized us as who we were and associated us as Mormon Yankees. And we were able to get in the home, leave the messages; and I know of specifically a couple of instances where people join the Church as a result. . . .

We had the Mormon Yankee basketball team already organized; the idea came to maybe play some of these Olympic teams in exhibition games. Of course, President Bingham's thought was this would be a good exposure into newspaper for the Church, to have that notoriety, if you want to term it that way, and expose the Church to that kind of public exposure, and it worked wonderfully well. The Olympic teams were anxious to play competitively against anyone, and to play a team that wasn't actually in the Olympics was a good experience for them. The competition level was very good. The Mormon Yankee team that we played on was comprised mostly of players who had either played college basketball in the United States before going to their mission—or, at least if not college, the other players had played some basketball in high school. And so the competition level was very, very good. And in fact, in my experience with Mormon Yankees playing Olympic teams, we were able to be victorious in virtually all of those games. . . .

I . . . was transferred from Perth to Melbourne. And upon arriving in Melbourne, President Bingham called me in the office and said, "We're calling you to be a supervising elder over this particular district with so many missionaries." But he said, "One of the other duties that you will assume is to coach the University of Melbourne basketball team." It was currently being coached by Harold Reeb, one of our other missionaries, who had [done it] in the months prior to me coming to Melbourne. . . . I was coaching there from February of '58 until the first part of July in '58. . . . And I might mention that there were actually three university basketball teams. There were different levels of competition that they were involved with. . . .

My experience in coaching the University of Melbourne was that of, "Boy, you have a challenge to coach these guys, teach them plays." Because you had to start first by teaching them skills. A lot of the guys couldn't even dribble down the court without looking at the ball. They had to physically watch as they were bouncing the ball down the court. And so there were a lot of very elementary basketball skills that you had teach along with plays and teamwork and how to rebound and how to do these other things. I remember we had some very athletic guys that could jump out of the gym physically, but they were terrible ball handlers. You know, you'd throw the ball to them, and they were just all over the place. So . . . from a coaching standpoint, you did a lot of coaching. Whereas some teams with a little more experience, you know, with more teaching plays and how to set up defense and so forth, but this was a lot of elementary basketball skills. . . . A lot of plays that we used were plays that I learned at BYU. . . .

At the time that I served my mission, the Mormon Yankees, wherever they were—whether it was in Melbourne or Perth or Adelaide—did a wondrous work in, first of all, exposing the Church through the Mormon Yankee basketball program to the Australian people. It was a wonderful way of putting the Church out in front . . . because as they wrote about our missionary basketball team, they always had to mention, "Well, we're here on a two-year mission, and we proselyte and so forth." And it did a lot towards softening the attitude of the Australian people towards the missionaries and towards the Church. Because there was little bit of negativism about people knocking on your door and, you know, trying to talk religion. And I think the Mormon Yankees did a lot to overcome that. It made people curious, and they wanted to know more about the Mormons. So I think it was a very, very positive missionary tool. . . .

I think the Mormon Yankee program was good for its time. There was a time when it was effective and a great missionary tool for the Church. And I was excited and proud to be a part of that program. It exposed the Australian people to the Church and to many positive aspects of the Church, as well as to America as a whole. I mean, there's two words that was on our uniform. One was *Mormon* and the other was *Yankees*. We were Americans, and we were there representing our country as well as our church. So I think it did a lot to bring a very positive exposure to the Australian people to both of those venues, the Church as well as our country.

EDWARD A. (TED) JOHNSON

BOISE, IDAHO, USA
JULY 7, 2010

1953. AT THAT time, the Church was allowed to send one missionary per ward at a time. I was privileged to go [from] Idaho, and consequently others in other places were able to go on missions because at that time there was a draft-all. I knew Loren [C. Dunn] at BYU playing basketball, and I was a sports editor at the time, so we knew each other quite well. When we arrived in Australia, . . . Loren was sent by President Liljenquist after he had been there to determine if it was a good place for sports, and incidentally the Harlem Globetrotters had just been through and lit everybody's fire. . . . We were sent to Adelaide and organized a basketball team. The basketball team, basically, was Loren Dunn at center, and he was a very tall man. I was one forward, and Norm Wietzel was the other forward, and [Bob] Steck and [Ted] Haynes were guards. It was a wonderful band of brothers. We just had a great time together, and we baptized as much as we played. . . . There were lots of different churches, and the introduction of the Mormon Church was not opposed but wary. At all of our ball games, we had a printing of "What Is a Mormon?" that we would pass out to the people in the group. The thing that really lit the fire of the members there was that they had something to cheer about. It was a focus. And the focus was absolutely delightful. . . .

I remember many times that we cautioned ourselves that we should not stand too close to the door [while tracting], because if you stand in front of the door and you see these big guys standing right there, you were not right sure what you were doing. So we learned how to approach them, and my way of activity not being too intense. . . . [We wore a] white shirt, a tie, and, in the summertime, a hat. We all wore hats. Mine was made by—I don't remember. It was a pork pie hat. That was the style that everybody wore hats at the time. . . .

Stan Watts was one of the best basketball coaches that BYU had ever had, and Loren learned the plays through Stan Watts, and consequently he taught them to us, and we taught them to the Australians. . . . Things like screens, things like overloading one side of the floor, things like when you take jump shots, that sort of thing. . . . I don't think there was a thing that was unsportsmanlike. We respected each other, and we still do, and the activities were made for a purpose. We were to teach the gospel through sports. . . . During the halftime or whenever it might have been, I had a little pamphlet, which I have here, called "What Is a Mormon?" That was passed out to the crowd, and [it] explained in detail the message of the gospel, and that was done at nearly every game. . . .

The legacy of the Mormon Yankees, in my mind, is this. The experience we had together, playing and teaching and converting and baptizing, is a great joy in my life. I know that we had success in many ways and have a large posterity in our lives; it's a joy. We feel like Australia would be our second home. . . . To all of my Australian friends, I want you to know, that you're really fair dinkum to me, and we love the Australians.

DR. DAVID A. KIMBALL

SALT LAKE CITY, UTAH, USA
FEBRUARY 15, 2011

WHEN I WAS called to Australia, I didn't realize that we would have an opportunity to play basketball. We were going down there, of course, to be missionaries, and I didn't realize that might be part of it. I did, however, take my basketball with me, so I must have had somewhere in the back of my mind that that might be possible. . . .

When I was first in Australia, I was assigned to Geelong, which is south of Australia by—oh, I don't know how many miles, but we had to take a train to get into Melbourne. At that time, I think President Bingham felt that the idea of having a basketball team was appropriate and that we could do some good by having one, and he decided to form a basketball team. DeLyle Condie, who was a basketball player from the University of Utah, was kind of given that assignment, and he and I knew each other a little bit—not a great deal—but he asked if I would like to be on the team, and of course I said yes. So they formed a basketball team in Melbourne and played in the local Melbourne league. . . . At that time I would travel from Geelong to Melbourne on days when we would have games, and we'd get to play. . . . We would play once a week, and that would be about it. We didn't practice a lot; we didn't get together a lot, but we did enjoy playing together and had a lot of fun playing together, and it looked like we would have a fairly decent team at that time. We had several players from college teams: University of Utah, Utah State, and BYU. . . .

DeLyle Condie . . . was an exceptional basketball player, and they invited him to come and see if he could help the Australian [Olympic] team to become a better team. And after they had formed their team and decided kind of who was going to be on their team and were again trying to get some competition so that they could improve, they invited us to play against them. I think we played against them four different times, most of those in Melbourne. We did have one trip where we went to Adelaide and played against them in Adelaide. . . . We got along very well with the Australian players. They were very friendly. They were very willing to learn what we could give them in knowledge of basketball. I think it was an excellent opportunity to just show these people that we were something besides just missionaries. . . .

I think the missionaries that were on the basketball team realized that this was a special opportunity, that not all missionaries were allowed to play basketball or were able to. I think that . . . for that reason, . . . the missionaries on the basketball team tried to work harder and tried to get more meetings with people than other missionaries were sometimes feeling that they needed to do. But I think that it made a difference. I think that as we played basketball and as the word got around that we were also basketball players, that you'd meet somebody at their door, and they'd say, "Oh yes, you're the Mormon Yankees." Where when we first got there, [they'd] say, "Oh yes, you're the polygamists." . . .

While the Olympics were still going on, the Formosa [Nationalist Chinese] team had been eliminated, and they decided that it would be an excellent time for us to be able to go on a tour with the Formosa team. So we were able to go with them to Tasmania. And there we toured Tasmania. I can remember taking a train. I remember a member picking us up and transporting us from place to place, and staying with members in Tasmania. . . . We got along extremely well with the Chinese; they are very friendly people. They spent a lot of time with us on the train and in travel. And I can remember talking to them a lot and occasionally even discussing religion with them. . . .

After the Olympics, I went to Tasmania, and we formed a basketball team there, the Mormon Yankees. We didn't have a lot of great players on our team, but we enjoyed playing in Hobart, and because we were Americans and because we probably knew more about basketball than most of the people there, we were invited to put on some clinics and to try to teach the people there how to shoot. . . .

I think that the Word of Wisdom did help us to stand out because, you know, the Word of Wisdom has a lot of guarantees in it: that if you live the Word of Wisdom, you can run and not be weary and walk and not faint. Of course, in basketball, you run until you are weary, and I think that because you live the Word of Wisdom—and because you're a missionary—that these people were amazed how long you could run and how long you could play before you became tired. . . .

I have a lot of great memories of people that we converted there and people that joined the Church, and some of those people I've been able to see since then. . . . I think the legacy of the missionary basketball program is just to show a different side of the Church, to show the people that there is a lot of fun in the Church and the Church accepts fun and accepts games and things like that, that people can enjoy besides the religious part of the Church. . . .

I have a great love of the Australians and for their country. It's a great country. I love the people there and think that they have a great attitude towards life and towards their enjoyment of life. And I think that they're a people that sometimes have been looked down on because they've been said that they came there because of the penal colony, that they were banished there, but I don't believe it for a minute.

DR. RICHARD IAN KIMBALL

MAPLETON, UTAH, USA
DECEMBER 8, 2010

NOTE: *Richard Kimball is a professor in the History Department at Brigham Young University.*

FOR MISSIONARIES, BASKETBALL proved to be an incredibly popular tool. It was something that was safe for them, a safe way that they could contact especially young men, which they could generate interest in a community. Basketball was popular. People wanted to learn how to play. Mormon missionaries . . . , especially American Mormon missionaries, had a skill that they could teach. . . . Sports was safe. It wasn't controversial. It provided an entrée into people's homes. It helped generate interest in communities, and once the kids got hooked on basketball, they saw how Church members lived. They got to know the missionaries, what it meant to be Mormon, and those were powerful lessons. . . . [Some] missionaries misused sports as a tool. They used it to manipulate potential converts. By about 1970 or so, with the end of the Church basketball tournaments, it probably marks a transition in the Church. Basketball was the American game. Mormonism was an American church, but by 1970 or so, with the worldwide growth of the Church, it was no longer an American church, that, and that wasn't something that the Church wanted to lead with. And because it was an international church, it didn't make nearly as much sense to focus on American games like basketball [with] the Church growing throughout the world and Latin America and Africa and in the Pacific; this was a worldwide movement. So basketball and other particularly American institutions may have fallen by the wayside. . . .

They say that you'll never be able to outlaw prayer in schools as long as there are exams in school. I think as long as young American men are called to go on missions that there will always be sports in the mission field. I remember as a missionary in the late 1980s in Queensland, basketball was still a big draw. We didn't have anything like the Mormon Yankees, but on preparation day you could always count on the elders, members of the local ward, and anyone else who was interested. Often potential converts and investigators would come and play in the church house on Monday or Tuesday morning, and they would be able to practice their basketball skills. It was still a great way to get people interested in the gospel. I'm not sure that's ever going to end. . . .

Although Mormons were building on a tradition that was used by other religious denominations, sports and physical activity for Mormons were special because they were treated in a unique way because sports, for Mormons, could be considered sacred. If you are teaching the gospel, if you a treating your body properly, if you are engaged in any of those activities, those are sacred for Mormons. It's based often in the United States, I think less so in Australia, but a gym will be attached to the back of the chapel area, the worship area. So there will just be a curtain that divides sacred space from what's thought of as secular space, a gymnasium. But in reality, for Mormons, it's all sacred space because it's all about building the kingdom, learning the gospel, getting others interested, and keeping members faithful. So basketball isn't a secular pursuit for Mormons; it's part of their sacred calling.

ERIC LEIVESLEY

MACKAY, QUEENSLAND, AUSTRALIA
JUNE 23, 2010

ELDERS PETERSON AND Skousen, I think, were the very first we had. And they played for a men's team called the Vikings, and they coached them and took them and won a premiership. . . . I [also] knew Elder Gunnel played for one of the opposition teams called Spirits, and I knew Elder Jordan played in an opposition team called Saints. And I had the unfortunate pleasure of having to guard him in a grand final, and as I said, he was very good. But essentially I didn't have much to do with the prize, or if I did, it might have been after a Mormon all-star game. We went to one of the people's place[s], and we had a few drinks and a few nibblies, and there was one little fellow that told a few jokes. Yes, so I don't remember much. I think Elder [Gary] Blackem [Blacker] might have been one of the ones that I had to guard in the all-star game. . . .

My feeling was they're pretty decent sorts of fellows, and they were out here to do a job, because they were good and enjoyed basketball; that was secondary. They did actually have to put their time [on a] missionary basis, and I would often see them riding around the streets in a car going to different places—and very well dressed, very presentable. We even had them knock on my door once. There weren't basketballs or anything, but that was the first thing I asked them. . . . They were really nice fellows and well presented. None of them had a car because they couldn't afford that sort of thing, but they had [a] push bike each. . . .

The crowd loved them. I think probably in those day[s] I'd just love listening to [the] American accent, and particularly when they're [they were] talking basketball, they had a sort of a tender voidance. And I don't remember much about the party we had after the game, not because I was drinking or anything, but I do remember the little fellow telling a couple of jokes, and they always had the blokes around them just trying to pick their brains and find out what we could. . . . I'd just say that they were great guys. They were pleasant to be with, and I was quite comfortable being around them, probably because we never had much social contact with them. They were non-drinkers. Sometimes after training we'd end up going somewhere and having a few. We didn't mix a lot socially with [them], but when we were at basketball, yeah, they always had an audience. . . .

I can only remember one occasion that they came to our place, introduced themselves, and were starting to tell their story, so to speak, and because I wasn't particularly interested, I wanted to talk basketball. So we had an amicable finish, and they told me that they weren't able to play basketball unless they put in their missionary work first, and I think there's some barrier on them playing basketball at that time, anyhow. . . .

I think they just showed us the skill and finesse that they had and, as I said before, they taught us the shot; they didn't teach us the shot, but they used the shot that we had to teach ourselves pretty quickly if we wanted to get up to any standard of play. . . .

In those days, the local paper and sport was, as you can see from the write-ups, they got quite a lot of coverage, and any sports-minded person, not necessarily basketballer, would have known that the Mormons were involved in basketball and probably for that reason might have opened a few doors. . . . I think the Mormons would have been known [and] probably more readily accepted in a lot of places, particularly if the residents were sports orientated, because they may not have been interested in basketball but because the Mackay *Daily Mercury* used to publish quite a lot of sporting features, particularly every Monday and Tuesday after the weekend. The general public would know, or the sports-minded public would know, that the Mormons were involved in basketball, and would readily be accepted at their doorstep[s].

PAT LEIVESLEY

MACKAY, QUEENSLAND, AUSTRALIA
JUNE 23, 2010

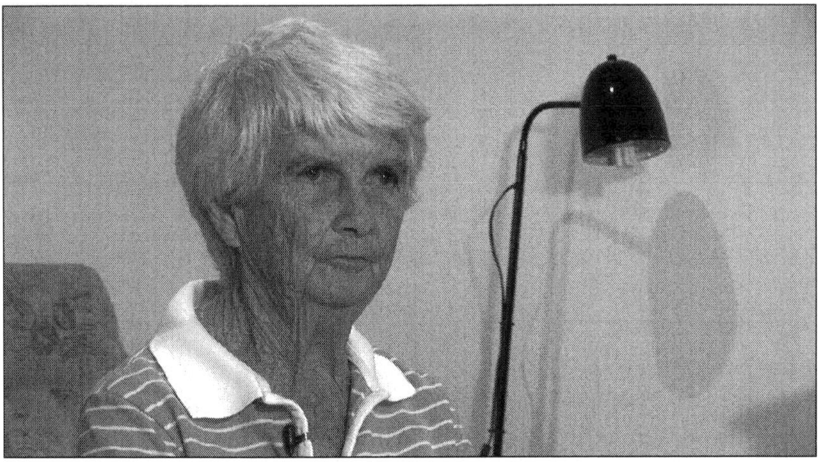

I THINK JUST the novelty of having strangers come to the town that seemed to have a lot higher skill than what the locals had—and really, the locals were a self-taught group because people like Denis Ryan taught most of us, you know, picked it up from books and taught us all the fundamentals and things of the game. And just to have these people come in—and they seemed to have so much more skill in ball control and at speed. And once again, with their American language and their different sort of way that they talked, and they used to have different names for their plays. You know, they'd have some sort of a play, and they'd have some sort of a name. And I can remember quite clearly when they played for the Vikings, one of their plays was "Utah." And they used to call out "Utah!" Whatever that was, but it was some scramble of play. But, you know, just the variety in play and their skills. . . .

I remember the taller man, Elder Skousen, . . . and Elder Peterson was the shorter one and raced around a lot. And then Elder Jordan; I can remember him as just a dead-hot shot. . . .

Denis Ryan was probably what you call self-taught from all the books and that that he used to read, and he passed on his knowledge, and he picked up a lot of knowledge from the American Mormons.

And he passed on a lot of knowledge to other teams that were playing. We always said that most original players in Mackay would have been taught by Denis Ryan, and then Denis taught people like Eric [Leivesley] and Neville Pearse, who in their turn coached people like me and went down through the grades. . . .

We started off with the Catholic priests, and they sort of started it off, and they also played most of them, and especially Father Michael Hayes and Father Tiddle. And they each had their teams, but in contrast to what we were to learn from the Mormons later, the Catholic priests were just self-taught, and they weren't stars. They were very enthusiastic. They probably didn't have a real good grasp for the finer points of the game, but they sort of got us going. Then people like Denis and his brothers and a lot of people joined up and furthered the game, and then came the Mormons with a little bit more finesse, and they passed on their tips, and so it goes. . . .

I don't think we probably knew about Mormons and that they came from Utah and they did have a church in town and these gentlemen used to ride around on their bikes and they always looked very neat and tidy, and apart from that—and another thing was, and I think Eric did say, that they were never pushy. A lot of—you have the missionaries coming around, and they're very hard to sort of—when you say you're not interested, it's hard to shake them off, but they never sort of pushed themselves. They sort of told you what they were about, and apart from that, I didn't know much about them until they played basketball.

JAMES WILLIAM LUNDAHL

LOGAN, UTAH, USA
JULY 8, 2010

IN AUSTRALIA, THE average tennis player could beat a really good American tennis player. In Australia, an average American basketball player was a pretty good basketball player in Australia, and so I just went up there [to Thursday Island] and tried to help Elder Blacker as he gave them lessons and as he coached them. And that—the good thing about it was that the kids were there, both men and women, really enjoyed the activities, that they came there. And Elder Blacker worked them hard, but they all appreciated it; they enjoyed it. . . .

When I think of the Cairns tournament of 1961, I think of all the preparations that went on: working with the players, you know, teach them how to play and to get them in condition and that sort of thing, and then going to Cairns and see some of the kids' eyes when they got on that airplane and flew. It was exciting to see the excitement they had and then to get in Cairns—and Thursday Island wasn't very big. . . .

I remember the day that Gary Blacker left Thursday Island and all the people came down to see him, but to be quite honest, I think I was the most sad of all because he had done such a good work there—such a great companion that I hated to see him go. I wasn't the only one. There were all these kids there that followed; there [were] all these basketball teams. There [were] parents of these kids as well. I mean, it's not a very big wharf, but it was certainly full, and I kind of compare that to when I left: there weren't anywhere near that many. It was just kind of like a Super Bowl team coming home, to have all those people there, and it was really gratifying, and they all had such a good experience and a good remembrance of Elder Blacker. He was great, and the nice thing about Elder Blacker, too, . . . was that he's kept in close contact with them since he's been home. . . .

I remember when I was told I was going up to Thursday Island. I was told by President Moore, "Your main purpose is to go there and just make friends with the people. Members have never been there. We just want you to make friends with them." And through basketball, the Church was able to do that because they all knew that these were the Mormons helping their kids play basketball. And they hadn't played very much before, and so that I think that was good, and I think that helping them improve their tennis skills, going to all their parties at night, it got to the point where they couldn't have a party unless they invited the elders. And even though there was a lot of drinking there, they were very respectful to us. . . .

The Word of Wisdom would come up, you know, as we were playing basketball and they were getting tired and they just kept playing and kept working. It would come up there when we'd go to these parties. At first, they would come up and say, "Would you like a drink?" And we'd explain, "No, we don't like drink." And then we'd explain to them about the Word of Wisdom, and after that, after a period of time, they didn't ask us anymore; they respected it.

ELSPETH LYON

MELBOURNE, VICTORIA, AUSTRALIA
DECEMBER 10, 2009

IT MUST HAVE been 1951 when the missionaries first came, because my mother was taught for about nine months. The Anderson plan, I believe it was called. So she was baptized in April in 1952, and my sister and I were baptized on November 1, 1952. . . . My first recollection of the Mormon Yankees basketball team was when Elder Bybee was still here, so it must have been '52, '53. . . .

Once we joined the Church, it became our life, and we used to go into East Melbourne . . . every Tuesday night. We'd go in there by train and walk quite a long distance to get there, and that was sort of part of our social life. . . . And they used to play basketball in this hall that was in the showgrounds, and you could get access to the hall from Epsin Road, so we used to go there quite regularly and became quite involved with the basketball team, and we felt very proud of them and sort of did our best to support them. . . .

I remember the basketball uniform they had, which was white, sort of a shiny material—I don't know what it was—with a pale blue trim. . . . The missionaries seemed to like us supporting them, because they taught us sort of a chant or whatever you call it: "Blue, white, blue, white! Mormon Yankees, fight, fight!" And we were happy to say that. . . .

Basketball, I would say, . . . was only very low key in Australia at that time, and I like to think that the missionary team sort of helped to promote it, because even though they came from all different places, and yet they played at a pretty high standard, I would say, and were very competitive with the best teams in Melbourne at the time, and I think that it was a very good missionary tool. I think it caused a good feeling amongst the general public, the part they played. . . .

I think that the missionaries, the Mormon Yankees team, did a great job as far as promoting the Church in the community and giving the Church a good name, I suppose you could say. . . . Striking-looking young men, polite and very pleasant young men. I think it made a good impact in Melbourne at the time, and a lot of people started listening to the missionaries in that time period. Really started to grow, the Church, but I'd never heard of them before 1951. . . .

I thought they were fine young men, and it gave me sort of a goal to look for something in the young man that I would end up marrying, to have some of the qualities that they had: the cleanness and the brightness. We thought that the missionaries were just—we put them on a pedestal, I suppose, back in those days—but we just thought they were wonderful, wonderful people.

CARL MCGAVIN

SALT LAKE CITY, UTAH, USA
OCTOBER 31, 2009

I HAD BEEN to the University of Utah for a couple of years and completed two years at the university and went in for my interview with Elder Duff [Marion D.] Hanks, who was a neighbor and a good friend, and I thought I was quite privileged to be asked where I wanted to go. I thought that was not the norm, that you went where you were assigned, but he said, "Where would you like to go?" And I said, "Australia," and so I ended up with a call to Australia. My first assignment in Australia was out in Perth, and shortly after arriving in Perth, we started playing basketball every Saturday morning. . . .

[We played on an] asphalt court, and it was a kind of a recreational league, and we'd play all of the various teams that were in the competition. It was a good experience. I don't remember ever getting in any fierce battles, but you would always come out feeling beat up. Just a good experience. Seems to me like I remember we had at one time some members that were playing, some younger members that were not missionaries. We'd have them help us out and participate and play for us. And I think it helped activate some of them that had not been very active, but they wanted to have a chance to play on the Mormon Yankee team, so they came out and supported us and helped out when needed and just had some real good experiences that way.

Later on, after leaving Perth, I had an assignment up in a little country town out of Melbourne called Hillsville, up in the mountains, and we were assigned to handle it a little differently. Rather than just going in and tracting the town out as fast as we could—it was only about three thousand people in the town, so we could've done it in a couple of weeks—President Bingham said, "I want you guys to take it real slow and get very well acquainted with as many people as you can and get active in the community and participate and see if that's not more effective than just trying to knock on doors all day." So we did: we got active in the Boy Scout program. . . . While we were involved in the Boy Scout troop there, they were trying to raise money to build a new hall for the Boy Scouts, and so we arranged to have the Mormon Yankees come up to Hillsville and put on an exhibition game and charged admission, and all of the money went towards the building of the Boy Scout building. That got us a great . . . many friends that became sympathetic with us because of that effort and the money that we were able to raise. All of the ministers that had preached against us previously, telling everybody to be wary of these guys that come in and look like they're trying to do good—watch out because they're not as good as they seem. So this was a good event that really turned the tide, and it got a lot of people very positive on our side. . . .

My experience was the Australians are wonderful, friendly people. Once you become a friend, you're a friend for life. They'd do anything for you. I have many people, former friends that I knew there, that every time they come over to America—which they do often; the Australians are great travelers—on their vacation, whenever they come over, they look us up, usually stay with us, and it's just lifetime friendships. But their attitude is, "I want to be your friend, but just please don't talk about religion."

JOAN MCNAIR

BENDIGO, VICTORIA, AUSTRALIA
JUNE 20, 2010

I FLEW FROM Sydney, Australia, to Adelaide—I was a nanny to a family of five children, and I was working with them in Adelaide when there was a knock on the door. My employer answered the door—I was busy with the children—but the next thing, she appeared in the doorway and said, "There is some young men you can talk to." And so I looked up and saw these two very tall, handsome young men standing there, and [I was] thinking, "What's happening?" They just spoke to me for a little while and made an appointment to come back and left. They came back a few days later and started teaching me the discussions; they were wonderful, the discussions. . . . I was . . . I kind of forgot about the young men; the discussions were just what I'd been praying for and looking for. And they asked me at one time, had I heard the discussions before, because I seemed to know the answers before they were telling me things. . . . So I went along, and I was baptized on . . . the seventeenth of September [1954]. But that's about how it all came about. . . . I was baptized, all of us, by Elder Loren C. Dunn, and Elder Johnson confirmed us. . . .

I had no idea of Mormons, Salt Lake City, Utah—never heard of those. And so that was all new to me, and the people I associated with didn't seem to have any opinion at all. . . . [Concerning the Mormon

Yankee basketball games,] it was very noisy, pop, and the music of "Sweet Georgie [Georgia] Brown," which was deafening and played on and off all through the night. There were a lot of people; the building was always packed full of people. . . . The games were played in Our Boys Institute in Adelaide; they were always crowded. The crowds were very noisy and very vocal. We had a small group of girls and boys that were with us, and we cheered loudly. There was, that I can recall, not anyone booing or, you know, bad feeling towards the missionaries or the missionary elders when they scored a goal or when anything bad happens, when there was a foul. Everybody seemed to be quite nice and polite and played really nice sportsmanship. . . .

They were always polite in the games, even though they wanted to win, and they worked hard, but they played fair. . . . I think it was a good influence. I think it has helped over the years; I think it was a good influence in the beginning, a good opening to presenting the Church to the local people. And I think it gave it a really good base and let them see that we're just ordinary people and we can have fun just like everybody else and still have the gospel in our lives, and I think it made a big . . . start of the gospel there in the Adelaide area.

MERVYN MOY

SYDNEY, NEW SOUTH WALES, AUSTRALIA
JUNE 25, 2010

NOTE: *Merv Moy played on the first Australian Olympic basketball team in the 1956 Melbourne Olympic Games.*

I KNEW VERY little about the Mormons until I played against their team—a team, and as it turned out, later a number of teams over the years—in basketball, which was started at the YMCA back in 1951. I've learned a lot about [them] since but have pleasant memories of them. . . . They were very formidable opponents; they usually won. Sometimes we might have grabbed a victory, but it was half court. They didn't, from the point of view of basketball, try to, as far as I was aware, impress anybody with any kind of doctrine, their religion, or anything else other than just play basketball, and they were respected by every team that played against them and with them. . . .

Well, we played against them . . . in the city of Sydney competition. There were several years in the 1950s, and as the Sydney team was being formed to represent the Olympics in Melbourne in 1956, they were years to try to put us that way. As a yardstick, to pick representatives for the 1956 Australian basketball team. Prior to that, in 1955, [an] Australian team [for] each state that was competing was allowed to have two or three Mormon players invited to play with that state for the purposes of the championships. I think this was only a one-odd situation; I don't think it ever happened before or after. . . . We had Elder Dunn and we had Elder North and Elder Day on our team as honored guests, guest players, if I could call it that. . . .

Elder Dunn, of course, had great advantage in his height, for a start. There weren't many first-rate or A-grade players with his height and athletic ability. But he was a typical center, even competed in modern game; he used new plays. He sometimes went by himself. He had all the shots, hook shots, types of things that were needed. There were a lot of plays that they did, structured plays that were based on each post, but generally when he's working, he was like the other Mormons that we played against. They were very athletic, very skillful, and raised the bar quite high, and that was the first introduction we ever had of international basketball, because there were teams from other nationalities that played in competitions. We had Latvians and other nationalities, but the Mormons were the tops; they were American, and the standard they set was very, very high, and it was a pleasure to play against them. . . .

As far as Elder Dunn, when he was opposed to George Dancis, it surprised me to have them. They were quartered at the same height because it appeared to me that, probably because of his athleticism, that Elder Dunn seemed to have much more control, much more ability, for reaching for the ball, for using extra plays, and for shots, than George Dancis had. But I wouldn't say—he was not a selfish player, Elder Dunn. He was [a] team player, and it wasn't so much that he was a star in his own right. He was very, very capable at scoring points if he chose to, but he was more a team player, and that's the way the Mormons were. Individually they were brilliant, but they were better as a team, and that's the way they presented themselves. And we played them the way we looked at them. . . .

Leading up to the '56 Olympics, a squad of about sixteen set[s] of players was selected to go through various selection games to be picked for the Olympic team, and we played the Mormon Yankees in Melbourne. And I remember Elder Condie. . . . I was wanting to get on that Olympic team and thankfully made it, but I remember it was a very hard, hectic game, and I haven't got much memory of points scored or who won it, as a matter of fact, but I'm pretty sure that the Mormons won that one. . . .

The Mormons, to me, as I've said before, were a bar you had to reach, and I saw them play well other teams, and we played them a lot of times over those years, in the fifties particularly. And never once did I see any kind of altercation or unsportsman behavior. There used to be four fouls in those days; I think they raised it to five at some stage, but my memory betrays me as to when that was. You have to [be] careful of your fouls, but sometimes in the hurly burly of the game, there were some awful smashes and calls and so on. But they'd be the first to put their hand down and pick you up if you were on the ground. There was always a respectful way in which they approached the game, and everybody regarded them the same way, as far as I can see, but from our point of view, when you get a body contact—and sometimes we did have some rugged games, not against the Mormons. They were rugged, but they weren't—there was nothing bitter about it at all. It was a part of the sport, and we didn't mix with them much, socially, after the game. We always talked and talked to one another in the dressing room before, and they were just a pleasure to play against. I felt very enriched for having known them and remembered some of their names. I haven't seen them since those days, but I still remember their names. And that says something. . . .

The Mormons to us represented class, and if you have to spell it, you'll never have it, that type of class. They were gentlemen; they were great athletes. They—I think, as far as I was concerned, it was a pleasure to play against them, and I think that they embodied that kind of spirit in all of it, in our team, anyhow. And I think all of the other teams, the majority of the other teams, were most anxious and pleased to play against the Mormons because they did things easily, they did them classily, and they did them well. . . .

As I look back now, I think they were the beginning of where we are today. In my opinion, they set the bar, and with the experience that the players have had—that came long after me, overseas competition. They've developed accordingly, but it was the Mormons, as far as I was concerned, in my era, that came out and showed us how it was done, and how to play the game without the . . . bitterness that sometimes occurred between players and between teams that played in that era; some of them were out of hand, sometimes. Not to any great extent, but bitterness. . . . But you could never say that about the Mormons. It was always a pleasure to play against them because even they—you knew you had that play of being on your best game. You had to bring your best game with you to beat them. It was no shame to lose because you enjoyed the game, and if you did the best you could, you enjoyed it a little bit more. So, . . . I think the Mormons and the YMCA, in another way, became the start of basketball in Australia as it is now played by the boomers.

DENISE MUTTON

ADELAIDE, SOUTH AUSTRALIA, AUSTRALIA
JUNE 19, 2010

WHEN I FIRST came in contact with Elder [Loren C.] Dunn and Elder [Ted] Johnson, they told me that they belonged to The Church of Jesus Christ of Latter-day Saints. They didn't mention the Mormons, you know, so I didn't know much about them. But as soon as I had the first discussion, . . . I just knew the plan of salvation is true. . . .

When I told people then that we had been visited by the missionaries, they said, "Oh, they're the Mormons; they come and take people away." And my mother-in-law was a smart woman; she said, "You shouldn't have let them in your house," because I was five months pregnant and I was on my own. And so I was a bit frightened, you know, and so I decided that when they knocked the next time, it was the day to them, I didn't answer it. But then the next time they came back at night, and my husband was home. . . .

Ever since we were baptized [on the] seventeenth of September 1954, we [have] kept in contact with the elders; we used to send a Christmas card every Christmas, and they would send one back to us. Loren Dunn, when he arrived home, was called into the army, and he went to Germany, and he'd write us a letter from there, and he told us his experience. And as I said, we kept in contact with them all those years, and then, we've been over to America a few times, and each time we went over, we would tell him we were coming over, and we went to dinner at Elder Dunn's place, and it was wonderful, met his family and his little boy. His father [Elder Dunn] had said to his son, "Would you like to go to Australia?" And he says, "No, because I wouldn't be out to learn the language." And we remembered that because he [Elder Dunn] said, "Well, these people are from Australia." And so we spoke to him, and he was quite surprised, and that was fun. And also Ted Johnson; we went up and we stayed with him in Boise, Idaho, and it was lovely. We had a lovely experience. And he was a lawyer then, and he took us to a judge, and he took us to his court, and we saw how he worked. . . .

Since the elders knocked on our door, we've held pretty well all the positions in the Church and that. We've loved it; we've just loved being a member of the Church, and it's been wonderful to be able to bring your children up, and all our children have been married in the temple and have served missions. They've all served missions but one daughter; the other daughter served a mission. . . . We are so grateful that the elders knocked on our door and brought the gospel of Jesus Christ to us.

PETER G. MUTTON

ADELAIDE, AUSTRALIA
JUNE 19, 2010

I HAD OTHER missionaries from other churches come before those, and I said, "I've never listened to this, too." But then I thought, "Well, I'm expecting a child, right? I don't know much about bringing up children." But then they told us about the family and so forth, and I thought, "Well, the things they believe in are what I believe in, too, and are what I need to do to raise my children." Of course, there were a lot of private things going around at that time. So I had some way knowing how to bring up my children, and so what they said about the Church appealed to me, and I thought, "We need to be together, too, work together." . . .

I spent years at that time—I'd never been to basketball camp, but I went in order to watch them play because I heard so much about it. Elder Dunn got so much publicity that they just had a chance of losing with the opposition on top of him. So some of the others got a chance to do something, too. I remember one of the small ones there got around there to get the goal while someone constrained Elder Dunn. He'd sneak around the back and got the goal, but I never had seen much before that. I got quite interested when they were going to start a basketball team of their own, but I never got to play that sport. . . .

I didn't have any worries about polygamy. It was a little bit strange when they called each other "Brother" and "Sister," so I thought. I met a couple, Brother and Sister Smith, and I thought they were brother and sister because they looked so much alike and sometimes couples adapt to each other's mannerisms and they look alike sometimes.

DENNIS O'RIORDAN

MELBOURNE, VICTORIA, AUSTRALIA
DECEMBER 14, 2009

[THE NAME MORMON YANKEES] was a combination to show the Church's actual involvement and secondly because the Americans were the majority of players. They put the term *Yankees* together, so we ended up with *Mormon Yankees* as a term rather than the Mormon [in] other areas. And the team down in Melbourne was the most-known team. Their participation also in training programs for the universities and some schools and some other activities was shown in the activities in the community. They were reaching into the community to make an involvement, and some of the people had involvement in programs, and they then attached to those programs and continued on. . . .

The [Mormon Yankee] school clinics were held because we had a number of teachers in the Church who were trying to introduce basketball into the school, and they brought the missionaries in to train the children at school in the games. And this was in the high school arena from ages thirteen to eighteen. . . .

My understanding from all the competition and by the advertising and by the media was that the Mormon Yankees played each team as a warm-up environment so that every nationality—the Russians, the Chinese, and other groups—all competed against the Mormon Yankees as part of the team. Ron Cutts was the manager of the team at that stage, and he took the team to the different locations and the venues. And in some competitions they wiped the floor; and other teams, they were wiped off the floor; but the games went on, and when it was all over, they then went to Tasmania and played a series of games against the [Nationalist] Chinese. . . .

They were focused, and it was a highlight on them, but the actual area was the presentation of their game. It was well conducted; they didn't break the rules, and they weren't violent. I think that stood out in more attention because a lot of the other teams were bringing violence in as a means of trying to win. Knock the man down rather than playing fairly. I think that the fairness and the etiquette on the court from the missionaries was part of setting the standard. . . .

Most of the missionaries that came had competition or practice at home, and they'd also played in the BYU and other university organizations, and they were of higher standard than what we had in Australia. So therefore, they brought [to] the game techniques and the various challenges and also the way people should conduct themselves in the court. So the information that you didn't think about. The Australians are a fairly rough group, and they played to win, and they just roll everybody over, and this wasn't sort of the way that this was to be done. So the court etiquette was improved. . . .

The followers that were there came to see the Mormon Yankees play because they were interesting to watch and they played nice techniques and even got to the stage of doing some slam dunks in the early days, which are a highlight these days. But the taller members could slam-dunk the ball without any sort of problem, as they would just leap up and then put the ball in, and they'd move on, and it was a very sort of outgoing stage. . . .

The techniques that they brought with them are the techniques that we didn't have. It is the same way today that if we were playing in the soccer match, we didn't have the coach, so we bought a coach. He came, the team played, the coach left; but the techniques were left behind. This is the same situation. The missionaries came, they played, they brought their techniques, and they left them behind. . . .

Australians are not a religious people. They have their beliefs and their practices, but we do allow people the right and the privilege to do what they like. And the Church came, and they seemed to be a little strange sometimes, but overall we have been left alone. We have had minutes where we have had in the early days—people were tarred and feathered in Australia or in New Zealand. They have been abused, they have had doors slammed in their faces, but there have been some accidents later on where people have been attacked. . . . But in general, I believe that the Australian people and the membership have a quiet existence relationship, and we go on doing what we are doing, and they go on with what they are doing, and where we can assist, we have assisted; where we can't, we can't. We today . . . focus on the community, small groups, because we are now growing larger. With six stakes and eighteen thousand people in membership, we just don't have the time to involve ourselves as much as we used to do when we were in small branches and small communities. . . .

They [the Mormon Yankees] set some standards, and they set some rules of behavior, and they have continued on, and the basketball communities that exist today in the small communities, before the larger teams [were formed], are still there. They still play Wednesday and Friday nights instead of Monday nights. . . . I would believe that the training, the missionary training at the universities, the other environment and areas have left threads behind which have been picked up, and I believe that the Australian coaches will probably visit overseas and take coaching clinics, and they will come back with what they find.

ALLAN PASCOE

MACKAY, QUEENSLAND, AUSTRALIA
JUNE 23, 2010

I KNEW VERY little about the Mormons before they . . . came into Mackay. . . . I didn't know too much about the Mormon religion or anything like that. . . .

Basketball was becoming very popular in those years in Mackay, and when those fellows come [came] to town, . . . they're quite good, entertaining basketball, or a little bit on the—if anything, on a Harlem Globetrotters sort of thing. So everyone was interested to see them and to see how they played. . . . [They were] very popular. They were good games of basketball, very entertaining, in a really tiny place, and good sportsmanship, mixed well with the players. They were much normal, very nice fellows, the fellows that we met. . . .

Elder Gary Blacker was sort of a stalwart player that I based myself on. I thought, you know, I like his style of playing, and I spoke to him while he was here about the game in general and how he trained and what he did, and I was always interested in new ideas to try and so forth because I was at that stage where arriving to basketball, and I think I stopped corresponding with him. When he went back to the US, he wrote me a nice letter and gave me some tips on training. A couple of things [that] have always stood in my mind is the skipping or jump rope, as you call it, which I sort of knew about in my training kit. It was probably in there, anyway, but one of the things that really stuck in my mind was he told me to do pushups on my fingers. . . . I used to do these pushups with my fingers. And people used to say to me, "You're doing pushups on your fingers. Where did you get that from?" I said, "From a Mormon." Elder Gary Blacker told me that years ago in a letter, that that was part of his training schedule to strengthen your hands, strengthen your fingers for basketball, so that was one of the things that I did, and it always sticks in my mind that he was the bloke that told me how to do that. . . .

I didn't have a lot to do with [the Mormon Yankees] when they were here, but as far as I remembered, their sportsmanship and their behavior and everything was exemplary. They were just nice young fellows. They blended in with the people here. . . . They were good sportsmen, and they played the game . . . fairly and they were—I think that what they've show[n] is not only good sportsmanship, but they had good skills, and it was obvious to me, being a high-rate basketballer at the time, that they all either attended universities or they played this more than universities as they do in America, or whatever. And I think they probably brought, they eventually—well, I know they did in the North. They did it here. There's no question about that, at that particular time. They [had], as I say, sportsmanship, and they played the game fairly, and they played it very well. So that was what we were mostly interested in, you know, at the time. And they were nice enough fellows, so they blended in very well.

NEVILLE PEARSE

MACKAY, QUEENSLAND, AUSTRALIA
JUNE 22, 2010

WHEN THEY [the Mormon elders] first came to Mackay, they had a lot to do with basketball, . . . so that's the way we met them, through basketball. We did not have a lot to do with them religiously. They weren't trying to push their religion on us at that stage. They were just mainly helping us with the basketball, and they really did help us with the basketball. I think they went a long way in Mackay, especially of promoting and strengthening the basketball, because we never had players like that before ever come to Mackay. We were just kids. . . . Elder Skousen and Elder Peterson were the first two that came to Mackay, and they came in 1955, '56, and we were just young kids in school, and they took over and helped us and coached us, and we won. Took us up into a higher grade and we won the . . . next year, through their support. . . .

Most of the games we've played on bitumen courts, at the back of the churches. Most of the Catholic churches have them. . . . They were the first ones to start the basketball in Mackay, and they would play on bitumen courts at the back of these churches, and they came, and the Mormons came and coached us there. . . . They mixed with people very well. . . .

They never preached to us about any Mormon religion or anything, but they did give us a Bible—their Book of Mormon, as they call it. And they did sign it for us, by Elder Skousen and Elder Peterson. I had a book here with it on. . . . It was signed by both of them. I think this might have been when they actually left, when they left the district; they signed it for us then. . . . The crowd really loved the Mormons playing here. . . . They were looked up to, for sure, as far as basketball players [go]. And their conduct was impeccable. There was no trouble at all with the Mormons, as far as I can remember. . . .

They [also] helped others, even though they played for us as a team. They also helped other younger children, but with their coaching and fundamental skills in the game, and that was really well appreciated. . . . They certainly raised the standard. The standard was never as high in later years as it was . . . mainly due to their coaching and their expertise, I suppose you'd say, and in the game they brought the local standard up to the higher grade. And then from there on, some of those players already made the Queensland team, and that was only mainly due to them.

ROBERT G. PEDERSEN

SALT LAKE CITY, UTAH, USA
DECEMBER 7, 2010

WE WERE ALL American, . . . and they would always sort of introduce us as "All-American Mormon Yankee Basketball Team." . . . When you get someone as athletic as each of our players were, take a special attention to each young man particularly, that would come up, showing them how to shoot, how to dribble, how to guard. That personal attention, I would imagine, if you were to check back now, fifty-one years later, that many of the young ball players that were there, they will remember that they were taught and shown a lot of attention by these American Mormon Yankees. . . .

I remember one town, we had a question mark: "Should we go to that town?" We'd heard there was a little bit of animosity. We thought, "Well, that's strange. We'll just go be who we are." While there, I remember there was a girl that seemed to be very shy and laid back, up in the stands. And somehow, someone suggested I go say hi to her. I went up into the stands, kneeled down on the steps there, and said hello to her. I said, "Come on down." She was reluctant, so I sort of picked her up and put her on my shoulder, and she held my hand, and I carried her down onto the floor, and I took her around, and she could sort of shake hands with some of the missionaries, and I thanked her, and I gave her the basketball after I put her down on the floor. I asked her for it back, and she went back up into the stands. Her parents had thanked us and gave us the old high-five, and I think from that point, Roger Bown, who was our MC, I think his jokes even got funnier because the people started to love him and us a lot more. That was a nice little moment that we all remember. . . .

Well, first and foremost, we knew we were missionaries. We weren't a traveling pre-NBA team on a lark. We were out to teach the gospel of Jesus Christ; that was our purpose, and we ship Books of Mormon ahead of time. We would take some, but we'd ship them by rail or whatever to the towns—always had plenty of them. The night before, or if we got there late, we would be sitting down together, and we would sign the name of every player we were going to play against the next day, and then all of us would sign the book to him, so as a part of the introductions—"And now the Mormon Yankees" introduction would be finished by Roger Bown. We would then go over and shake hands with all opposing players, and we would present them with a personally signed Book of Mormon from all the players. . . .

It's obvious, I would hope, to everyone, that we didn't go to Australia to be basketball players. We went to Australia to be missionaries for the Mormon [church], or The Church of Jesus Christ of Latter-day Saints. That's the truth. That was our assignment, and we were playing basketball for a few weeks; a lot of games, few weeks. Then we'd be reassigned with the companionships throughout the cities of New South Wales and Queensland, and then we'd go back to knocking on doors, asking people for referrals. Our primary purpose as Mormon Yankee basketball players was to preach the gospel of Jesus Christ, and that it had been restored to the earth through the Prophet Joseph Smith. That was the purpose of Mormon Yankees, and the reason we played was to let the people know that we were normal, caring, hardworking young men who felt enough about that message that they would give everything up to go on a mission. . . .

As the story of the Mormon Yankees was shared when we came back from our missions, then throughout our years, I think it was very unique in all the world. I don't know of anywhere else in the world that basketball played such an important part in building relationships between the community, the Church, the Church members, and with missionaries. . . . We were there to be missionaries, and we also were there, I'm sure, brought together in the way we were called by inspiration to have a team that was quality enough that we could really represent the word *basketball*, the word *Yankees*, and the word *Mormons*. . . .

Sometimes a question comes, "What do you think is the legacy of the Mormon Yankees?" And I always think the legacy of the Mormon Yankees is that we did it. We went there. We only had two years: we had limited time, limited opportunities, and we didn't miss the opportunity. We made friends throughout the whole Australian continent, particularly as our mission related to at that time—we were New South Wales and Brisbane—but we made friends. Today, many of our ball players have been back to Australia or have met Australians who can remember those Mormon Yankees came to our town fifty years ago. And maybe the kid that we played with was at that time eight years old or ten years old, but we were remembered. I can't think of a single instance where we were not representing the Church, in basketball, in the friendship between our countries, in a very upbeat way. . . .

To even have the opportunity to have the Mormon Yankees to even perform or to have such a tour required the inspiration and the love and support of President Weldon V. Moore, who was our mission president. Because of his background, maybe as opposed to other mission presidents in other areas, he loved the idea of taking good news to people in a very positive way. Now the gospel of Jesus Christ is referred to as "good news," "the glad tidings." But basketball, it's sort of like a little bit of sugar makes the goodness and the medicine go down. Basketball was a door opener; it was a heart opener, and Weldon V. Moore, our mission president, will long be remembered by all of us as how grateful we are that he would give us 100 percent support. He said to Elder Peterson—speaking for myself and Elder Day and all the missionaries and Elder Rampton (who was one of the counselors in the mission [presidency])—he says, "Do it, boys, do it. . . . Whatever you do, we support you. Go for it." And we did.

DON PEMBERTON

MELBOURNE, VICTORIA, AUSTRALIA
DECEMBER 14, 2009

NOTE: *Don Pemberton was on the University of Melbourne 1957 basketball team, which was coached by Mormon missionary Harold (Hal) Reeb.*

I'M A MELBOURNE boy. I was born in September 1936, raised mainly in the suburbs except during the war, when I had a bit of a country experience. . . . My earliest experiences with basketball were at the exhibition buildings in Melbourne, probably on Saturday mornings, when the American members of the Church and some locals were practicing. And it's very interesting that the exhibition buildings became a venue for the '56 Olympics. And in those days, they had competition basketball on two levels, downstairs and upstairs at the exhibition buildings, and the Church had teams. . . . They practiced at the exhibition buildings, one of their venues. . . .

Of the Mormon teams that I saw playing matches at the YMCA, I'd be pretty sure I had never seen an unsportsmanlike act. They were models. That's honest; they were models. . . .

[Elder] Reeb came at some time in my university years. I was at the University of Melbourne from . . . I was playing basketball at the University of Melbourne from 1955 to 1958, somewhere along that timeline. [Elder] Harold Reeb spent maybe two years coaching us. We used to play at two places that I remember, not the YMCA. . . . Now, Harold Reeb would work us out at practices, and he would coach us through games. I particularly remember, I guess he'd been coaching us for a while, and I remember one practice day, after the practice, he said, "Now look, I want you to come in here and sit down. We're going to have a talk." The lines of his talk were, "Look, playing basketball is one thing, but how you live your life is another. I'm just saying to you guys, if you're smoking, if you're drinking, if you're wasting your bodies, you're wasting your lives." Now I'm not going to make a song a dance, he didn't use those words, but the tone of it was, "I'm not going to make a big thing of this, but this is good sense." My sense of Harold Reeb—I'm saying this perfectly honestly; please believe it—he was a guy I looked up to tremendously. He was so clean cut; he was so good at his basketball moves, but he was just an exemplary human being, and I'm still a kid in a sense, and I thought he was just a magnificent person. . . . My sense of Elder Reeb was that he was the basketball coach. He was right up front, "I'm a Latter-day Saint." We knew exactly what he was, but I never heard him, that I can remember, nudge any of us towards a view of Jesus or a view of Joseph Smith or a sense of the Mormon Church being something that we should think about. I don't think that was a neglect in him; I think it was a very wise tact. . . .

Elder Harold Reeb, I just enjoyed being a young man, seeing how good you were as a slightly older young man. I think we always look to the people a little bit older than ourselves if they're really good, and that's how he was for me. He was a mentor and a good human being. But I'd be pretty sure that the guys that I remember on the team . . . would all want to look him in the eye and say those were great days and that was a very honorable period.

JAMES RICHARD (RICH) RAMPTON

SALT LAKE CITY, UTAH, USA
DECEMBER 7, 2010

WE WOULD GO into a town, and we were met usually by the Volkswagen representatives or the athletic companies that were sponsoring us and the mayor and the powers that be in that particular area, and they would interview us, and it was quite an experience. And then we would go over to the field house or where we were going to play the game, and we would usually have, give seminars to the high schools, the smaller grade-school kids. We also did an air force base; we gave clinics to them, and it was just a real good opportunity to spread the gospel through the tour and through the publicity that we were getting through our sponsors. We would then go to the area prior to the game, set up a table, and we would have the missionaries that were going to stay in that particular town set up, stand where they would give out Book of Mormons to the people and take addresses and so forth. And they got a tremendous start; a lot of times we would open a town that way. We would go into the town, and we would say, "We're going to leave a couple of elders here for a while," to explain what we were doing. . . .

I played football—the Australians called it gridiron—at the University of Utah under scholarship, and so when I got called on a mission, I played my junior year at the university, and I still had that mentality, kind of a contact mentality, from football. We were playing a game, and the [mission] president and his wife, Sister Moore, would always be there on the front row. There was this big bully that played gridiron, or Australian-rules soccer, and he was roughing up our little guard, just bumping into him, and finally Pres[ident] Moore called me aside and says, "Elder Rampton, see if you can't slow that guy down a little bit. He's roughing up our players." So I thought I had permission from the mission president to kind of quiet this guy down, so I went in and laid a couple hard blocks on him—nothing offensive at all, in my mind—but it worked. He calmed down, and we were able to play, and the fans loved it.

HAROLD (HAL) REEB

SPRINGVILLE, UTAH, USA
OCTOBER 31, 2009

I WAS INTERVIEWED by the General Authority. . . . We had to see a General Authority to get interviewed before we could be accepted [as a full-time missionary]. He also asked me where I'd like to go, and I told him Australia, because I had always read about the great cattle ranches in Australia and I'd always thought that'd be a great place to go, and I was too dumb to learn a language anyways. . . . There was never any mention of basketball or anything that alluded to it, so when I arrived, they sent me to Tasmania, and my first experience was the missionaries down there had jerseys that said Mormon Yankees. And so we got together and started playing in some games, and then later the Mormon Yankees, the Olympic group, came down and played. I remember in my journal noting that they came down, and they won, and I got to dress out with them; I didn't get to play with them. I played in the preliminary game, and I noted in my journal that I got the most applause. But anyway, I came back to Melbourne for Christmas conference and was assigned to Melbourne, and that's where I labored until the middle of February of '57. President Bingham called me in and asked me if I'd coach University of Melbourne basketball. . . . They'd had a request from the university for somebody to come and do that. So that was when I started working with those kids, and it was a great experience. It was a lot of fun, and they treated me very well, and I'd take whoever my companion was, . . . and we'd go out and practice with them, and then we had games, at least one game during the week. So I got a double dose of basketball. I got to [play] with the Mormon Yankees, and I got to play with, or practice and play with, some kids from the university. . . . They were respectful, and they were responsive. . . .

I remember when a navy ship would come to port, we would try to get a basketball game with them. Three of us had been picked to play on the Victoria state team. The way they played their basketball in those days, it was like the same way they played their football. They had clubs, and that's how you remembered it: they had clubs. So it was like a big intramural arrangement. But we played this US Navy team, and these kids were cocky—gee, they were cocky—and they were down about 50–20 at the half. This kid's going off shaking his head; he says, "I can't understand this. How could all these Australians beat us?" And I said, "Well, don't feel too bad. Four of us are Americans." . . .

We were still just kids, and I don't know that we had any, in general, any grandiose ideas about what this all was going to accomplish. It was just a great outlet for us to play ball and maybe ingratiate ourselves a little bit. I don't think that we saw the big picture. I mean, I didn't, even coaching the university [team].

DENIS RYAN

MACKAY, QUEENSLAND, AUSTRALIA
JUNE 22, 2010

I REMEMBER . . . THAT THEY [Elder Skousen and Elder Peterson] were very good guys. And they said they were looking to play basketball, so I immediately put them into my team; it was called the Trojans at the time. They were very, very good players. . . . They were exemplary. . . . I couldn't fault them. I thought, well, these are two handpicked guys to promote the Mormon religion, and they did a great job. . . .

We all just thought that they [the Mormons] were a religion that was popular in Utah and they were practicing polygamy. That was the general theme. None of us had much idea on what else. . . .

They were the talk of the town [in] . . . Mackay. . . . It was certainly a good way of getting them well known. . . . They just arrived, and straightaway basketball picked up, because most of us were just triers compared to the Melbourne people. . . . All the basketball was centered on church parish tennis courts originally, and then they covered them with [asphalt], . . . and I can remember Elder Jordan and Elder Peterson playing out at [the] West Mackay court. It was a very small court. I understand that our tennis court wasn't that big compared to the hospital court, but that was basically it, and then they started to build . . . [and] started playing in the skating rink; [it had] concrete walls. . . .

[Skousen and Peterson] coached the Trojans because they knew more about basketball than any of us did. . . . They [the Mormon elders] were genuine people—well-mannered . . . they were just really nice people. . . . I think they gave me a leaflet, but I knew a little bit about the Mormons at that time. I think I looked it up somewhere. But that was the only thing. No, they didn't mention anything. Skousen and Peterson [said], "Would you like to say a prayer?" And that was it. . . .

They taught us how to actually play the game properly and how to shoot and pass and all the fundamentals of basketball, and basically they were showing us how to play with them. . . . In other words, we learned more by playing with them than probably what they taught us. They didn't spend a lot of time with us. It was just a training session, and then they'd come and play, but they couldn't play on Sundays. . . .

[The fans] . . . really loved them . . . [and their] courteous behavior. . . . We never had any problems that I know of. . . . [The Mormon Yankees] were very well behaved and [showed] good manners to everyone. And that was the most noticeable, that they were [a] first-class type of people.

After the parishes had got these games going, there became great interest in the game from all over the Mackay city. So they opened up the game to the whole town, and teams were nominated, and we had quite a lot of teams in all parts of the district playing basketball on these courts. This went on for a few years, but the game really picked up when the Mormon missionaries came to Mackay. I was fortunate in meeting Elder Skousen and Elder Peterson; they were looking to play, and I got them to play on my team for a short period, and later on they moved out to help the younger players, and they taught most of the younger boys how to play the game properly. I had learned the game on my own from reading books. . . .

The main thing that the Americans did in Mackay was to get intense interest, because the local *Daily Mercury* was supporting the game and riding it, and when the Mormons came to town, it was quite a big headline for the paper. Crowds began to build up because at that time basketball was unknown in Mackay. . . .

[The Mormon Yankees] being accomplished players, the basketball people looked up to them. They all knew that they knew how to play. In . . . those days, we were all beginners. They used to basically idolize them to a degree; that's because they had all the interest. They weren't involved in basketball to the degree that they were [involved] there all the time. They went about doing their missionary work, and I don't think that they were overly employed in teaching; they were valuable. They taught me quite a lot of the finer points, and then when I went to help the juniors, the younger players, they were well listened to because some of my friends said they could explain things very well. . . .

When I first met Elder Skousen and Peterson, they gave me a booklet on their religion, and they came around and visited me at my home. . . . They gave me this booklet, and they said, "Would you like to say a prayer with us?" I said I could do that, so we said a short prayer, and I enjoyed that quite certainly. . . . They were just good guys. . . .

When the Mormons stopped playing basketball in Mackay, I was myself very disappointed because these were the only players that we could learn from. Mostly at that time, every one of us wasn't good at basketball, and we, myself and others, were disappointed that they were not playing. I offered one of them, you know, "Why did this happen?" All I heard was everybody may have been getting too involved with the basketball, so, which was understandable because they were getting a lot of support from the local community. . . . I remember people coming to me and saying, "The Mormons came to my place today; gee, they're nice guys." But they knew them through the basketball. . . .

I think one of the reasons that the game picked up in the women's game, too, would be the effect of the Americans involved. In the war here, this was a base for recreation for the troops, and Mackay got very, very much popular with Americans, and all the girls here were crazy on their accent, the way they spoke, and the way they dressed, and just generally how well-known they were. This was just a follow-up when the Mormons came here, but they were [a] similar type of people, and their accents attracted the girls, and I didn't have a lot to do with that side of them, but I know that that was one of the reasons we got a great following from the female side of the game. . . .

I think the main legacy [the Mormon Yankees] brought was the fact that they had the knowledge [of] how to play the game, and their behavior was exemplary. I can't say that there were any bad impressions in the local community. They certainly promoted basketballing by their ability to play the game. . . . I think that the Church of the Latter-day Saints . . . was greatly boosted by the presence of the Mormons playing basketball . . . to promote themselves through sport, and I know that the Mormon religion went ahead in leaping bounds. . . . When [the Mormon Yankees] arrived, we knew very little about the Mormons and their religion, so it was a great boost to themselves and to their church.

BOB SKOUSEN

MESA, ARIZONA, USA
FEBRUARY 11, 2011

I ARRIVED AT BYU [Brigham Young University] in 1959—was it '59 or '58? And I played on the freshman team and enjoyed that very much. Played under Stan Watts and one of his assistants there at BYU, and we had a good season; I don't think we lost a game when we were at BYU our freshman year. . . . I had never planned on going on a mission. And my sophomore year I had a real good year, sophomore year, and made the all-conference team; I was averaging about almost eighteen points a game. And I really enjoyed playing at BYU. . . . After the last game of the year, we'd played our last game, and that night I went home, we went home, went to the dance that night, and then we went home and had a good night's rest. And about six o'clock in the morning, the phone rang. And I, "What in the world? Who's calling me at six o' clock in the morning?" So I picked up the phone, I says, "Who is this?" He says, "This is Delbert L. Stapley of the Quorum of the Twelve. . . . Bob, I need to talk to you. I want you to come up to Salt Lake today." . . . So I jumped in my car and drove up to Salt Lake, got there about nine o'clock or so. And he said, "Have a seat." And I said, "What's this all about?" And he says, well, he said, "Bob, I'm calling you on a mission." I said, "A mission?" You know, I says, "I don't figure I'm going on a mission. I'm going to play professional basketball.

I don't want to go on a mission." And he said, "Well, the Lord wants you to [go]." . . .

So I went back to BYU and met with this girl, and she said, "Gee, if the apostle calls you on a mission, well, you can't turn it down." I says, "But I don't want to go on a mission. What do I want to go on a mission for?" She says, "You need to go on this mission if he calls you on this mission." And he told me, "Well, you guys discuss it, pray about it, and then call me in the morning." So we called him, and I said, "Okay, I'll go." And he said, "Well, I knew you would," but he said, "I just wanted you to be sure yourself." And it was irresistible. I mean, I couldn't turn it down. I mean, there just wasn't any way I could do that. So anyway, we called him up and said, "I'll go." And he said, "Okay, the call will come through your bishop at BYU" and told me all what was going to happen and everything, so I said, "Okay, let's do it." So that's the way it started out, going on this mission. Then he says, "Is there anything [at] all that I can promise you if you'll accept this call?" He said, "It's that important." And I said, "Well, if I go on this mission, my basketball career's through. I know a lot of guys go, but you just aren't the same when you get back." And he said, "Well, what can I promise you?" And I said, "Well," I said, "If I could just do one thing. If I could just hold the record for one game at BYU, I'll feel it's worthwhile." And he said, "I can promise you, you will do that. You will hold the record for one game." . . .

Well, when I returned from my mission, I went back to BYU, and of course Stan Watts says, "I don't even know if I'm going to give you the scholarship for leaving." I says, "Okay, . . . I'll just go back and play for the University of Arizona, or UCLA wants me to play for them." And he says, "Oh well, forget with that. You just come and play, you know, come and play." So I said, "Okay." So my parents took me up there, but first game of the year was UCLA, and they were the number-one team in the nation. And they'd been in the Final Four for the past two years, as far as I could remember, anyway. So it was kind of a—this was our first game of the year. In fact, we played back-to-back games against UCLA. And the first night we played, you know, and know the rules, and we beat them—it was really a great game—but only by three points. And anyway, that was it: we beat them. So the next night was Saturday night, and we played them, but in the first game I got a real bad charley horse on my leg. I couldn't hardly walk or anything. It was a really bad deal, but I said, "Well, I'll . . ." And I never even thought, really thought, about the record, never thought about it. And so when we got out on the floor, and everything, started warming up, I couldn't hardly warm up because my leg was hurting so bad. But anyway . . . the game started, and I went into a—some people in athletics will tell you they go into a zone. . . . It's an unbelievable feeling. Everything goes in slow motion, completely slow motion. And as you go through the whole thing, it's difficult to explain the feeling you have, but everything I threw up there went in, I can tell you that. And I just went through the whole game, and I heard them announce that I had broke the school record. . . . And never thought much about it because I really hadn't thought about the record ever since he told me that I would hold the record. Anyway, after the game was over, you know, I didn't realize that I'd even broken the record. And that's it. . . . "Man! The promise came true!" So that was about the way it went. . . .Well, it lasted until this last year [2010], when Jimmer Fredette broke it. And he scored forty-nine points; I scored forty-seven. He had the shot clock and all that stuff, too, so three-point shot and everything, but I didn't. But I don't know; if I'd had the rules they had today, I would have scored—I think they said fifty-six or fifty-eight points. So I guess I still hold the record in one way or another, but the Lord's true to His promise. And I can testify to that. . . .

The Mormon Church was not even well known, as far as I could see. Most people had never even heard of the Mormon Church; they didn't even know what it was. And when we came in and started playing ball, you know, then they took notice of us and everything else because we had some real good ball players in our mission—real good ball players. And so, you know, we won everything, you know. We were in there because they just hadn't played basketball long enough to compete with us. . . . I think that's the main thing: the legacy that's left of the Mormon Yankees is the fact that we were good ball players, and we played clean; we played good. And I think that it was a great thing to do. . . .

Well, I love the Australian people. I really do. Val Williams is one of the great ones that I met. And she was on the Australian Olympic team in the '56 track and field Olympics. She was a sprinter. And at that time she had seven children, and she ended up having seventeen children. . . . She wrote me the other day, "Just want you to know that the amount of converts to the Church because of me coming into the Church through your efforts was over three hundred people." She said, "I just want you to know that." . . .

The basketball team was good to give them [Australian Latter-day Saints] all a sense of pride in the Church and everything. And the members there were so glad that we were playing, and everybody was just—it just boosted everybody's spirits that we would win and play in most games. . . . I appreciate the privilege the Lord has given me to go on a mission and to go to Australia and to be with those people.

ROBERT (BOB) STECK

SAN FRANCISCO, CALIFORNIA, USA
APRIL 15, 2011

MY MISSION CALL was a surprise because it was in the Korean War era, and they were only taking one missionary per ward. So I sort of said, "I'm safe." And then I did receive a mission call from President [David O.] McKay. . . . My bishop said, "Robert, you'll be a changed man. This will be the best experience of your life." . . .

I grew up in a family of sportsmen. . . . I played high-school sports; I played junior-high sports. I played basketball, football, played quarterback for Weber High School, and my last year of high school, I took a state championship in wrestling, much to my surprise. So I grew up with an athletic family with my two brothers. . . . I wrestled three years in college. . . . I wrestled and played football at the Y [and] played Church-ball basketball all the time. . . . I went to the all-Church tournament in basketball. . . .

I'd been there [in Australia] about three months. I got a telegram from the mission president saying, "You're being transferred to Adelaide." I didn't know why. I went to the mission home; I met with President Liljenquist; he said they were forming a basketball team. . . . He told me the other elders that would be playing, and one of the elders, of course, I came to Australia with: Loren Dunn. . . .

I . . . started practicing with each of them. Elder Haynes was already there; Elder Dunn; Elder Johnson—Elder Ted Johnson; Elder Wietzel; Elder Thayer; and then Brother [Arthur Emery], who was an Australian—he played with us the first three or four months. So we started immediately, and we practiced every Tuesday or Wednesday and Saturday, and we played on Thursdays most of the time, Thursday evening. . . .

[Basketball] was there for a reason; it was a means to an end, and so we were very clear on our mission call as basketball players that it was to teach the gospel. That was made very clear to all of us, and we took that very seriously. We led the mission in baptisms in Adelaide while we were playing [on] the Mormon Yankees. So we never lost focus on missionary work. We tracted every day; we held our meetings. I didn't see that basketball really impacted our time as far as missionary work was concerned because when we were playing, we were doing missionary work. But I have to say it was a lot of fun; it was gratifying, but our mission was to preach the gospel. That was very clear, and we all knew that. . . .

We competed as sportsmen. We knew that we were being watched—we knew that we had to be an example, so sportsmanship was very high on our priority list. Whether we won or lost, we were good sportsmen, and I think that carried a lot of weight with those we competed against and [with] the fans. But we were all competitive: we wanted to win, the Church members wanted us to win, and so we were very competitive, but the main theme was to do it as gentlemen and be good sportsmen. . . . We were registered as a state team, and that was the state of South Australia, so we were registered as a state team, and we competed with all of those teams that were registered as a state team. . . .

When we got there, the [Harlem] Globetrotters had just been to Adelaide, and that got everyone stirred up. . . . We played at the OBI, Our Boys Institute—a lot of Australians, and they had a team. . . . Very good competition. We didn't win every game. We thought we could. I mean, Loren Dunn was the only one who could dunk the ball; he was [six feet six inches], and when we'd warm up, after warming up a while, he would dunk the ball. They'd never seen that except [with] the Globetrotters. And every game, before we started, they'd start asking, "Loren, Elder, dunk, dunk, dunk!" And then that was a kind of fun for us. So we lost some games, but we won most of our games; we were that much better, more advanced in basketball than they were. They didn't have the basics down like we did. Then, just growing up, we knew the basics. And then Loren, of course, played college ball at BYU, and he coached us. . . .

The press was very favorable to us. They covered most of the games. We had our names and pictures in the paper; we had signs in some of the stores; the action, our pictures were in some of the stores. And so the media was very, very friendly towards us. . . . Elder Dunn and I were both on the radio and had at least two interviews on the radio. . . . Every conversation was a missionary conversation, and it opened the door for us to talk about the gospel. It started with basketball; it ended up with missionary work. First of all, they knew we didn't smoke, we didn't drink; that was a door-opener. . . . When we tracted, sometimes they knew we were Mormon Yankees, and they would let us in. But most of the converts, we tracted, and they knew very little about our playing until they got to know us, and then basketball would come up, and then they [would say], "Oh, these are the Mormon Yankees. These are the young men on a mission for their church." That's basically, I think, how the gospel was spread. . . .

The Australian people, when they found out that . . . we paid our own way, that we were not paid to be there to play basketball and then were missionaries—it was hard for them to believe that we were not paid to do that. Because the Church of England, Episcopal Church here—paid ministry. All they knew was paid ministry, and so that was a real door-opener. Really, basketball led us to the Word of Wisdom, led us to no paid ministry; they're the two things that basketball opened the doors for us. And then it was straight missionary work. We taught the lessons and challenged for baptism, but they were the two door-openers from basketball. . . .

I think we were tops [in baptizing], and the elders that played basketball managed their time better. We knew that we were playing. We knew that we wanted to do our missionary work first; it came first, and so we worked very diligently to make sure that our time was spent wisely. And so I think time management, if you will, was a big part of it. And then I have to say that if you're playing basketball—you're playing athletics—you're physically fit, you have more energy, and you have that enthusiasm that maybe sometimes [is] a little lacking in other missionaries. . . .

Basketball was significant because it was a new sport. It was an exciting sport. [The Australians] were anxious to learn this sport. The other thing is that we were Americans. In Australia, they looked up to the Americans. That was the place to be; that's where all of the action was. And so when a basketball player—when we were there and we were Americans and basketball, the two came together, and that's why it was so popular. . . .

I was asked by the mission president to go to Queensland, to Brisbane, to coach a team. I was surprised at that. I was a zone leader in Adelaide, continued there three months, and then the mission president asked me to go to Queensland to organize a team, and he said that because it was so popular in Adelaide, they felt that it would open up Queensland, and Brisbane particularly, and [we had] a couple of ball players up there. And so I went to Brisbane, organized a basketball team up there; we participated similar to what we did in [South] Australia. Totally different players. The caliber of basketball was not nearly as high there as in Adelaide, but the enthusiasm was there. And it was the same pattern: we knew what we were there for. We taught the gospel, but basketball did give us entry into a lot of the media and then the homes, particularly the homes of the members. I think that that encouraged the members to know that basketball was part of the Church, and they felt an enthusiastic attitude toward the missionaries and towards basketball. And I think that probably is the key to have basketball spread the gospel as much with the members as it did with the missionaries doing the missionary work. I think it spread. I think that's what ignited the members in Australia. . . .

The members were . . . proud of the missionaries, . . . but they were also proud to see that the media picked up on the basketball and, through basketball, talked about the Church. No one knew about the Church in those days; in the fifties, very few people knew about the Church, and it was a little difficult for the members. You know, every member a missionary—they weren't that enthusiastic about it. You know, we were there to do the job. But when the media picked up on basketball, I think it lifted the Saints, and they felt more comfortable talking about the Church. . . .

That's how basketball developed in Australia from Adelaide. It started in Adelaide, and the players were dispersed; they went to all of the different states in Australia. And it was so successful that—I didn't have the perspective of the mission president—but obviously it was doing so well that all of the other states formed a Mormon Yankee basketball team. . . . It ignited basketball all through Australia, and then it ended up that we played the Australian Olympic team. And so every missionary that had played basketball before, and those who came in, like Don Hull and DeLyle Condie—they just kept it going. . . .

I think the Mormon Yankees should be known historically as igniting, first of all, the members of the Church. They felt more comfortable talking about the Church; they had an enthusiasm regarding basketball, and that spread to them being enthusiastic about talking to friends and neighbors, even their own family members. Many of the members were split-member families, and I think this gave them a chance to show the other family members that we're not just ministers of the gospel, that we were regular people, that we could be approached. And the media was very friendly, and before we got there, I know there was some negative publicity—particularly they rubbed the Short Creeks hairs on the polygamy, and that hit the papers. And so this media, the great media coverage we had, and positive, that seemed just—again, to repeat, I think it really helped the members of the Church, and I know that from the Mormon Yankees, the gospel expanded rapidly after that. . . .

In Australia, the members that were baptized that were interested in basketball were lifetime members. We didn't see many, if any, fall away from the Church when I was there. Basketball was an entry. The gospel was firm in their minds; they had a testimony before they were baptized, and they remained faithful.

RAYMOND ARTHUR STEEN

MACKAY, QUEENSLAND, AUSTRALIA
JUNE 24, 2010

I HAD NO knowledge of the Mormons whatsoever, and so when they did arrive . . . to . . . our community, and then especially on the basketball court, we befriended them because they were so easy to befriend; they really were. . . . When they took to the basketball court, we were in awe because we'd never seen that standard of basketball in our lives. Plus, you can watch it on some movie cameras. When we saw them in the flesh, and they were so [ready] to sort of demonstrate to us and encourage us, and it was a really nice feeling. . . . They had definite set plays, set moves, which we—we used to run up and down the court like kangaroos, but those guys actually brought set moves. And Denis Ryan, who was our coach, he then took that on board, and we would do set moves in just about every game we played. And that's probably why we were so successful playing Adelaide and Mackay, because after watching them—the Mormons—play, and the set moves which looks so graceful and so good, we decided to copy that. . . . Denis . . . could take them on board readily. What the Mormons illustrated to him, he could very easily demonstrate to us, so we'd follow those moves on. And then he would actually—we pieced up getting some American basketball magazines and then books, and we developed our own moves. . . .

The Mormons were very warmly accepted in the community, very warmly, because they were such approachable sort of people. Well, they're so much better than the rest of us. That didn't show [off] at all; they just took us on board, prepared to show us the skills they had, and it was a really warm relationship. It was really wonderful. . . .

The girls couldn't get anywhere near them. But that didn't stop them from still mingling with everybody. They would interact with their social activities, like barbecues. . . . They mixed with that; they'd come to our homes. My parents actually invited them to dinner. So they were taken into the community and taken into our lives very, very easily, and very warmly, too. . . .

They just mixed with the rest of us. We used to have a few drinks, just to be sociable, of course, but they didn't. That didn't make a scare of a difference because they would be just as happy-go-lucky and interactive just as well, like some of my other friends who didn't drink anyhow. . . . That doesn't make a difference to any person whatsoever, no. They joined in; they were accepted. It was a wonderful time. . . .

They played as hard as we played; they were just clipper than us. There was no give and take. We mixed it with them, and they mixed it back, but same as we do; it was all taking the right approach. It was played with good sportsmanship. There was good, solid, hard basketball, and that's what we needed, and they probably realized that as well. . . .

When they mixed with the community outside the basketball environment, they had a very positive sort of atmosphere about them. But it was an honest atmosphere, and I think that's why they were so well accepted. They were respected—that's what they really were. They were respected for their values, and no one put them after that. . . . They definitely mixed well with the community once they played basketball, because you'd feel like you were close to them rather than being the Mormons, the elders walking down the street and talking over the fence outside the yard with their white shirt[s] and black ties on. Always very well dressed, very neat. That was because we have other religions who also walk down the street on weekends as well, and they can sort of be a bit of a pain sometimes, but these guys, once they played basketball, the community sort of accepted them a lot better; they were invited to functions, as I said earlier. They came home for dinner, and they explained about Mormonism to us, and they gave us a Mormon book as well, which we still have. So we were paid to listen to them a lot because you felt like they were one of the group, one of the community. You've already had redirection with them, and they weren't preaching down to you. You took them into your homes, and they were great. We were really disappointed . . . when they weren't allowed to play basketball anymore. I think we lost something, and they definitely lost something as far as the community is concerned. . . .

The Mormons were accepted for who they were. The fact they went out of their way to actually mix with our community—the community readily accepted them. They were really sort of pure blokes. . . . The girls always felt safe around them. They mixed so well with our parents, so they would take them—the junior, the little people—up to my mother, and treat everybody the same, and I think that's why they were taken so warm in the hearts of the people here in Mackay. And we were really disappointed when they stopped, you know, really disappointed.

KEITH STRINGER

MELBOURNE, VICTORIA, AUSTRALIA
DECEMBER 12, 2009

WE WERE LIVING in Blackburn, and . . . when I came home in the evening from work, my dear wife said to me, . . . "There's some American boys coming to see us." And she said, "I invited them because I know how over-the-top you are about Americans." . . . They came back in January, . . . and from then on, they started talking to us. . . . And so we came to a point where the Word of Wisdom was discussed. And that point was a sore point with me because I liked the alcoholic beverage, and I said, "You nineteen-year-old kids, here's me forty-two. You haven't been around; you don't know anything." And so after the first night on the Word of Wisdom, then they came back a week later, and I was to talk to them about the Word of Wisdom. And when they came back, in that week later, and I started to parade myself, and again, "You don't know what you're talking about. I need alcohol in my business. I need it because I go out with everybody and we talk business over the bar of the hotel." And one of the elders stood up . . . and said, "Mr. Stringer, when the prophet of the Lord speaks, what should we do?" I went down like a pricked balloon, because I said, "We should obey what the prophet says." And I went to work the next day, and we used to go across for a favorite pastime of most people in Australia. And I went across, and we got to the hotel, and I said, "I'm finished drinking.

This was my last drink." One of my fellows said, "I'll give you a week." Another one said, "I'll give you a month." Another one said, "I'll give you three months." I haven't touched a drink for sixty-odd years. That was all there was to it, really. And Kay and our son that's deceased, Ian, were all in favor of getting baptized . . . on the nineteenth of March in 1960. . . .

We used to go down to the Albert Park stadium at the invitation of our mission president at the time, which was John O. Simonsen, and from there we wanted to go every week, every time there was a game, and there was quite a crowd of us there. I don't know how many, but there were a lot of people there, and we had a very enjoyable time, yelling and screaming and carrying on, barracking for the Mormon missionaries. . . . Mostly members of the Church were doing all the cheering, . . . and particularly my daughter, Kay, here is doubly vocal, insomuch as she cheered like anything. . . .

They passed out quite a large number of Books of Mormon to the opposition, and we had pamphlets which sometimes we would take around to nonmembers, and generally the whole atmosphere was directed as a missionary activity. . . .

When the Mormon Yankees were abolished by the order given by Bruce McConkie, I felt a little bit disappointed because I thought it was a great promotional situation, where we could be seen not only as preachers of the gospel, but as preachers of the good rules in basketball. But we tried. He just said, "Oh, it's got to stop," and that's all there was to it. It was explained to us that it was from Salt Lake, from the General Presidency, and so as we learned in the early stages of being totally obedient to everything that's said from Salt Lake, we just accepted it and went on with life just the same. But by that time I was stake mission president and being tutored by him inadvertently. . . .

I think they made the Church a good deal better known than previously because again, as I've said earlier in the piece, people tend to look on Mormons with the big hats and the long beards and all that sort of stuff that was in the early days of the Church and sort of didn't believe that they could play sport of any sort, despite the fact that, as we know today, many of them are filling top-line professional football and basketball players. . . .

When the basketball was stopped, it didn't have an impact, really, on the degree of conversions that were taking place. Bruce McConkie stirred the pot quite a lot, and by and large the way he handled the situation, the way he taught the missionaries, the way they were educated as to how to be obedient to the instructions about missionary work, we had an increase, a very big increase, in baptisms. All things improved, increased, and it was under the . . . basic leadership of President Bruce McConkie.

HAROLD E. TURLEY JR.

SALT LAKE CITY, UTAH, USA
SEPTEMBER 7, 2010

I'LL TAKE MACKAY [in Queensland] as an example. We would get there in the early afternoon, and we would have a clinic, and we would teach them all the basketball skills, to the kids first and then to the adults. But throughout that whole thing, we would also share the Word of Wisdom and also other principles of the gospel as we could fit them in. Also, part of us would do the clinic; the other part would go to one or two of the stores in the downtown part of the town, and we would have a signing and an exposure to people where they could come in and talk to us, and we could talk to them about who we were, what we were doing, and why we were here. And they just flocked to this because all of a sudden this Mormon Yankee team is coming to town; they're going to play their all-star team, and so they were hoping so much that they could beat us, but they wanted to get acquainted with us as well. So now we go and we have the game. We not only play the game, but we do something else that they can't resist, and that is we give them a token of friendship, and that was a Book of Mormon that we would give to each of the players as we would start the game. And then Roger Bown was our entertainer, and he was phenomenal in putting this whole thing together, and so he would then—and as we went through this tour, he started to give us all nicknames, and he would use those nicknames as he would have us playing, and then he would do the halftime show. And he would have them just going crazy because he could do these impersonations that were just fantastic, and so the crowd just loved him.

And Mackay's a good example because we beat their team, and that really upset them, but they pleaded with us to come and play them again. And so we were able to work it out at the end of the tour to come back and play—and it was packed the first time, eight hundred people or so. The next time, they had over nine hundred people. That kind of gives you a feel of what happened. All of a sudden, we break out [of] all these bands that are put around us of negativism, and now people will let us talk to them, and we can tell them about what we are, and we're not poylgs [polygamists]. We're not here to take their wives or their girls or anything else like that. We're here to share Christlike virtues with them that we have and that we know they have and put it all together and have a real family experience, where they can raise their family as it should be raised. . . .

Mackay was probably our focal point, and the main reason is because the missionaries had been treated so poorly by the people in that town just very recently, just a few months before. So we were a bit concerned when we got to Mackay: how were we going to be treated? Well, this Big Jim [Connolly], he was so happy to have us there, and he had prepared the town to take us all in and to make us feel really at home. That was such a great thing for us that on the second run when we came back—that's when I remember—we had the store appearance, which was massive: the people coming and wanting to see us and talking to us, getting autographs, and then with our clinics for the young people and then also for the men and women, older. We had just hundreds of people wanting to be a part of this whole experience. It just totally unraveled their hatred and their bad feelings for our church. They could see we're just regular guys and that we loved life and we loved to play sports—and the Aussies, they loved sports. . . . So sports really made a difference in helping us to get through and to help teach the gospel of Jesus Christ to all these wonderful people. . . .

I would say that place that the sports had the greatest influence in helping to open up the missionary work was more in the smaller towns because in the smaller towns, they were really enclosed, and so when you're enclosed like that, it's harder to break in as missionaries.

When you'd send missionaries up there, they were scared to death of them. But by going there and playing basketball, we totally opened up the town, and so now the people would say, "Oh yes, we'd love to have you come and visit with us." They may not join the Church, but they're willing to talk with us and develop friendships, and in many cases, they joined the Church. So [in] the smaller towns, we found even greater success by using the sport of basketball. Now the beautiful thing here was in the late fifties and early sixties, all of a sudden basketball caught fire in Australia, and they were just accelerating the development of it. We were so far ahead of them that we could even beat their Olympic team. We'd get our very best players; we could beat their very best players in all of Australia, and so that really helped develop credibility for the Church, with their missionaries, themselves. Now in the city, like Sydney, we'd play on a team there and everything else, but it was so big, it would affect some areas, but it's not like it would [be] with the smaller towns.

DELL TUTTLE

LEHI, UTAH, USA
JULY 9, 2010

I WAS RAISED on a row crop farm and a fruit farm in Bountiful—very, very hard work. Dad would roll us out long before daylight, and we wouldn't quit until the sun had gone down, and as a result of that, I was probably stronger than most young people my age, and as a result of that, that kind of gave me an edge in the athletic field, and I participated in four consecutive years of pentathlon, played a lot of basketball ever since junior high school. . . .

I went into the mission field on March 12, 1959, and I was released on March 12 two years later. I really don't remember a time on my mission that I wasn't playing basketball. All of my companions enjoyed it, and we was always able to find enough missionaries that we could field a team, and because Australia was such great lovers of sports and especially basketball, it was never a problem in fielding a team. We had tryouts for the Mormon Yankee team, and fortunately I was able to make that team, and other than those spiritual aspects of the mission, that was indeed a highlight of my missionary experience, and I think basketball used as a proselytizing tool was excellent. We would put missionaries into the area where we played about two weeks after we played, and we had a lot of success from it, and so basketball has been a big part of my life. . . . There was a lot of special, spiritual memories, but the basketball was extremely choice in my mind. Those men that I was fortunate enough to travel with were some of the finest men that you could ever want to meet, and they bring back so many pleasant memories as I reflect back on the experience. . . .

We started out tour in Brisbane, and we rented an older-model Volkswagen van. The van itself looked just a little bit scary to me. I've been around a lot of old agricultural equipment, but this ranked right up to the top with all of them. Prior to starting, one of the sweet members said, "Well, you brethren cannot be missionaries when you are traveling without everybody knowing who you are." So she went and made a banner that was as long and about half as wide as what the van was that said, "Mormon Yankees on Tour." And as we would be driving down the road, an individual would come up alongside of us and motion for us to roll down the window, and they would yell at us, "What's a Mormon Yankee?" And we would lean out of the van as far as we could lean with a pamphlet that had a picture of all of the players on it and then told what we were doing and that we were on a basketball tour. So we literally proselyted as we were driving down the highways, and that was a fun experience.

Another experience that I remember was that the majority of the roads that we traveled on were dirt. They were rough roads and consequently, if my memory serves me correctly, we went through five tires during that basketball tour, which again, if my memory serves me correctly, was about ten thousand miles. We were constantly changing tires and constantly getting lost, and when we would pull into a town, the auditorium or the bleachers would be chock full. All the dignitaries would be there, and we would jump off the van and change our clothes and frantically run out on the court without any time to even hardly collect your thoughts. So that was a memorable experience. . . .

When we would come into a community, we were treated like royalty, and my whole life I was just a farm boy and I had never been treated like anything special, so that was a little bit difficult for me to get used to thinking that somebody else thought that we might be special. But they were always so kind to us, and what was interesting is that we had so many dignitaries there; the mayor would probably be there. The chief of police would be there; all of the ball players would be there, and the bleachers would be loaded with people who wanted to watch the game. We were kind of sneaky as missionaries, because we would bring the mayor and the chief of police and the other dignitaries out onto the floor, and at that time we would give them a Book of Mormon and other appropriate literature about the Church, and we kind of had them between a rock and a hard spot because they couldn't refuse. If they had have done, it would have been embarrassing for them and the Australian people, and so we kind of took advantage of that, and I don't know who came up with that brilliant idea, but it was a good one. The players and the fans treated us with great respect. . . . They would take us to their homes or to a large room in a motel that they had rented for us, and there they would feed us and talk with us, and we could talk about the Church; we could talk about our athletic experiences and just had a wonderful, wonderful time. . . .

When we were driving down the highway, we would hand out our brochures. People would want to know who we were and what Mormon Yankees were, and so we would hand them brochures, and we proselyted all the time, even when we were driving. It was fun for the first time in my life to feel like a dignitary because people would come and want your autograph. Never in my life had anybody ever wanted my autograph, and I figured I've never done anything that was good enough to have somebody come and ask for that autograph, but they did, and that just really made me feel very special. It gave me a great love for those people because they did that. We would hand literature, Joseph Smith pamphlets that we would hand out. If we felt like we had an individual that we could pull aside and talk to and if they ever ask any questions about the Church, we made sure that we always had plenty of Books of Mormon. We took cases of Books of Mormon with us so that we could hand them out, and from the time we got home, we never had a Book of Mormon left and we never had any pamphlets left and never did have a single person refuse a Book of Mormon or refuse any of our literature that we handed out while we were playing. They were just so gentle and so kind. . . .

The media was very kind to us, and that's one of the first things that we did when we went into a new area was go to the newspaper and go to the radio, just to let them know who we were. We wanted the people to know who it was that was knocking on their door. Because of the way we were dressed, we didn't want them to think we were the CIA or some other government agency was there trying to pump information out of them. We were always treated graciously, and the newspaper reports were always favorable.

Basketball was a great proselyting tool because after we had been in that town, then we would always send missionaries in right after as a follow-up, and I would have liked to have been one of the missionaries that went into one [of] those towns, because from all reports that we got, they were always treated very, very well. . . .

I think the Mormon Yankee basketball team helped the Church in that it broke down any prejudices that people might have. We showed people that we as missionaries, that we really were not any different than they were. We were just normal people. We had strong beliefs—we had core beliefs, and they found out, at least the players that we played, they found out that we would not deviate from those core beliefs. So because of that, we were respected. I think the Church was elevated in the eyes of the Australian people because they could see that we were genuine. We were not putting on airs; we were just young people, there at our own expense, which impressed them, and that we bled the same as they did. We laughed the same as they did. We showed emotions, sincere emotions, the same as they did. Consequently, it elevated us in the eyes of the Australian people, and I think we gained a great deal of respect as a church because of a simple tool, the Mormon Yankee basketball team. . . .

It is difficult for me to talk about those men that I went on tour with because they hold such a special place in my heart, and [I] feel that it was such a privilege to be associated with men of that great character. They were veritable giants, every one of them, and coupled with the fond memories that I have with those brethren, it's my prayer that I will be privileged to spend the eternities with men like that.

GARWOOD WALTON

LOGAN, UTAH, USA
OCTOBER 31, 2009

WHEN I GOT my papers ready to go to apply for my mission, I had to be interviewed, and in those days we all had to be interviewed by a General Authority, so I was directed to have that interview with Carl Beaner, who I believe at the time was [an] assistant to the Twelve. I went into his business office, and before I even sat down, he asked me a question: "Where would you want to go on your mission, young man?" And I said, "I'd like to go to Australia." First thing he said immediately was, "You're tall enough." I don't think I understood the significance of what that was all about. I really don't think I had much information about the Mormon Yankee team until I arrived in Australia, but it became apparent to me why he had made that comment after I got down there and my first companion told me a great deal about the Olympics and all the things that took place and particularly about the Mormon Yankee experience and all of the games they played. It was pretty obvious throughout my mission that basketball had definitely raised the profile of the Church in a positive way. . . .

I know a lot of the comments were that the Church, particularly in the media, did not have a very positive image. But that did change, and there were many good things that happened because of the basketball program, which, of course, was very much secondary to the missionary work. . . . My first experience really playing regularly with the Mormon Yankee team was over in Adelaide, after I'd been in Australia about a year. That was a good experience, and I think some of the gentlemen who played at the time of the Olympics mentioned that Adelaide had been a time, [a] place where there wasn't a real good feeling about the Church, but it definitely changed. There were quite a few baptisms about a year and a half later, when I was over there, and we had a lot of positive impact from our playing. We were—in comparison to the team that played at the time of the Olympics—we were pretty much the second or third string, but we enjoyed it, and the Australians seemed to enjoy it. . . .

When I was out in the country east of Melbourne in a town called Sale, Carl [McGavin] was my supervising elder. . . . We got very much involved in the community, and we also invited the Mormon Yankee team to come out and play, and the team that we set up to play against them was the Royal Australian Air Force team. Just three miles out of town, there was a Royal Australian Air Force base. My companion and I, Elder Jim Moorhead, played on the Royal Australian Air Force team. Unfortunately, Elder Moorhead got transferred, I think, one day before we had the big exhibition game, and I inherited a brand-new green companion. He was from California, and I was hoping that, when we heard that there was going to be a transfer, that he would be as good as Elder Moorhead; he was a better ball player than I was. So here comes this elder—he was one foot shorter than I am, and because of that he wasn't much of a basketball player, so that part of it was a little bit of a disaster. We also charged admission for that game; they printed programs. The radio station came down to the hall [to] broadcast the game as best they could with the rudimentary knowledge they had of basketball, but they played that game on the radio for weeks, again and again. Everybody knew the outcome, but it was one of the major things that happened in the town that year, maybe for several years. Our reception when we knocked on doors, when we finally did start to do some tracting, was really much improved over the experiences I'd had in the previous year and a quarter or so that I'd been a missionary. It really had made a remarkable difference. . . .

It wasn't easy when you broached the subject of religion on somebody's front porch. I always felt—maybe I'm the eternal optimist—but I always felt like the Australians had a great interest in us because we were Americans, and maybe that was a carryover from the Second World War. . . . I always felt that they were interested in Americans and interested in American sports, aside from religion; but when it came to religion, they definitely (most of them) were not interested. . . .

You know, I've heard my own children—both of my boys and one of my three girls served missions, and they continue to make comments because I still talk about my mission after fifty years—and they frequently observe that they have never heard anybody talk about their missions like this group from Australia. I think it was a special time, and there were some special things that took place. . . .

When you mention the fifties being special, I remember the first letter that I wrote when I got Perce Davis's [Australian LDS Church leader] address. . . . When he responded to my first letter, I asked him, "I don't know if you remember me, but we served in the mission presidency together," but the first sentence of his letter was, "Oh, the roaring fifties. I definitely remember you during the roaring fifties." So the Australians felt the same way about the fifties, I think.

KAY WATTS

MELBOURNE, VICTORIA, AUSTRALIA
DECEMBER 12, 2009

WHEN WE FIRST met the American missionaries, I was absolutely gobsmacked because I'd never met Americans before. I'd only ever seen them on television, and I felt in love with them because I was fifteen and a half, nearly sixteen, and I was just, "Oh! They're gorgeous!" And I remember I loved all the discussions that we had. . . .

The perception of Latter-day Saints was that no one really knew who they were or what they believed in. Once I joined the Church, I remember getting a lot of animosity, a lot of lost friends, because I believed in a strange religion. The fact that I didn't drink tea or coffee . . . I was very fiercely defendant of the Church and would give as good as I got, in a nice way, but I would set them straight. Because I used to get asked, "Why did you join that church? Why do you even want to go to church?" . . .

The Mormon Yankees introduced me to basketball. I had never seen it in my life. The first time I went along, they were just magnificent. They had the most wonderful uniforms. That is what I really remember was these American-styled uniforms because our guys used to just wear shorts and a singlet, . . . and when the Mormon Yankees first came out on the court, it was like, "Wow! They look top-notch!" They played really well; their standard of play was a lot higher than what we had in Australia because the basketball in Australia was such a fledgling sport. . . . I think they brought the Church up in the eyes of the public to the next level, and there was a lot of publicity of the games, and we used to go along, and we would have pom-poms and cheer and, you know, that sort of thing. It just made you so proud of being a Latter-day Saint. . . .

Going to see the Mormon Yankees was a big deal for me. I had fallen in love with basketball, and women didn't play it very much back then; it was just the guys. I wasn't actually in any of the cheer squads, but I had my own little cheers. I used to sit about halfway up the court, and I always had my pom-poms. I didn't care where I sat. I sat with nonmembers; I remember having religious discussions with the people next to me, particularly if they started dishing out any nasty stuff. I used to just [use] my testimony to them. I tried to get them to understand that we were just normal people, not some weirdo. I loved the way the Mormon Yankees gave out Books of Mormon: they used to line the two teams up, introduce the teams, and then the missionaries would go along and would give a Book of Mormon to all the other players. I used to love watching the players' faces at the shock of getting this book. . . . It also started the culture of the members becoming parts of basketball teams, to the point where we had a basketball competition going in the Melbourne Stake if we tried to become a referee for. So it was a great start to getting that athletic program going in the Church, and I really appreciate them having it and being part of it. . . .

The Mormon Yankees were very sportsmanlike. That was one thing that really stood out compared to the Australian teams. Of course, this is always—whatever country you have got basketball in, there is a slight interpretation of rules, and so our rules were slightly different to what the Americans were used to on the court. I found and what I observed was that they just rode over the top of any difficulties. If they did something wrong, they would apologize to the ref, to the player that they bumped into. Or some of the things that are allowed in American basketball are not allowed here in Australia or in that stage. So it was very impressive to watch their level of sportsmanship because I think they got a lot of aggression from the other players just because they were missionaries; the other team was out to down these Yanks to prove that Australians were better than Yanks and that these religious guys were just a bunch of no-hopers. And the Mormon Yankees ran rings around them, did things that our guys couldn't even do, they didn't even know how to do. That was a real learning curve for everyone, I think. . . .

I think the pride that I had in being a Latter-day Saint was enormous. Being a little girl in a church that wasn't known, having so much flack at the school—just to be a member and to go along and be able to cheer a team that was good and was worthwhile and was having an impact on people was just terrific, very building, very uplifting. It made me want to be a basketball player and to get involved, and that was the push that came when they finished, that we were encouraged in Young Women's to get out. So we formed a basketball team in my ward, in Blackburn Ward. We called ourselves the Blackburn MGs, the Blackburn Mormon Girls, and we registered at Albert Park, and we had a really smart uniform. Three of the girls on the team were members, and they got three or four of their friends. . . . Then we had a missionary, Elder [H. David] Burton, who became our coach, and he is now the presiding bishop [of the Church], and he had a huge impact on us girls. And I think out of our group, two of the girls joined the Church through the activity that we had. . . .

[When the Mormon Yankees] program was stopped, . . . I remember that I was devastated. But I think it was because I just enjoyed going along to the games and cheering and being proud of these young men. I could see the wisdom later because I believe the Church had moved to the next level and needed to go into the public in a different way. And it established young people in the Church getting into basketball teams, because now just about all the kids in the Church play some sort of basketball competition, and we are role models in those competitions because we're different and we bring a standard. I remember President McConkie when he announced it; he didn't want to stop it either, but he was teaching us to be obedient to the leaders, and as a fledgling church and fledgling members, obedience and sacrifice were part of growing up in the Church. And that's what the members needed to learn then was the sacrifice you make for the gospel, because we weren't pioneers, so we didn't have to make that sacrifice. And by giving up something that we all loved to go to, we transferred that into being obedient to President McConkie, enjoying him as a person, and moving on and finding other avenues for the love that we had. . . . So his personality and his obedience and his determination to move the Church forward took away the upset that you felt when the Mormon Yankees stopped. We all understood it was part of the program and we needed to be obedient to the program.

NORMAN L. WEITZEIL

MOUNTAIN GREEN, UTAH, USA
APRIL 16, 2011

AT THE TIME I was called in 1953, or through '54, there was only one elder that could go [on a mission] per ward because of the Korean War. . . . I was thrilled because I was under the impression I would probably never go on a mission, so it was a real blessing. . . . My first thought of basketball was when we landed in Australia, in Brisbane. We'd been thirty-three days on a freighter from New Orleans, coming, and Elder Francis, who was the first counselor or the second counselor in the mission presidency, he met us at the ship, and he said—the other two elders, he told one to stay in Brisbane, the other one went to go to Sydney. And he said, "Elder Weitzel, you're going to Adelaide to play basketball as part of your missionary assignment. And so when you stop in Sydney, get a hold of Bob Steck, who's a missionary, and you'll travel together," and so that was all a surprise to me. I had no idea, but the thirty-three days that we had spent on the ship, the good old USS *Pioneer* freighter, was nothing to do except skip the rope and practice a basketball dribbling on the deck. So we were in pretty good shape, as far as—I don't know how many times a day we'd go out and skip the rope and dribble—and so it was amazing that that just fell into place. . . .

Our mission president, President Charles V. Liljenquist, had gone to all five cities in Australia [Brisbane, Sydney, Melbourne, Adelaide, and Perth] and told them that if they would put . . . a short article in their papers once a week on basketball, and then if they would put—and I don't remember—a larger article once a month, he would bring the best basketball team they'd ever seen to their city, and he'd had no team at that time. . . . He was very adamant about how much time we spent: just our practice time, two hours on a weeknight, and then we did on four hours on Saturday mornings because that was our P-day [preparation day], and then we played on Thursday nights. That was it. . . . In our report meetings, when he came, he'd say, "Elders, you're slothful," and we had more tracting hours, more contacts than anybody in the mission, but he just expected us to be more than the average because of what we were involved in. He didn't want us to lose track of who we were. We were missionaries of The Church of Jesus Christ of Latter-day Saints, and that was what we were there for, not to play basketball. . . .

We'd get on a tram to go somewhere, a companion[ship] or maybe four of us or something, and they'd always say, "Elder, who's going to win the ball game this week?" We didn't even know these people. You go into a department store, and the clerks would all come, and we were just ordinary guys, other than we were tall and wore hats and suits, but we had no tags at that time. But in Adelaide, I think there was, what, two million people in the city of Adelaide, and it was amazing. But our pictures were in the paper from what President Liljenquist asked for, and the ball games and so on. And of course all these Latvians and Estonians, the Eastern European countries were all coming there because Australia would give them land; they would give them so many acres of land if they came. And so they were all trying to get out of Eastern Europe and get to a land of freedom, and so, and they were good ball players. . . .

They're such a sports-minded country. I mean, they love sports, anything. I think even just the fact that, "Oh, you're one of those Mormon Yankees. Come on in and talk to us." So it opened doors. It opened—I mean, when you can go down the street in a business district or on the tram, and people say, "Elder, how are you?" They know who you are. And we didn't have any badges; sometimes we were just in white shirt sleeves, sometimes we had suit coats on, all depending on how the weather was. They didn't know who we were other than pictures in the paper or going to the ball games. They were always so friendly. They never, ever [said], "Well, who do you think you are?" or whatever. They always were very courteous, and that was, that was the main thing, I think, to get the Church out. I don't know what kind of different articles they read about polygamy and all, and on and on and on. I don't know. But I think if nothing else, we probably brought them to the point where we were just normal young men, and I hope they found out that we had integrity; we didn't do anything that would bring any shame on the Church. . . .

I just hope that my actions didn't deter the gospel in any way, that I did some good and that we did some good just in that silly game of basketball. It was a tool in our Heavenly Father's hands in bringing the gospel more to light, and how grateful I am I could be part of that. When I left Brisbane, there's a little lady that was a member of the Church, and she said to me, "Elder, I'll be at the train tracks when you go by." I stood on the back of the train as we left Brisbane, and there she was as we went by, waving, and to me that was kind of the fulfillment of my mission. "Good-bye, Elder. Thank you for all that you've done."

WILBURN WEST

COTTONWOOD HEIGHTS, UTAH, USA
MAY 4, 2011

WHEN I GREW up, my dad had been on a mission, and we had a great ward where the boys were prepared and wanted to go on missions, and I did too. So in June, actually a little before June of 1956, I put in my papers and got my call. But back then, after we were interviewed by the bishop and whatnot, then we had to go and see a General Authority. And I remember going downtown and going into the Church Office Building, and I met with Marion D. Hanks, and he was the one that interviewed me. And I've thought since—he asked me about playing basketball and some things like that—and I've thought since that maybe he was inspired that not only myself, maybe some others that were called that played ball, because maybe he had an inkling of what would occur. . . . This was in the early fifties. I remember in our ward, there were a number of priests that were made elders that wanted to go on missions, but at that time it was limited; they would only let two go from a ward, so that was a tough choice for a bishop, I'm sure, so some did not get to go. But I think by the time that I left in '56, that had passed, and whoever wanted to go could go. . . .

[Prior to my mission] I had the privilege of getting a scholarship at the University of Utah, and back then, freshmen could not play varsity, and so we had a freshmen team that . . . played BYU; we played the community college; we played Utah State freshmen; there was kind of a freshman [league]. . . .

Basketball was quite a new sport in Australia, and I think the servicemen in World War II, if they didn't introduce it, kind of put it to the forefront a little bit, more than it ever had been. And so the Olympic teams, they needed some teams to warm up with before the Olympics, and in Australia. . . . And so somehow the word got out that, "Hey, we've got a bunch of Latter-day Saint missionaries that play ball, and they're playing, and they have a pretty good team in the Melbourne league, and maybe they could do some scrimmages and play some games against the international teams." Now I don't know how all that came about, but apparently our president, President Bingham, was approached, maybe by the International Olympic Committee for all I know, and then he got permission from Salt Lake. . . . He brought ball players in and teamed them up as companionships, and—like, David Kimball was my companion—and there were probably a nucleus of maybe ten—not ten but probably five or six companionships. . . .

You know, you kind of wonder, "Man, these are Olympic teams. Can we be in the same class with them? Can we give them the competition they need?" And at first it was kind of—I won't say overwhelming—but it was an exciting moment, and then as we got playing, then we realized that they're very good, but we're not too bad either, and we can give them a run for their money and warm them up like they wanted to be. . . .

Australian members of the Church loved it, and they would come out. In fact, some of them would help to, as I recall, help to put out a brochure or tract to people. . . . It was an exciting game, basketball, and I think the members of the Church enjoyed watching it, and then felt that this was putting the Church in the limelight. I never heard any negative from the members; they loved it! . . .

The players on the different teams that we met in Melbourne, they had a little different lifestyle, and when they came to know that we were not consuming alcohol or using tobacco, to them, I think, they stood in admiration and realized that, "Okay, we respect you." It didn't necessarily change how they were living, but we had the respect, and I think that they knew where we stood. . . .

There was a YMCA in Bendigo, and my companion and I and other elders that were there, we had a team that we played in that league in Bendigo. And then also, my companion and I helped to coach one team that was there. So it was something that—it was on a weekly basis. And we were able to practice with that team, and those members of the teams became familiar with the LDS Church. . . .

I don't recall President Bingham ever calling us in and giving us something specific, except that he always said, "Remember who you are, and you have to live the standards of being a missionary. You have to live those standards and remember that other people are always watching you." But I don't remember that he ever called us in and gave us any specific instruction. . . . He had a lot of faith in us as individuals that we would hold to the standards that we needed. . . .

I think at the particular time, in the mid-fifties, it was a means of getting people to recognize that The Church of Jesus Christ of Latter-day Saints was in Australia. And I think it caused people to say, "Well, what about this?" And they were curious. And I think at that time, you'd read about, in the papers a little bit, maybe about the Mormon Yankees, and people would wonder, "Okay, what about it?" So some people, I think, at that particular time, it was important to help the Church come more in the limelight, and that's what I think the benefit was. Plus, I think it gave a sense of—if I can use the word "pride" in the right way—to members of the Church, that here is something that is going on, that we're like you Australians. We love our sports, and we can do it in a very positive, sportsmanship-like way, and I think it was a source of pride for members of the Church. . . .

It was a privilege, a privilege to have been part of it, and I look back with fond memories because I know that it had a positive influence for the Church in Australia. And we got rubbing shoulders with players on other teams; we got so that we actually loved them, and so I have fond memories. I remember there was one player that his wife had this fantastic recipe for scallops in a beautiful, tasty white sauce. And they invited us over, and I remember, man, I thought, "I'm in heaven," eating that dish, because I love fish. And just things like that, just fond memories and the association with the different players. Though I can't remember their names per se now, but we could rub shoulders with them, and it was more than on court. There were other things that happened like that that we enjoyed. . . .

I just admire the Australian people. . . . They're a wholesome, wonderful people, and I just hope that this project . . . will just have a positive influence. And I'm sure it will. I'm sure it will, and it's exciting to me to be a part of it, and I'm sure it is to all the other Mormon Yankees and missionaries that played, and I just think it will be great to—hopefully we can get it to where people in Australia can . . . relate, and some people that weren't there at that time, they can say, "Gee, that really happened, didn't it?" And especially the Church, I think, Church members again, even though they're younger now, guys that are members of the Church that are playing ball, I think, will get excited about, "This actually happened back in our country with the missionaries," and it will be a positive thing.

ENDNOTES

1. Richard Ian Kimball, interview by Fred E. Woods and Martin L. Andersen, Brigham Young University, December 7, 2010. On the role of sports in LDS culture during the early twentieth century, see Richard Ian Kimball, *Sports in Zion: Mormon Recreation, 1900–1940* (Urbana: University of Illinois Press, 2003).
2. "History of Basketball," Basketball Victoria, last modified 2010, http://www.basketballvictoria.com.au/index.php?id=61.
3. In *Sports in Zion*, 4, 17, Kimball notes that the Church followed the model of muscular Christianity to help activate young Mormon men.
4. Jessie L. Embry and John H. Brambaugh, "Preaching through Playing: Using Sports and Recreation in Missionary Work, 1911–64," *Journal of Mormon History* 35, no. 4 (Fall 2009): 60; Jessie L. Embry, interview by Fred E. Woods and Martin L. Andersen, Brigham Young University, September 10, 2010. On the topic of spiritualized recreation, see Jessie L. Embry, *Spiritualized Recreation: Mormon All-Church Athletic Tournaments and Dance Festivals* (Provo, Utah: Brigham Young University, 2008).
5. "Elder" is a term used by the LDS Church to refer to a man who holds the priesthood office of elder, regardless of his age.
6. Embry and Brambaugh, "Preaching through Playing," 54; "History of Basketball." This service is certainly not to infer that the missionaries were in support of Hitler's regime.
7. *Portals of Opportunity, 66th Annual Report Young Men's Christian Association of Melbourne* (1937), 16, University of Melbourne Library, Melbourne, Australia.
8. *Citizens of To-day and To-morrow, 67th Annual Report Young Men's Christian Association of Melbourne* (1938), 19, University of Melbourne Library, Melbourne, Australia. In the LDS periodical the *Austral Star* (published out of Sydney), an article titled "Victorian District" shows more evidence of Mormon basketball players, possibly including members of the championship team: "The 'M Men' are showing excellent

form in the basketball tournament. They have won four games out of four. The team is ardently supported by the Saints and friends, and one of the consistent visitors is the team's mascot, a squirrel presented by Sister Rawolle." See "Victorian District," *Austral Star*, June 20, 1938, 8.

9. *Weaving the Fabric for the Future, 68th Annual Report Young Men's Christian Association of Melbourne* (1939), 18, University of Melbourne Library, Melbourne, Australia.

10. Elder D. Forrest Greene, "Victoria Champions," *Improvement Era*, June 1940, 369.

11. Greene, "Victoria Champions," 369–70. The name of this newspaper is not given in the *Improvement Era* article. However, the newspaper may be the Melbourne *Argus*, which contains several mentions of the American Mormons playing basketball in Melbourne at this time. (See, for example, these articles in the *Argus*: May 27, 1938, 20; July 14, 1938; May 13, 1939, 15; June 24, 1939, 19). On page 370 of "Victoria Champions" is a picture of the missionaries on the Victoria championship team. Nine young men are pictured in uniform with the word "Mormon" written across their jerseys, although the names of the elders are not given. However, the mission president is listed as James Judd, who is seated in the middle of the photograph on the front row.

12. "Basketball," in *Christian Democracy for Today, Sixty-Ninth Annual Report and Financial Statement of the Young Men's Christian Association of Melbourne for the Year Ending 31st December, 1940*, 17–18, University of Melbourne Library, Melbourne, Australia. "Victorian District," *Austral Star*, September 1940, 10, notes, "Basketball is [the] main sport among members here, all teams have had much success. The Elders playing as Y.M.C.A. No[.] 2 defeated the Church of England No. 1, 64 to 32, to take the Victorian State Championship for the second year in succession." Marjorie Newton, *Southern Cross Saints: The Mormons in Australia*, Mormons in the Pacific Series (Laie, Hawaii: Institute for Polynesian Studies, 1991), 186, notes that because of World War II, the American missionaries were evacuated from Australia in October 1940.

13. Elder D. Forrest Greene, "Australian Mission Basketball," *Improvement Era*, May 1941, 305.

14. Greene, "Australian Mission Basketball," 305. Alongside this article, the eight members of the Mormon Colts team are pictured with the following caption: "Sydney Mormon Colts, New South Wales Champions. Left to right: C. Collard, R. Hannat, F. Greene, W. McCall (Capt.), R. Walker, L. Bowren, J. McDonough, R. Thorup." Six of the young men have "Mormon Colts" written on their uniforms, whereas

R. Walker has only "Mormon" written on his jersey and C. Collard does not have "Mormon Colts" or "Mormon" written on his uniform, only the number fourteen.

15. Newton, *Southern Cross Saints*, 38, explains that the *Austral Star* was a monthly periodical launched in 1929 by mission president Clarence H. Tingey to compensate for the long distances that separated the Australian Saints. Modeled after the *Latter-day Saints' Millennial Star*, the *Austral Star* was published each month for nearly three decades, with its last monthly issue in December 1958. This periodical published news about various Australian branches as well as information related to missionary work. The *Austral Star* issue of August 23, 1947, 9, noted that the "A" Grade basketball team of the Adelaide Branch was composed of the M-Men (members of the LDS church male youth organization) and that the team captain was Elder Gibb. This reference suggests that Gibb, an American missionary, was leading a group of local youth at this time and notes that he "has chosen to represent the Mormons in the interstate team which will probably visit the other States." The following month, the Adelaide Branch section of the *Austral Star*, September 23, 1947, 8, reports, "Perhaps it is just as well that the basketball season is over. What with our A team coming up to be in the final four and then being defeated and the general collapse of the Mutual barrackers, not to mention the departure of the captain of the team, Elder Gibb." Apparently Gibb was a very talented player and was influential in local basketball, for the article further notes that "before arriving in Sydney, Elder Gibb will play in the Interstate Basketball matches at present being played in Melbourne." Two years later, there is also evidence of what appears to be another influential LDS American. The *Austral Star*, April 1949, 2–3, notes that Elder Mecham has "become well-known in sports, and made good contribution to basketball acceptance out here."

16. See, for example, *Austral Star*, August 23, 1946, 9, in which Fred Crane, a member of the Adelaide Branch, is listed as "the latest victim of the basketball team. He sustained a cut under his right eye which necessitated two stitches." *Austral Star*, November 23, 1946, 11, further notes that the Adelaide Branch "young men's Basketball team narrowly missed the final four, although their play throughout the season has been consistent." *Austral Star*, September 23, 1946, 9, notes that the Melbourne Branch's "M. Men basketball team has concluded its season." *Austral Star*, September 23, 1947, 6, observed that "many local members [of the Hurstville Branch] have been suffering from troubles caused through 'yelling' our champs to victory as the State Basketball

Champions."

17. *Austral Star*, August 23, 1947, insert between pages 6 and 7. The players on this team were listed as follows: "Elders Arlin, Mecham, Richard Hicks, Fred Osterloh, Wallace Devey, Joseph Porter, Brothers Bill McCall and Bob Hannant."
18. *Austral Star*, May 1949, 5.
19. Tingey Hall was named after Clarence H. Tingey, who served as a mission president in Australia from 1928 to 1935. See Newton, *Southern Cross Saints*, 183.
20. Kathleen Rawolle, "Melbourne Branch," *Austral Star*, November 1949, 6.
21. Elder J. Bennion, "Bendigo Branch," *Austral Star*, July 1950, 8.
22. "Victoria Missionary Record Australia[n] Mission [1950–1953] Historical Record of Victorian District," August 28, September 4, and September 11, 1950 (unpublished manuscript), Church History Library, The Church of Jesus Christ of Latter-day Saints, Salt Lake City, Utah (hereafter cited as Church History Library).
23. June Trost, "Brisbane Branch," *Austral Star*, July 1950, 9. This article also points out that "much credit is due Brother Mike Feeney[,] the organizer and manager of both teams." Thus, it is evident that although an American missionary was apparently a member of the team, a local Latter-day Saint was running the program.
24. June Trost, "Brisbane Branch," *Austral Star*, August 1950, 8.
25. Nancy Mitchell, "Hobart Branch," *Austral Star*, August 1950, 10.
26. Elder Douglas Brian, "New South Wales Elders' Basketball Team," *Austral Star*, August 1950, 14. On this page is also a picture of the team with each of the ten players named, along with the mission secretary, Elder Delmer F. Howell. Elder Douglas G. Brian, who wrote the article, is noted as a co-captain of the team. The others named are Elders John E. Meyers, captain; George E. Collard; Gordon K. Anderson; George H. Fairbanks; Orson D. Wright; Glenn R. Blatter; John E. Bean; Robert E. Griffin; and Warren V. Judd.
27. Loris Holzworth, "Toowoomba Branch," *Austral Star*, December 1950, 8. Loris Holzworth, "Toowoomba Branch," *Austral Star*, April 1951, 8, reveals where the four visiting elders may have come from. Holzworth reported, "The Toowoomba Elders and Brisbane Elders played a basketball match last month against a Toowoomba team and beat the latter by 36 points to 18."
28. Marjorie Burnett, "Bankstown Branch," *Austral Star*, June 1951, 10.
29. "Missionary Items," *Austral Star*, August 1951, 12. "Victoria Missionary Record Australian Mission [1950–1953] Historical Record

of Victorian District," December 3, 1951, notes, "The Elders basketball team defeated the Dainas tonight in the grand finals to win the [YMCA] championships & it proved to be a very joyous occasion. The game was tied at the finish so we played an extra five minutes & beat them by a score of 50–47. Each of the team received a very fine illustrated book of Australia."

30. Loris Holzworth, "Toowoomba Branch," *Austral Star*, October 1951, 8.
31. June Trost, "Brisbane Branch," *Austral Star*, November 1951, 11.
32. Peggy Whitehead, "Melbourne Branch," *Austral Star*, January 1952, 11.
33. Peggy Whitehead, "Melbourne Branch," *Austral Star*, June 1952, 12.
34. Ruth Nash, "Bankstown Branch," *Austral Star*, August 1953, 15. See also Ruth Nash, "Bankstown Branch," *Austral Star*, April 1953, 12, in which Nash had previously noted that the young men in the Bankstown Branch had formed a new basketball team, "and they seem to be really in earnest."
35. Mary Bellott, "Melbourne Branch," *Austral Star*, August 1953, 17. Yet the previous month, Bellott had written that the players in the Melbourne Branch "had occasion to be elated, having won several games over non-LDS opponents."
36. Marie Cray, interview by Fred E. Woods and Martin L. Andersen, Graham and Marie Cray home, Melbourne, Australia, December 14, 2009.
37. Arthur Emery, interview by Fred E. Woods and Martin L. Andersen, Arthur Emery home, Adelaide, Australia, June 18, 2010.
38. Ted E. Haynes, the only Canadian to play on this elite Mormon Yankees team, remembered, "In Adelaide we played in their premier league for the season of 1954, and we were successful in winning the state, senior men's basketball championship there, and received a lot of publicity and good will. . . . The members benefitted, and also it opened doors for us, and we were able to meet quite a number of people through that particular method." Ted E. Haynes, interview by Martin L. Andersen, Ted E. Haynes home, Magrath, Alberta, Canada, April 8, 2011.
39. Elder Loren C. Dunn, interview, typescript, 24–25, by Matt Heiss, 1991, Church History Library.
40. Zita Margaret Gage, "Prospect Branch," *Austral Star*, May 1954, 19.
41. "Mormon Yankees," *Austral Star*, June 1954, 10; boldface original. In reality, Liljenquist visted five major city centers in Australia to determine which city would provide the best coverage of the Mormon Yankees team. Norm Weitzel recalled, "He went first to Brisbane, Sydney,

Melbourne, Adelaide, and Perth and he said if you'll put so much in the paper each week on the ball games, and then . . . an article once a month in your paper about the Church and what we are trying to do, he said, 'I'll bring the best basketball team you've ever seen,' and Adelaide took him up on it." Norm Weitzel, interview by Martin L. Andersen, home of Norm Weitzel, Mountain Green, Utah, April 16, 2011.

42. "Mormon Yankees," *Austral Star*, June 1954, 11; boldface original. Besides Arthur Emery, who was an Australian, the only player on this team who was not an American was Haynes. Concerning the team, Haynes noted, "All except two, were Yankees . . . and one player from Adelaide who was a local member of the Church[;] of course [he] was Australian. I was Canadian." Ted E. Haynes, interview by Martin L. Andersen, Ted E. Haynes home, Magrath, Alberta, Canada, April 8, 2011.

43. Charles Bruce Flick, a former member of the Australian Olympic basketball team, whom Dunn had played against as a missionary, also recalled Dunn's compassion two decades later. During an emotional point of an interview, Flick recalled, "Twenty years after we stopped playing, I was in a hospital having a hip replacement and Loren Dunn actually came. . . . It was just something." Charles Bruce Flick, interview by Fred E. Woods and Martin L. Andersen, Charles Bruce and Barbara Flick home, Sydney, Australia, June 26, 2010.

44. Arthur Emery, interview by Fred E. Woods and Martin L. Andersen, Arthur Emery home, Adelaide, Australia, June 18, 2010.

45. Various interviews reveal that "Sweet Georgia Brown" continued to be played for warm-up music, while "When the Saints Go Marching In" was used when the Mormon Yankees first entered the court.

46. Ted Johnson, interview by Fred E. Woods and Martin L. Andersen, Ted Johnson home, Boise, Idaho, July 7, 2010.

47. Ted Johnson recalled, "Stan Watts was one of the best basketball coaches that BYU had ever had and Loren learned the plays through Stan Watts and consequently he taught us and we taught them to the Australians." Ted Johnson, interview by Fred E. Woods and Martin L. Andersen, Ted Johnson home, Boise, Idaho, July 7, 2010. Dunn was a member of the BYU basketball team which won the 1951 National Invitational Tournament, http://en.wikipedia.org/wiki/Loren_C._Dunn. An article published after the Mormon Yankees had made their mark in Adelaide, "Elder Dunn Appointed Mission Counselor," *Austral Star*, November 1955, 5, notes, "Prior to his mission call to Australia, Elder Dunn attended Brigham Young University for four years, working on

his composite major in Journalism and Economics, and while there also played basketball for the varsity team. . . . Since being on his mission, Elder Dunn has been an invaluable aid in publicizing the Church in Australia, serving respectively as Publicity Aid, Mission Editor, and Public Relations Aid to the mission president." Newton, *Southern Cross Saints*, 67, adds, "Loren C. Dunn, later became a General Authority of the Church, Australia Sydney Mission president and Area Executive Administrator for the South Pacific."

48. Mikelis Dancis, interview by Fred E. Woods and Martin L. Andersen, George Dancis home, Adelaide, Australia, June 17, 2010.
49. Colin J. Burdett, interview by Fred E. Woods and Martin L. Andersen, Colin J. Burdett home, Adelaide, Australia, June 18, 2010.
50. Ted Johnson, interview by Fred E. Woods and Martin L. Andersen, Ted Johnson home, Boise, Idaho, July 7, 2010.
51. Denise Helen Mutton, interview by Fred E. Woods and Martin L. Andersen, Peter G. and Denise Helen Mutton home, Adelaide, Australia, June 19, 2010. Elder Rodney Burt, who commenced serving a mission in Australia about this same time, described how some Australians viewed the Mormon missionaries in the mid-twentieth century: "A Mormon was someone who came to Australia to kidnap a girl; they would lock her in the Salt Lake Temple, and the only way she could escape was to jump out of the temple into the Great Salt Lake and swim to safety. I don't know how many times the missionaries heard that story and [heard that] they wore hats to hide their horns. . . . I remember one time I took my hat off, it was a hot day, and there were a group of kids following us around, and when they saw me take my hat off they broke and ran, and we didn't know why. Come to find out, they actually believed that Mormons had horns. It was interesting how rumors, and falsehoods, and that type of thing got started." Rodney Burt, interview by Fred E. Woods and Martin L. Andersen, Rodney Burt home, Springville, Utah, February 17, 2011.
52. Denise Mutton further noted in an interview with Fred E. Woods and Martin L. Andersen, Peter G. and Denise Helen Mutton home, Adelaide, Australia, June 19, 2010, "Ever since we were baptized in [on] 17th of September, 1954, we kept in contact with the elders, we used to send a Christmas card every Christmas, and they would send one back to us." The Muttons are currently serving as temple workers at the Adelaide Australia Temple.
53. Gunars Esins Berzzarins, interview by Fred E. Woods and Martin L. Andersen, Gunars Esins Berzzarins home, Adelaide, Australia, June 18, 2010.

54. "The Mormon Yankees Basketball Champs Lead in Baptisms," *Church News*, April 30, 1955, 12. These famous tennis players included Pancho Segura, Pancho Gonzales, Frank Sedgman, and Ken McGregor, as noted in an interview with Norm Weitzel by Martin L. Andersen, home of Norm Weitzel, Mountain Green, Utah, April 16, 2011.
55. "Elders Close Season with Exhibition," *Austral Star*, January 1955, 11.
56. "The Mormon Yankees Basketball Champs Lead in Baptisms," *Church News*, April 30, 1955, 12.
57. Program titled *Australian Basketball Championships Sydney*, 1955. Yet this was not the first time that Mormon elders had played for a state Australian team. For example, Al Ramsay, *Basketball in New South Wales: A History: 50 Years of Achievement and Development, 1938–1988* (Flemington Markets, New South Wales: NSW Basketball Association, 1989), 427, notes that A. T. Mecham and G. Walker played on the 1948 New South Wales state team and that they were players from the "Mormons" team.
58. Charles Bruce Flick, interview by Fred E. Woods and Martin L. Andersen, Charles Bruce and Barbara Flick home, Sydney, Australia, June 26, 2010.
59. Mervyn Moy, interview by Fred E. Woods and Martin L. Andersen, Mervyn Moy home, Sydney, Australia, June 25, 2010. The program titled *Australian Basketball Championships Sydney, 1955* indicates that it was Elder Smith, not Elder Day, who was on the New South Wales 1955 team. Flick and Moy also played together on the first Australian Olympic basketball team in 1956.
60. "The Mormon Yankees Basketball Breaks Australia Barriers," *Church News*, November 19, 1955, 11.
61. "The Mormon Yankees Basketball Breaks Australia Barriers," *Church News*, November 19, 1955, 11.
62. Ronald L. Bouck, interview by Fred E. Woods and Martin L. Andersen, Ronald L. Bouck home, Salt Lake City, Utah, December 27, 2010. DeLyle H. Condie, who commenced playing as a Mormon Yankee in 1956, was also a student who knew Bouck at the University of Utah. Condie remembered other performances by the former cheerleader: "He commonly would run up what they called a chain-link fence that [was] around the ends, behind the baskets. He'd run and climb up like a monkey, and swing back and forth, like a monkey. I mean, he just was a character." DeLyle H. Condie, interview by Fred E. Woods and Martin L. Andersen, DeLyle H. Condie home, Salt Lake City, Utah, July 7, 2010.
63. Ray Feeney, interview by Fred E. Woods and Martin L. Andersen, Ray Feeney home, Sydney, Australia, June 26, 2010.

64. Elder Loren C. Dunn, interview, typescript, 26–27, by Matt Heiss, 1991, Church History Library.
65. Newton, *Southern Cross Saints*, 190–91. This division occurred four months later. The "Australia Melbourne Mission General Minutes, July 3, 1955" (unpublished manuscript), Church History Library, notes, "Today a new mission was formed in the Church of Jesus Christ of Latter[-]Day Saints, called the South Australia Mission."
66. Newton, *Southern Cross Saints*, 191. Newton also points out that Elder Marion G. Romney of the Quorum of the Twelve Apostles had been a missionary in Australia from 1920 to 1923.
67. DeLyle H. Condie, interview by Fred E. Woods and Martin L. Andersen, DeLyle H. Condie home, Salt Lake City, Utah, July 7, 2010. Condie worked closely with Burt, who was at this time the second counselor in the mission presidency. Burt noted that President Bingham had told him that when the newly arrived missionaries disembarked, Burt was to ask them, "'Are you a basketball player?'" And of course if they had had experiences of basketball we would ask Elder Condie to talk to this missionary." Rodney Burt, interview by Fred E. Woods and Martin L. Andersen, Rodney Burt home, Springville, Utah, February 17, 2011.
68. DeLyle H. Condie, interview by Fred E. Woods and Martin L. Andersen, DeLyle H. Condie home, Salt Lake City, Utah, July 7, 2010.
69. Rodney Burt, interview by Fred E. Woods and Martin L. Andersen, Rodney Burt home, Springville, Utah, February 17, 2011. Burt also mentioned that prior to Watson's contacting of President Bingham, "When I came to Melbourne I was under the distinct impression that basketball was not going to be a priority. In other words, we weren't going to press sports, we wanted the missionaries to do missionary work." Burt also noted that as a counselor to President Bingham, he helped recruit players along with Condie. President Bingham told Burt that when the new missionaries would disembark from the ship, Burt was to ask them, "Are you a basketball player?" which sometimes brought a "dumbfounded look" from the missionaries. Additionally, Burt assisted with writing news releases for a radio announcer's weekly broadcasts of the Mormon Yankee games. Further, in his role as counselor in the mission presidency, Burt would receive weekly letters from the missionaries and noted, "Invariably many of them would say, 'The Mormon Yankees must have played this week. Someone saw your blurb in the newspaper and they were very willing to talk.'"
70. DeLyle H. Condie, interview by Fred E. Woods and Martin L. Andersen, DeLyle H. Condie home, Salt Lake City, Utah, July 7, 2010.
71. "The Victorian Mormon Yankees," *Austral Star*, April 1956, 10.

72. "Missionaries Win Latvian Basketball Tournament," *Austral Star*, August 1956, 11.
73. Elspeth Archibald, "Bentleigh Branch," *Austral Star*, July 1956, 20.
74. Newton also observed, "The Church building program, which began in 1956[,] . . . probably brought the greatest amount of good publicity to the Church, as occasionally national and state newspapers and, more frequently, suburban or regional papers reported ground-breaking ceremonies, plaque-laying ceremonies and opening days." Newton, *Southern Cross Saints*, 87, 192.
75. Zita Margaret Gage, "Prospect Branch," *Austral Star*, September 1956, 15. The following year, Lily M. Whitworth, "Whyalla Branch," *Austral Star*, June 1957, 18, reported, "The 'Mormon Yankees' came to Whyalla from Adelaide and played a well contested game against the Hungarian Basketball Team, which they won. The proceeds of the evening were in aid of our building fund."
76. Rodney Burt, interview by Fred E. Woods and Martin L. Andersen, Rodney Burt home, Springville, Utah, February 17, 2011.
77. Brian Duthie, "Condie Is Colossal," *The Sporting Globe All-Sport Magazine*, September 8, 1956. Duthie also commented, "The [LDS] [C]hurch runs what is thought to be one of the largest tournaments in the world."
78. Lindsay Gaze, interview by Fred E. Woods and Martin L. Andersen, Lindsay Gaze home, Melbourne, Australia, December 10, 2009.
79. Inga Freidenfelds, interview by Fred E. Woods and Martin L. Andersen, Lindsay Gaze home, Melbourne, Australia, June 18, 2010.
80. Geoff Heskett, interview by Fred E. Woods and Martin L. Andersen, Geoff Heskett home, Melbourne, Australia, December 13, 2009.
81. Dr. Donald F. Hull, interview by Martin L. Andersen, San Francisco, California, April 15, 2011. Hull was impressed when he went back to Australia in 2002 for the World Games and learned, "The Mormon Yankees were remembered by those players that were our age, and I remember one of them said, 'Yes, I remember I used to play against Elder Condie and Elder Hull.' And I said, 'Well, I'm Elder Hull.'"
82. Mervyn Moy, interview by Fred E. Woods and Martin L. Andersen, Mervyn Moy home, Sydney, Australia, June 25, 2010.
83. The "Australia Melbourne Mission General Minutes," July 28, 1956 (unpublished manuscript), Church History Library, noted that the Mormon Yankees had beaten the Australian Olympic team earlier in the year. "It proved to be very colorful. It was a tough game, but the 'Yankees' defeated them 72–62. Remarkable sportsmanship was shown."

84. "Basketball Scores—Melbourne," *Austral Star*, December 1956, 10. The point margin may actually have been wider in the second game against Russia; the "Australia Melbourne Mission General Minutes," November 17, 1956, note, "Mormon Yankees played Russia today. Lost 60–81 Very close and good game. It got world publicity."
85. Delmar H. Bjork, "Freed, At Last from Spirit Prison, Unusual LDS Missionary Experience(s), Autobiography: Delmar H. Bjork" (unpublished manuscript), 12.
86. Apparently the Mormon Yankees played the Russian team a third time, an event that proved effective for the exposure of the Church. The "Australia Melbourne Mission General Minutes," November 12, 1956, noted, "This morning the Mormon Yankees Basketball Team played the Russian Olympic Team in an exhibition game. The Russians won 90–56. Very good advertizement [*sic*] for our missionary work; also a privilege to play one of the top basketball team[s] of the world. Afterwards Elder DeLyle Condie talked to a group of Army personal [personnel] who were physical education instructors assigned to the Olympic Games." These minutes also demonstrate that the mission kept an official record of Mormon Yankees play, a practice that shows the concerted effort to use the team as a channel for proselytizing. See, for example, the "Minutes" for May 16; July 4, 11, 13, 18, 20, 27–28; and August 8, 12, 22.
87. Mark J. Frodsham, interview by Fred E. Woods and Martin L. Andersen, Mark J. Frodsham home, Murray, Utah, July 9, 2010.
88. Paul Grant, interview by Martin L. Andersen, Jackson Hole, Wyoming, August 28, 2010. James Nyle Garn, in an interview with Martin L. Andersen, St. George, Utah, April 13, 2011, clarified that although Garn was athletic and played football at Ricks College, he did not play on the basketball team, though he did play a great deal of competitive church basketball.
89. "Basketball Scores – Melbourne," *Austral Star*, December 1956, 10.
90. DeLyle H. Condie, interview by Fred E. Woods and Martin L. Andersen, DeLyle H. Condie home, Salt Lake City, Utah, July 7, 2010. The "Australia Melbourne Mission General Minutes," December 4, 1956, note, "Elders Condie, Grant, D. Kimball, Garn, Frodsham and Hull, members of the Mormon Yankees Basketball squad, left for Tasmania to play a series of basketball games in Devonport, Launceston, Hobart, with the Nationalist Chinese Team."
91. Paul Grant, interview by Martin L. Andersen, Jackson Hole, Wyoming, August 28, 2010.
92. James Nyle Garn, interview by Martin L. Andersen, St. George, Utah, April 13, 2011.

93. DeLyle H. Condie, interview by Fred E. Woods and Martin L. Andersen, DeLyle H. Condie home, Salt Lake City, Utah, July 7, 2010.
94. Dr. Donald F. Hull, interview by Martin L. Andersen, San Francisco, California, April 15, 2011.
95. "Manuscript History of the South Australia Mission," *Quarterly Report* (June 30, 1957), Church History Library, cited in Newton, *Southern Cross Saints*, 67, 235.
96. Harold Reeb, interview by Fred E. Woods and Martin L. Andersen, Harold and Janice Reeb home, Hobble Creek Canyon, Springville, Utah, October 31, 2009.
97. Journal of Harold Reeb, in possession of Harold Reeb, Springville, Utah.
98. Don Pemberton, interview by Fred E. Woods and Martin L. Andersen, Pemberton home, Melbourne, Australia, December 14, 2009. Apparently Reeb also influenced another University of Melbourne basketball player, Trevor Reid, who met with another set of elders to learn more about the Church. The journal of Harold Reeb, May 9, 1957, notes that Elders Lawlor and Blaizer had "met with Trevor Ried [Reid] & have a future appointment."
99. Journal of Harold Reeb, June 9, 2011, notes, "Got a telegram from Andy [Kalkaus] yesterday, they're joint winners with Sydney." In conversations with Fred E. Woods, April 25, 2011, Reeb explained that Andy Kalkaus was a member of the University of Melbourne basketball team and that President Bingham did not want Reeb to go to Perth.
100. Journal of Harold Reeb, September 19, 1957.
101. Journal of Harold Reeb, February 25, 1958. In a conversation with Fred E. Woods at the Woods home, Springville, Utah, April 25, 2011, Harold Reeb indicated that he was replaced as coach of the University of Melbourne team by Eldon J. Huntsman. This change was confirmed in a phone conversation between Fred E. Woods and Eldon J. Huntsman, May 5, 2011; Huntsman said that he was the coach at the University of Melbourne for about six months after Reeb's departure.
102. "Mormon Yankees," *Austral Star*, July 1957, 4.
103. G. Lamont Christensen, "Spotlight on Australian Mission," *Austral Star*, September 1957, 8. This same article was published under the name Elder G. LaMont Christensen in the *Church News* as "Mormon Yankees: Australians View Play on TV," August 17, 1957, 2.
104. "Mormon Yankees," *Austral Star*, September 1958, 222.
105. Newton, *Southern Cross Saints*, 191, notes the territories included in this mission.
106. Sherm Day, interview by Fred E. Woods and Martin L. Andersen,

Robert G. Pedersen home, Salt Lake City, Utah, February 15, 2011. Following his mission, Day served as a planner for the 1996 Olympic Games, which were held in Atlanta, Georgia. He has also been the president of four different universities; he noted that he received his leadership training for these assignments as a young man in the mission field. The 1959 Mormon Yankees program, 10, notes that Weldon V. Moore "arrived April 11, 1959, where he succeeded President Zelph Y. Erekson as mission president."

107. Sherm Day, interview by Fred E. Woods and Martin L. Andersen, Robert G. Pedersen home, Salt Lake City, Utah, February 15, 2011. Pedersen recalled, "Now before I went to Australia, we were selling, as young college kids, trousseau items and various assorted things. Diamond rings for boys and silver and crystal cookware for girls. That background sort of led us to when we got to Australia [and when I] had the opportunity of meeting and having as a companion Sherm Day." Robert G. Pedersen, interview by Fred E. Woods and Martin L. Andersen, Robert G. Pedersen home, Salt Lake City, Utah, December 7, 2010.
108. Robert G. Pedersen, interview by Fred E. Woods and Martin L. Andersen, Robert G. Pedersen home, Salt Lake City, Utah, December 7, 2010
109. Sherm Day, interview by Fred E. Woods and Martin L. Andersen, Robert G. Pedersen home, Salt Lake City, Utah, February 15, 2011. Both the 1959 and 1960 Mormon Yankees tour programs addressed the issue of plural marriage. The Mormon Yankees 1959 program noted on page 9, "Mormons do not practice polygamy and have not done so for nearly 70 years. The practice was begun in 1843 by commandment from the Lord and in 1890, by direct revelation, the Latter-day Saints were commanded that the practice should cease." The 1959 program (page 4) also talked about the Latter-day Saints' M-Men basketball tournament, which at the time was the largest in the world—its participants included 55,000 players from more than 3,500 teams in all fifty states as well as teams from Mexico and Canada. The program further noted, "Only the boys who are morally clean and who live a strict health code known as the Word of Wisdom are allowed to play. Mormons do not smoke or drink."
110. Robert G. Pedersen, interview by Fred E. Woods and Martin L. Andersen, Robert G. Pedersen home, Salt Lake City, Utah, December 7, 2010.
111. Robert G. Pedersen, interview by Fred E. Woods and Martin L. Andersen, Robert G. Pedersen home, Salt Lake City, Utah, December 7, 2010.

112. G. LaMont Christensen, "Basketball Australian Mission" July 24, 1959 (unpublished manuscript), Church History Library, 1–2.
113. The 1959 Mormon Yankees program, 9, depicts Elder Roger L. Bown wearing a bow tie and with a microphone in his hand. Bown also wrote the explanation that appears under the caption "The True Life Story": "My act consists of Singing and Impersonations of well-known movie and radio stars." On pages 6–8 of the program, the names and images of the other members of the Mormon Yankees team are shown as well as information concerning their ages, heights, positions, and homes in the United States. Their names are as follows: Dick Madsen, Snellen Johnson, Noel Stoker, Sherm Day, Bob Pedersen, Rich Rampton, and Lanny Nalder.
114. Sherm Day, interview by Fred E. Woods and Martin L. Andersen, Robert G. Pedersen home, Salt Lake City, Utah, February 15, 2011.
115. Robert G. Pedersen and James Richard Rampton, interviews by Fred E. Woods and Martin L. Andersen, Robert G. Pedersen home, Salt Lake City, Utah, December 7, 2010.
116. Roger L. Bown, interview by Fred E. Woods and Martin L. Andersen, Roger L. Bown home, Salt Lake City, Utah, July 9, 2010.
117. The excerpts noted below from April 22 to May 8, 1960, are taken from the journal of Harold Turley, excerpts from journal in possession of the author; emphasis original. Turley's journal also evidences that he went on another Mormon Yankees tour with different players in the New South Wales region. This tour, also a success, commenced on October 1, 1960, and concluded on October 23. Turley noted, "We've got a bunch of fellows to travel with in Elders Snellen Johnson of Roosevelt, Utah; Tony Cannon of Salt Lake; Ed Sharp of Glendale, Calif; Sherell Berrett of Cottonwood Heights, Utah; David Jones of Byron, Wyoming; Lynn Mathie of North Ogden; Reid Goldsberry of Brigham City; Glenn Capps of Hartsville, South Carolina; and myself. All of us have a lot in common and are very good friends." Journal of Harold Turley, October 1, 1960.
118. In a journal entry dated April 25, 1960, Elder Gary H. Blacker noted, "Picked up two beautiful signs that had our names 'Mormon Yankees' on them. We put one on the front & said goodby." Journal of Gary H. Blacker, April 25, 1960, excerpt copy in possession of author.
119. In his journal entry dated April 25, 1960, Blacker also mentioned, "Before arriving in Rockhampton we had 3 blow outs, that really put us behind schedule. Then Elder Mac took a wrong rode & we went 100 miles out of the way. We finally arrived in Rocky at 4AM, about 8 hrs. late." Journal of Gary H. Blacker, April 26, 1960, excerpt copy in possession of author.

120. In his journal entry dated April 26, 1960, Blacker noted, "There were 800 people there & the crowd was really great. We gave signed Books of Mormon to each player as we were introduced on the floor. I had to give a small speech on behalf of the whole team. Elder Bown then announced the game & we played them. We finally beat them 59 to 36. . . . Everyone there got a programme of the game & many got Books of Mormon." The following day, the local Mackay newspaper, the *Daily Mercury* (April 27, 1960), announced in bold headlines, "Mormons' Classic Basketball Win Over Mackay Team," and reported, "The visiting Mormon Yankees basketball team beat a Mackay representative side 59–36 at the Skating Rink last night. Their scintillating display thrilled a crowd of more than 1000 people—a record attendance for a basketball match in Mackay." Journal of Gary H. Blacker, excerpt copy in possession of author.

121. Concerning this day of the tour, Blacker wrote in his journal (entry dated April 27, 1960), "Had another blow out [*sic*] because of weight & rocks. . . . Elder Bown did another excellent job of singing & impersonations at half time. We beat them quite easily. Same routine Books & programmes. I am certainly getting tired of signing my name. They just swarm us after each game for autographs." Journal of Gary H. Blacker, excerpt copy in possession of author. In an interview with Harold Turley by Fred E. Woods and Martin L. Andersen in Turley's home in Sandy, Utah, September 7, 2010, Turley noted that the Mormon Yankees basketball program had the greatest impact in opening doors for missionary work in smaller towns "because in the smaller towns, they were really enclosed, and so, when you're enclosed like that, it's harder to break in as missionaries. When you'd send missionaries up there, they were scared of them. But by going there and playing basketball, we totally opened up the town, and so now the people would say, 'Oh, we'd love to have you come and visit with us.'"

122. Blacker's journal, entry dated April 28, 1960, states, "The paper said 2,500 people were there. Townsville had 2 or 3 players who were all-state players & were very good." Journal of Gary H. Blacker, excerpt copy in possession of author.

123. Blacker's journal entry dated April 29, 1960, notes, "In the 2nd half we started clowning around. We had the crowd in stitches. . . . After the game . . . autographs." Journal of Gary H. Blacker, excerpt copy in possession of author.

124. In an interview by Fred E. Woods and Martin L. Andersen, September 7, 2010, Turley noted, "Probably the greatest experiences that I recall were from the clinics with the children and the teenagers. . . . We'd

talk about the Word of Wisdom. And they'd say, 'You mean, you don't smoke? You don't drink? You're not serious, are you?' And we'd say, 'Yes, and that helps us to keep our energy level, to keep our competitive spirit, and be able to have the durability in the games.' So the teenage boys especially, we saw a lot of them stop smoking. We would see that happen almost immediately in these experiences. That was probably the thing that I remember the most, is seeing them making changes, and then they would come and talk to me at the game, after the game and say, 'I want you to know, Elder Turley, I've stopped smoking.'"

125. Turley also notes here that Jim "weighs 350 lbs." Blacker's journal entry for May 2, 1960, also gives Jim's last name: "Talked to Jim Connolly about tomorrow. He's sure a great guy." Blacker's journal entry for May 3, 1960, adds, "We were at the biggest Dept. store on personal display. We gave out programmes. . . . Met lots of fine people. Lots of the girls were in who play basketball." Journal of Gary H. Blacker, excerpt copy in possession of author. A local Mackay newspaper ran an article with the headline "Mormons Play Dazzling Basketball to Win" in the *Daily Mercury* (May 4, 1960), in which it was reported that the Mormon Yankees beat the Mackay team 59 to 43. The writer also noted, "Their clever stepping, handling, and passing at times left the Mackay players bewildered. Sportsmanship was superb. The touring Mormons had the 700 spectators cheering wildly in the second half when they turned on a sustained exhibition of 'clowning.'" That Blacker really cared about the people of Mackay and "desired to be one of the Elders . . . to open McKay [Mackay] when it is reopened," as noted above from his journal, is also evident from an interview with one of the Mackay basketball players, Allan Pascoe. Fifty years after playing against Blacker, Pascoe recalled, "Elder Gary Blacker was sort of a stalwart player that I based myself on, . . . how he trained and what he did. . . . When he went back to the U.S. he wrote me a nice letter, and gave me some tips on training. A couple of things [that] have always stood in my mind is [*sic*] the skipping or jump rope. . . . One of the things that really stuck in my mind was he told me to do pushups on my fingers." Allan Pascoe, interview by Fred E. Woods and Martin L. Andersen, Allan Pascoe home, Mackay, Queensland, Australia, June 23, 2010.

126. Lindsay Gaze, interview by Fred E. Woods and Martin L. Andersen, Lindsay Gaze home, Melbourne, Australia, June 21, 2010. Bob Skousen, interview by Fred E. Woods and Martin L. Andersen, Bob Skousen home, Mesa, Arizona, February 11, 2011. Skousen mentioned that he played at BYU under Stan Watts before being called as a missionary. Further, Skousen explained that he had planned on serving a mission

but instead had become engaged and had set his mind on professional basketball. This outlook was all changed by an early-morning phone call from Elder Delbert L. Stapley of the Church's Quorum of the Twelve Apostles, who invited Skousen to come that very day to Elder Stapley's office in Salt Lake City. When Skousen arrived, he was told that the Lord wanted him to serve a mission. During the interview Elder Stapley said, "'Is there anything at all that I can promise you if you'll accept this call?' He said, 'It's that important.' And I said, 'Well, if I go on this mission, my basketball career's through. I know a lot of guys go, but you just aren't the same when you get back.' And he said, 'Well, what can I promise you?' And I said, 'Well,' I said, 'If I could just do one thing. If I could just hold the record for one game at BYU, I'll feel it's worthwhile.' And he said, 'I can promise you, you will do that.'" In BYU's first game of the 1961 season against number-one ranked UCLA (January 1, 1961), Skousen scored forty-seven points, a school record that was not broken until Jimmer Fredette scored forty-nine points in a game in 2010. Skousen noted, "The Lord's true to his promise[s]."

127. Newton, *Southern Cross Saints*, 40. The word *stake* is used by Latter-day Saints to describe an ecclesiastical region made up of congregations (usually numbering several hundred), which are referred to as ward units. This is similar to the Catholics employing the word *diocese* to represent a district that is made up of parishes.

128. Harold R. Turley, interview by Fred E. Woods and Martin L. Andersen, Harold Turley home, Sandy, Utah, September 7, 2010.

129. Gordon Holt, interview by Fred E. Woods and Martin L. Andersen, business office of Gordon Holt, Utah County, Utah, July 6, 2010.

130. James William Lundahl, interview by Fred E. Woods and Martin L. Andersen, Gary H. Blacker home, North Ogden, Utah, July 8, 2010. It was common for the Mormon Yankees to include a discussion of the Word of Wisdom in their basketball clinics. As noted previously, this issue was also addressed in the 1959 Mormon Yankees tour program. According to Lindsay Gaze, by living their health code, the Mormon Yankees made an impression about their religion without even opening their mouths. He noted that by "observing the Mormon players who were noted for not drinking or smoking, and playing really well, just as role models, I thought, 'That might be a good idea, not to indulge in these sorts of things.' So without the proselytizing, just merely their behavior was an influence on me, personally, to say this might be worthwhile to be a non-drinker, a non-smoker, and have a fairly decent appearance, which at that time I'd never had." Lindsay Gaze, interview

by Fred E. Woods and Martin L. Andersen, Lindsay Gaze home, Melbourne, Australia, December 10, 2009.

131. Gary H. Blacker, interview by Fred E. Woods and Martin L. Andersen, Gary H. Blacker home, North Ogden, Utah, July 8, 2010. John Turner, who was one of Blacker's players at the Cairns tournament, remembered, "The ladies . . . played the final against Cairns, and they went down by one point. . . . We played against Townsville in the Final and I think went down by five points in the end." Ben Watson, "The Mormon Yankees," (unpublished manuscript, undated), 63, in possession of the author. (The author expresses appreciation to Ben Watson, a former LDS missionary to Brisbane, Australia, for allowing him to use this manuscript). Turner was correct about the outcome of the women's game. In fact, "Stop Press From Cairns," *Torres News*, June 13, 1961, 6, notes that the final score was 23–22. However, Turner must have confused the men's final with another tournament game that the men's Wongais played in, as this same article reveals that the men's Wongais lost to Townsville by a score of 46–27.

The fair-skinned Blacker was a player-coach for the men's team and was smitten by the heat of the sun which probably contributed to the men's team losing the Cairns tournament championship. Lundahl, who journeyed with Blacker from Thursday Island to Cairns, remembered that the parents of the players worked hard to raise funds for the team's travel because they "just wanted to give their kids that opportunity to go and say that they had gone to a basketball tournament in Cairns, . . . [as] some of the kids had never been off Thursday Island." James William Lundahl, interview by Fred E. Woods and Martin L. Andersen, Gary H. Blacker home, North Ogden, Utah, July 8, 2010.

132. For the full story, see Fred E. Woods, "Making Friends Down Under: The Beginnings of LDS Missionary Work on Thursday Island, Queensland, Australia, 1961," *Mormon Historical Studies* 11, no. 1 (Spring 2011): 105–23.

133. Keith Stringer, interview by Fred E. Woods and Martin L. Andersen, Keith Stringer home, Melbourne, Australia, December 12, 2009. Stringer also noted, "When the basketball was stopped, it didn't have an impact really on the degree of conversions that were taking place. Bruce McConkie stirred the pot, quite a lot, and by and large the way he handled the situation, the way he taught the missionaries, the way they were educated as to how to be obedient to the instructions about missionary work, we had an increase, a very big increase in baptisms."

134. Watts and other Australian LDS teenage girls found the Mormon Yankees quite attractive. Watts said, "When we first met the American missionaries, I was absolutely gob spanked, because I'd never met

Americans before. I'd only ever seen them on television, and I fell in love with them, because I was fifteen and a half, nearly sixteen, and I was just [thinking,] 'Oh! They're gorgeous! . . . The missionaries were definitely a huge part of my desire to join the Church. I knew it was true, but I also loved the missionaries, and was very impressed with them." Kay Watts, interview by Fred E. Woods and Martin L. Andersen, Keith Stringer home, Melbourne, Australia, December 12, 2009.

135. Kay Watts, interview by Fred E. Woods and Martin L. Andersen, Keith Stringer home, Melbourne, Australia, December 12, 2009. Elspeth Lyon, an Australian convert, remembered, "During the [1960s], . . . a lot of the wards used to play basketball and form teams." Elspeth Lyon, interview by Fred E. Woods and Martin L. Andersen, Elspeth Lyon home, Melbourne, Australia, December 10, 2009.

136. Lindsay Gaze, interview by Fred E. Woods and Martin L. Andersen, Lindsay Gaze home, Melbourne, Australia, December 10, 2009.

137. Recording of 1961 Mission Presidents' Seminar, audio cassette, Church History Library.

138. Bishop H. David Burton, interview by Fred E. Woods and Martin L. Andersen, Burton's office in the Church Office Building, Salt Lake City, Utah, September 7, 2010. Richard Christensen, a Mormon Yankee who served in Australia from 1955 to 1957, provides a glimpse of the hard work these elders put into their ecclesiastical efforts along with their basketball: "Of course the fact of the matter is, we didn't have any spare time. During the time that I served . . . eight of my fourteen months in Ipswich, Queensland, I was also the branch president, and we were building a building. I didn't have a P-day [preparation day] for the first fourteen months of my mission. . . . We didn't have any freebies, there weren't movies on the side, and [there weren't] extra luncheon engagements." Richard Christensen, interview by Martin L. Andersen, Richard Christensen home, Salt Lake City, Utah, February 17, 2011.

139. This impact is unlike the negative one that resulted from the infamous "baseball baptisms" performed by some Mormon missionaries governed by ulterior motives. In the late 1950s and 1960s, some elders laboring in Great Britain required that young people be baptized in order to play on baseball teams. For more information on this issue, see Michael D. Quinn, "I-Thou vs. I-It Conversions: The Mormon 'Baseball Baptism' Era," *Sunstone* 16 (December 1993): 30–44; and Richard Mavin, "The Woodbury Years: An Insider's Look at Baseball Baptisms in Britain," *Sunstone* 19 (March 1996): 56–60.

140. Lindsay Gaze, interview by Fred E. Woods and Martin L. Andersen, Lindsay Gaze home, Melbourne, Australia, December 10, 2009.

BIBLIOGRAPHY

Archibald, Elspeth. "Bentleigh Branch." *Austral Star*, July 1956, 20.

"Australia Melbourne Mission General Minutes." July 3, 1955 (unpublished manuscript), Church History Library, The Church of Jesus Christ of Latter-day Saints, Salt Lake City, Utah.

"Australia Melbourne Mission General Minutes." July 28, 1956 (unpublished manuscript), Church History Library.

"Australia Melbourne Mission General Minutes." November 12, 1956.

"Australia Melbourne Mission General Minutes." December 4, 1956.

Australian Basketball Championships Sydney, 1955 [Program].

Bain, Elder Douglas. "New South Wales Elders' Basketball Team." *Austral Star*, August 1950, 14.

"Basketball Scores—Melbourne." *Austral Star*, December 1956, 10.

Bellott, Mary. "Melbourne Branch." *Austral Star*, August 1953, 17.

Bennion, Elder J. "Bendigo Branch." *Austral Star*, July 1950, 8.

Benson, Betty. Interview by Fred E. Woods and Martin L. Andersen, city park, Sydney, New South Wales, Australia, June 26, 2010.

Berzzarins, Gunars Esins, (GEB). Interview by Fred E. Woods and Martin L. Andersen, Gunars Esins Berzzarins home, Adelaide, Australia, June 18, 2010.

Bjork, Delmar H. "Freed at Last from Spirit Prison, Unusual LDS Missionary Experience(s), Autobiography: Delmar H. Bjork" (unpublished manuscript), 12.

———. Interview by Fred E. Woods and Martin L. Andersen, home of Delmar Bjork, Taylorsville, Utah, USA, April 16, 2011.

Blacker, Gary H. Interview by Fred E. Woods and Martin L. Andersen, Gary H. Blacker home, North Ogden, Utah, USA, July 8, 2010.

———. Journal of Gary H. Blacker, 1960, excerpt copy in possession of author.

Bouma, Gary D. interview by Fred E. Woods and Martin L. Andersen, home of Gary D. Bouma, Melbourne, Victoria, Australia, June 26, 2010.

Bouck, Ronald L. Interview by Fred E. Woods and Martin L. Andersen, Ronald L. Bouck home, Salt Lake City, Utah, USA, December 27, 2010.

———. Interview by Fred E. Woods and Martin L. Andersen, Roger L. Bown home, Salt Lake City, Utah, USA, July 9, 2010.

Bradley, Shawn. Interview by Fred E. Woods, West Jordan, Utah, USA, March 25, 2011.

Brooks, Betty. Interview by Fred E. Woods and Martin L. Andersen, home of Keith and Betty Brooks, Melbourne, Victoria, Australia, December 11, 2009.

Brooks, Keith. Interview by Fred E. Woods and Martin L. Andersen, home of Keith and Betty Brooks, Melbourne, Victoria, Australia, December 11, 2009.

Burdett, Colin J. Interview by Fred E. Woods and Martin L. Andersen, Colin J. Burdett home, Adelaide, Australia, June 18, 2010.

Burnett, Marjorie. "Bankstown Branch." *Austral Star*, June 1951, 10.

Burns, Cliff. Interview by Fred E. Woods and Martin L. Andersen, home of Cliff Burns, Melbourne, Victoria, Australia, December 11, 2009.

Burt, Rodney. Interview by Fred E. Woods and Martin L. Andersen, Rodney Burt home, Springville, Utah, USA, February 17, 2011.

Burton, Bishop H. David. Interview by Fred E. Woods and Martin L. Andersen, Burton's office in the Church Office Building, Salt Lake City, Utah, USA, September 7, 2010.

Christensen, G. Lamont. "Basketball Australian Mission." July 24, 1959 (unpublished manuscript), Church History Library, 1–2.

———. *Church News* as "Mormon Yankees: Australians View Play on TV," August 17, 1957, 2.

———. "Spotlight on Australian Mission," *Austral Star*, September 1957, 8.

Christensen, Richard D. Interview by Martin L. Andersen, Richard Christensen home, Salt Lake City, Utah, USA, February 17, 2011.

"*Christian Democracy for Today, Sixth-Ninth Annual Report and Financial Statement of the Young Men's Christian Association of Melbourne for the Year Ending 31st December, 1940*, 17–18. University of Melbourne Library, Melbourne, Australia.

Citizens of To-day and To-morrow, 67th Annual Report Young Men's Christian Association of Melbourne (1938). University of Melbourne Library, Melbourne, Australia.

Condie, DeLyle H. Interview by Fred E. Woods and Martin L. Andersen, DeLyle H. Condie home, Salt Lake City, Utah, USA, July 7, 2010.

Cray, Marie. Interview by Fred E. Woods and Martin L. Andersen, Graham and Marie Cray home, Melbourne, Victoria, Australia, December 14, 2009.

Cullis, Lorna. Interview by Fred E. Woods and Martin L. Andersen, home of Lorna Cullis, Melbourne, Australia, December 10, 2009.

Dancis, Mikelis (Mike). Interview by Fred E. Woods and Martin L. Andersen, George Dancis home, Adelaide, Australia, June 17, 2010.

Dancis, George. Interview by Fred E. Woods and Martin L. Andersen, George Dancis home, Adelaide, Australia, June 17, 2010.

Davis, William Frederick Percival (Perce). Interview by Fred E. Woods and Martin L. Andersen, home of Perce Davis, Melbourne, Victoria, Australia, December 11, 2009.

Day, Sherman (Sherm). Interview by Fred E. Woods and Martin L. Andersen, Robert G. Pedersen home, Salt Lake City, Utah, USA, February 15, 2011.

Dodd, Heather. Interview by Fred E. Woods and Martin L. Andersen, Heather Dodd home, Brisbane, Queensland, Australia, June 25, 2010.

Dunn, Elder Loren C. Interview, typescript, 24–27, by Matt Heiss, 1991, Church History Library, Salt Lake City, Utah, USA.

Duthie, Brian. "Condie Is Colossal." *The Sporting Globe All-Sport Magazine*, September 8, 1956.

"Elder Dunn Appointed Mission Counselor." *Austral Star*, November 1955, 5.

"Elders Close Season with Exhibition." *Austral Star*, January 1955, 11.

Embry, Jessie L. Interview by Fred E. Woods and Martin L. Andersen, Brigham Young University, Provo, Utah, USA, September 10, 2010.

———. *Spiritualized Recreation: Mormon All-Church Athletic Tournaments and Dance Festivals*. Provo, Utah: Brigham Young University, 2008.

Embry, Jessie L. and John H. Brambaugh. "Preaching through Playing: Using Sports and Recreation in Missionary Work, 1911–64." *Journal of Mormon History* 35, no. 4 (Fall 2009): 60.

Emery, Arthur. Interview by Fred E. Woods and Martin L. Andersen, Arthur Emery home, Adelaide, Australia, June 18, 2010.

Feeney, Ray. Interview by Fred E. Woods and Martin L. Andersen, Ray Feeney home, Sydney, Australia, June 26, 2010.

Flick, Charles Bruce. Interview by Fred E. Woods and Martin L. Andersen, Charles Bruce and Barbara Flick home, Sydney, Australia, June 26, 2010.

Freidenfelds, Inga. Interview by Fred E. Woods and Martin L. Andersen,

Lindsay Gaze home, Melbourne, Australia, June 18, 2010.
Freidenfelds, Lolita. Interview by Fred E. Woods and Martin L. Andersen, Lindsay Gaze home, Melbourne, Australia, June 18, 2010.
Frodsham, Mark J. Interview by Fred E. Woods and Martin L. Andersen, Mark J. Frodsham home, Murray, Utah, USA, July 9, 2010.
Gage, Zita Margaret. "Prospect Branch." *Austral Star*, May 1954, 19.
———. "Prospect Branch." *Austral Star*, September 1956, 15.
Garn, James Nyle. Interview with Martin L. Andersen, St. George, Utah, USA, April 13, 2011.
Gaze, Lindsay. Interview by Fred E. Woods and Martin L. Andersen, Lindsay Gaze home, Melbourne, Australia, June, 15, 2009; December 10, 2009; June 21, 2010.
Grant, Paul G. Interview by Martin L. Andersen, Jackson Hole, Wyoming, USA, August 28, 2010.
Greene, Elder D. Forrest. "Victoria Champions." *Improvement Era*, June 1940, 369.
———. "Australian Mission Basketball." *Improvement Era*, May 1941, 305.
Hampson, Gayle. Interview by Fred E. Woods and Martin L. Andersen, in front of work place of Gayle Hampson and her husband, Brisbane, Queensland, Australia, June 24, 2010.
Haynes, Ted E. Interview by Martin L. Andersen, Ted E. Haynes home, Magrath, Alberta, Canada, April 8, 2011.
Heskett, Geoff. Interview by Fred E. Woods and Martin L. Andersen, Geoff Heskett home, Melbourne, Australia, December 13, 2009.
"History of Basketball." Basketball Victoria, last modified 2010, http://www.basketballvictoria.com.au/index.php?id=61.
Holt, Gordon. Interview by Fred E. Woods and Martin L. Andersen, business office of Gordon Holt, Utah County, Utah, USA, July 6, 2010.
Holzworth, Loris. "Toowoomba Branch." *Austral Star*, December 1950, 8.
———. "Toowoomba Branch." *Austral Star,* April 1951, 8.
———. "Toowoomba Branch." *Austral Star*, October 1951, 8.
Hughan, Owen. Interview by Fred E. Woods and Martin L. Andersen, home of Owen Hughan, Horsham, Victoria, Australia, June 16, 2010.
Hull, Dr. Donald F. Interview by Martin L. Andersen, San Francisco, California, USA, April 15, 2011.
Huntsman, Eldon J. Interview by Martin L. Andersen, home of Eldon J. Huntsman, American Fork, Utah, USA, May 5, 2011.
Johnson, Edward A. (Ted). Interview by Fred E. Woods and Martin L. Andersen, Ted Johnson home, Boise, Idaho, July 7, 2010.

Kimball, Dr. David A. Interview by Fred E. Woods and Martin L. Andersen, Dr. David A. Kimball home, Salt Lake City, Utah, USA, February 15, 2011.

Kimball, Richard Ian. Interview by Fred E. Woods and Martin L. Andersen, Joseph Smith Building, Brigham Young University, Provo, Utah, USA, December 8, 2010.

———. *Sports in Zion: Mormon Recreation, 1900–1940*. Urbana: University of Illinois Press, 2003.

Leivesley, Eric. Interview by Fred E. Woods and Martin L. Andersen, home of Eric and Pat Leivesley, Mackay, Queensland, Australia, June 23, 2010.

Leivesley, Pat. Interview by Fred E. Woods and Martin L. Andersen, home of Eric and Pat Leivesley, Mackay, Queensland, Australia, June 23, 2010.

"Loren C. Dunn." http://en.wikipedia.org/wiki/Loren_C._Dunn.

Lundahl, James William. Interview by Fred E. Woods and Martin L. Andersen, Gary H. Blacker home, North Ogden, Utah, USA, July 8, 2010.

Lyon, Elspeth. Interview by Fred E. Woods and Martin L. Andersen, Elspeth Lyon home, Melbourne, Australia, December 10, 2009.

"Manuscript History of the South Australia Mission." *Quarterly Report* (June 30, 1957). Church History Library, cited in Newton, *Southern Cross Saints*, 67, 235.

Mavin, Richard. "The Woodbury Years: An Insider's Look at Baseball Baptisms in Britain." *Sunstone* 19 (March 1996): 56–60.

McGavin, Carl. Interview by Fred E. Woods and Martin L. Andersen, home of Harold and Janice Reeb, Hobble Creek Canyon, Springville, Utah, USA, October, 31, 2009.

McNair, Joan. Interview by Fred E. Woods and Martin L. Andersen, home of Joan McNair, Bendigo, Victoria, Australia, June 20, 2010.

"Missionaries Win Latvian Basketball Tournament." *Austral Star*, August 1956, 11.

"Missionary Items." *Austral Star*, August 1951, 12.

Mitchell, Nancy. "Hobart Branch." *Austral Star*, August 1950, 10.

"Mormon Yankees." *Austral Star*, June 1954, 10.

"Mormon Yankees." *Austral Star*, July 1957, 4.

"Mormon Yankees." *Austral Star*, September 1958, 222.

"Mormon Yankees Basketball Breaks Australia Barriers, The." *Church News*, November 19, 1955, 11.

"Mormon Yankees Basketball Champs Lead in Baptisms, The." *Church*

News, April 30, 1955, 12.

"Mormons Play Dazzling Basketball to Win." in the *Daily Mercury* (May 4, 1960).

"Mormons' Classic Basketball Win over Mackay Team." *Daily Mercury* (April 27, 1960).

Moy, Mervyn (Merv). Interview by Fred E. Woods and Martin L. Andersen, Mervyn Moy home, Sydney, Australia, June 25, 2010.

Mutton, Denise Helen. Interview by Fred E. Woods and Martin L. Andersen, Peter G. and Denise Helen Mutton home, Adelaide, Australia, June 19, 2010.

Mutton, Peter G. Interview by Fred E. Woods and Martin L. Andersen, Peter G. and Denise Helen Mutton home, Adelaide, Australia, June 19, 2010.

Nash, Ruth. "Bankstown Branch." *Austral Star*, April 1953, 12.

———. "Bankstown Branch." *Austral Star*, August 1953, 15.

Newton, Marjorie. *Southern Cross Saints: The Mormons in Australia*, Mormons in the Pacific Series. Laie, Hawaii: Institute for Polynesian Studies, 1991.

O'Riordan, Dennis. Interview by Fred E. Woods and Martin L. Andersen, home of Graeme and Marie Cray, Melbourne, Victoria, Australia, December 14, 2009.

Pascoe, Allan. Interview by Fred E. Woods and Martin L. Andersen, home of Allan Pascoe, Mackay, Queenslands, Australia, June 23, 2010.

Pearse, Neville. Interview by Fred E. Woods and Martin L. Andersen, home of Neville Pearse, Mackay, Queenslands, Australia, June 22, 2010.

Pedersen, Robert G. Interview by Fred E. Woods and Martin L. Andersen, Robert G. Pedersen home, Salt Lake City, Utah, USA, December 7, 2010.

Pemberton, Don. Interview by Fred E. Woods and Martin L. Andersen, Pemberton home, Melbourne, Australia, December 14, 2009.

Portals of Opportunity, 66th Annual Report Young Men's Christian Association of Melbourne (1937), 16. University of Melbourne Library, Melbourne, Australia.

Quinn, Michael D. "I-Thou vs. I-It Conversions: The Mormon 'Baseball Baptism' Era." *Sunstone* 16 (December 1993): 30–44.

Rampton, James Richard (Rich). Interview by Fred E. Woods and Martin L. Andersen, Robert G. Pedersen home, Salt Lake City, Utah, USA, December 7, 2010.

Ramsay, Al. *Basketball in New South Wales: A History: 50 Years of*

Achievement and Development, 1938–1988. Flemington Markets, New South Wales: NSW Basketball Association, 1989.

Rawolle, Sister [Kathleen]. "Victorian District." *Austral Star*, June 20, 1938, 8.

———. "Melbourne Branch." *Austral Star*, November 1949, 6.

Recording of 1961 Mission Presidents' Seminar, audio cassette, Church History Library.

Reeb, Harold (Hal). Interview by Fred E. Woods and Martin L. Andersen, Harold and Janice Reeb home, Hobble Creek Canyon, Springville, Utah, USA, October 31, 2009.

———. Journal of Harold Reeb, in possession of Harold Reeb, Springville, Utah.

Ryan, Denis. Interview by Fred E. Woods and Martin L. Andersen, Mackay, Queensland, Australia, June 22, 2010.

Skousen, Bob. Interview by Fred E. Woods and Martin L. Andersen, Bob Skousen home, Mesa, Arizona, USA, February 11, 2011.

Steck, Robert (Bob). Interview by Martin L. Andersen, home of Bob Steck, San Francisco, California, USA, April 15, 2011.

Steen, Raymond Arthur. Interview by Fred E. Woods and Martin L. Andersen, home of Raymond Arthur Steen, Mackay, Queensland, Australia, June 24, 2010.

"Stop Press From Cairns." *Torres News*, June 13, 1961, 6.

Stringer, Keith. Interview by Fred E. Woods and Martin L. Andersen, Keith Stringer home, Melbourne, Victoria, Australia, December 12, 2009.

Trost, June. "Brisbane Branch." *Austral Star*, July 1950, 9.

———. "Brisbane Branch." *Austral Star*, November 1951, 11.

Turley, Harold E., Jr. Interview by Fred E. Woods and Martin L. Andersen, Harold Turley home, Sandy, Utah, USA, September 7, 2010.

———. Journal of Harold E. Turley Jr., 1960, excerpt copy in possession of author.

Tuttle, Dell. Interview by Fred E. Woods and Martin L. Andersen, Dell Tuttle home, Lehi, Utah, USA, July 9, 2010.

Victoria Missionary Record Australia[n] Mission [1950–1953] Historical Record of Victorian District" (unpublished manuscript), Church History Library, The Church of Jesus Christ of Latter-day Saints, Salt Lake City, Utah.

"Victorian District." *Austral Star*, September 1940, 10.

"Victorian Mormon Yankees, The." *Austral Star*, April 1956, 10.

Walton, Garwood. Interview by Fred E. Woods and Martin L. Andersen, home of Hal and Janice Reeb, Hobble Creek Canyon, Springville, Utah, USA, October 31, 2009.

Watson, Ben. "The Mormon Yankees." (unpublished manuscript, undated), in possession of the author.

Watts, Kay. Interview by Fred E. Woods and Martin L. Andersen, Keith Stringer home, Melbourne, Victoria Australia, December 12, 2009.

Weaving the Fabric for the Future, 68th Annual Report Young Men's Christian Association of Melbourne (1939), 18. University of Melbourne Library, Melbourne, Australia.

Weitzeil, Norman (Norm). Interview by Martin L. Andersen, home of Norm Weitzel, Mountain Green, Utah, USA, April 16, 2011.

West, Wilburn. Interview by Martin L. Andersen, Cottonwood Heights, Utah, USA, May 4, 2011.

Whitehead, Peggy. "Melbourne Branch." *Austral Star*, January 1952, 11.

———. "Melbourne Branch." *Austral Star*, June 1952, 12.

Whitworth, Lily M. "Whyalla Branch." *Austral Star*, June 1957, 18.

Woods, Fred E. "Making Friends Down Under: The Beginnings of LDS Missionary Work on Thursday Island, Queensland, Australia, 1961." *Mormon Historical Studies* 11, no. 1 (Spring 2011): 105–23.

INDEX

A

Adelaide 4, 9–12, 14–16, 19, 23, 54–57, 86, 109, 124, 134–35, 140, 143, 153–54, 158–60, 173, 175, 177, 180, 194–95, 228–29, 231, 233, 247, 252–53
Adelaide Advertiser 14
advertise 34, 113
alcohol 45, 56, 100, 147, 236, 256
Australian Tennis Association 15
Austral Star 4–5, 7–8, 10, 22, 25, 31

B

Bankstown 7–8, 59
baptism 15, 123, 229–30, 238, 247
behavior 4, 24, 50, 119, 145, 148, 150, 152, 198, 206, 208, 221–22
beliefs 147, 205, 245
Bendigo 5, 100–101, 256
Benson, Betty 51
Bentleigh Branch 22–23
Berzzarins, Gunars Esins 14, 54
betting 101
Bible 103, 210
Bingham, Thomas S. 20–21, 28, 29, 31, 86–87, 89, 96–98, 111–12, 143, 173–75, 179, 193, 218, 256–57
Bjork, Delmar 22, 26, 58
Blackburn 47, 236, 251
Blacker, Gary H. 39–40, 43–46, 62, 65, 165–66, 184, 188–89, 207–8
Book of Mormon 15, 36, 40, 57, 72–73, 102, 114, 169, 210, 212, 216, 239, 244, 250
Bouck, Ronald L. 18, 36, 66, 126
Bouma, Gary D. 69
Bown, Roger L. 36–43, 64, 71–72, 114, 212, 239
Bradley, Shawn 74
Brigham Young University 11, 224
Brisbane Branch 5, 7
Brooks, Betty 76
Brooks, Keith 79
Burdett, Colin J. 13, 81
Burns, Cliff 83
Burton, H. David 47–48, 91, 251
Burt, Rodney 21–23, 85
BYU 11–12, 26, 43, 74, 113, 149, 152, 172–75, 177–78, 180, 205, 224–25, 230, 255

C

Cairns 45, 65, 166, 188
Canadian 158
Castlemaine 5
Catholic 57, 67, 69, 83, 187, 209
Catholics 70
championship 2–8, 16–17, 20, 22, 32, 59, 97, 118, 127, 134, 137, 143–44, 146, 154, 159, 197, 228
chapel 22–23, 49, 64, 73, 88, 98
Charters Towers 40
cheer 18, 52, 60–61, 67, 76–77, 111, 126, 144, 177, 195, 237, 250–51
cheerleader 18, 66, 76

Chile 25, 100, 171
Chinese 27, 93, 100, 140, 153, 171, 180, 204–5
Christensen, G. LaMont 32, 36
Christensen, Hal 20, 56–57, 96
Christensen, Richard D. 93
Christianity 1, 69, 122–23
Church News 16–17
Church of Jesus Christ of Latter-day Saints, The ix, xi–xii, 1–2, 7–8, 23, 28, 32, 35–36, 48, 50, 61, 72, 88–89, 104, 117, 141, 167, 182, 200, 212, 234, 253, 257
clinic 3, 34, 38–40, 42, 73, 75, 115, 152, 181, 204, 206, 216, 239–40
club 4, 30, 54, 81–83, 126–27, 149, 219
coach 2, 9–12, 21–22, 24–25, 27, 29–31, 44–45, 47, 57, 60, 63, 65, 81, 86–87, 96–97, 124, 134, 137, 140, 142–43, 151, 153–54, 158–59, 175, 178, 184, 187–88, 205–6, 209–10, 214–15, 218–19, 221, 230–31, 233, 251, 256
Colts 4
Condie, DeLyle H. 20–22, 24–28, 31–32, 60, 79, 86–87, 89, 96, 111–12, 130–31, 143, 146, 148, 151, 162–64, 170, 179, 180, 197, 232
Connolly, Jim 42, 240
convert 2–3, 9, 28, 35, 49, 56, 92, 104, 108, 127, 153, 156, 178, 181–83, 227, 230
convict 69
courts 64, 118, 209, 220
Cray, Marie 8, 103
Cullis, Lorna 105

D

Dancis, George 12–13, 55, 81, 107, 134, 197
Dancis, Mike 12–13, 107, 109
Davis, William Frederick Percival 22, 110, 248
Day, Sherman (Sherm) 32–34, 36, 113–14, 130–31, 197, 213
Dodd, Heather 117
drinking 31, 147, 185, 189, 215, 236
Dunn, Loren C. xii, 9–13, 16–19, 22, 55–57, 81, 108, 124, 127, 130–31, 134, 157–58, 177–78, 194, 197, 200–202, 228–30

E

Embry, Jessie L. 121, 259, 281
Emery, Arthur 9, 11, 124, 229
Erekson, Zelph Y. 32–33, 68, 114
Europeans 69, 84, 143, 148, 162, 163, 253

F

Feeney, Ray 18, 126
Flick, Charles Bruce 16–17, 115, 128–29
football 9, 41, 62, 73, 104, 111, 144–46, 174, 216–17, 219, 228, 237
Formosa 27, 100, 140, 180
France 25, 60, 100, 111, 142
Fredette, Jimmer 226
Freidenfelds, Inga 25, 133, 135–36, 154
Freidenfelds, Lola 135
friends 28, 39, 46, 49, 52–53, 93, 99, 105, 116, 119, 140, 144, 147, 154, 170, 178, 189, 193, 213, 222, 232, 234, 249, 251
Frodsham, Mark J. 26, 32, 79, 106, 137, 150, 152–53, 170, 172

G

Gardner, Jack 22, 96, 114, 148, 151
Garn, James Nyle 22, 27–28, 87, 139, 152, 170
Gaze, Lindsay 20–21, 24–25, 43, 48–50, 63, 83, 97, 105, 112, 142
GEB 14, 54
Germany 2, 54, 60, 121–22, 200
Globetrotters. See Harlem Globetrotters
Grant, Paul G. 26–27, 32, 79, 101, 134–36, 148–49, 151, 170

H

halftime shows 17, 36, 41–42, 64, 67, 72, 94, 240
Hampson, Gayle 156
Harlem Globetrotters 9, 11, 37, 64, 81, 101, 146, 177, 207
Haynes, Ted E. 11, 56, 157, 177, 228
Heskett, Geoff 25, 161
Hobart Branch 6
Holt, Gordon 44–45, 165
Hughan, Owen 40, 168
Hull, Dr. Donald F. 22, 25–26, 28, 32, 87, 152, 170–71, 173, 232
Huntsman, Eldon J. 172

I

impersonation 36–38, 41, 71–72, 240

J

Johnson, Edward A. (Ted) 8, 10–13, 20, 56, 93, 96, 165, 177, 194, 200–201, 229

K

Kimball, David A. 22, 87–88, 142, 148–49, 170, 179, 256
Kimball, Dr. Richard Ian 182
Kombi 34, 113

L

Latvians 12–14, 22, 25, 54–57, 81–84, 107–9, 133, 135, 143, 147, 154, 197, 253
league 5–7, 10–11, 20–21, 30, 74, 86–87, 97–101, 108, 118, 122, 126, 146, 158–59, 179, 192, 256
Leivesley, Eric 184, 187
Leivesley, Pat 186
Liljenquist, Charles V. 8–10, 16, 19–20, 58, 68, 177, 228, 252–53
Lithuanians 14, 54–55, 82, 109, 143, 147
Longley, Luke 155
Lundahl, James William 45–46, 166, 188
Lutheran 57, 108
Lyon, Elspeth 190, 277

M

Mackay 39, 41–42, 185–87, 207, 209, 220–22, 233, 235, 239–40
mayor 5, 35, 72, 216, 243–44
McConkie, Bruce R. 46–48, 145, 237–38, 251
McGavin, Carl 192, 247
McKay, David O. 18–19, 22, 88, 98, 228
McNair, Joan 194, 283
Melbourne ix, 2–5, 7–8, 19–24, 26–29, 31–32, 44, 46, 58, 60–61, 83–84, 86–88, 93, 97, 101, 104–6, 110–11, 130–31, 135–36, 140,

145–46, 152–54, 159, 168, 172–73, 175, 179–80, 190–91, 193, 196–97, 204, 214, 218, 220, 247, 250, 252, 256
Moore, Weldon V. 4, 33–34, 63, 189, 213, 217
Mormonism. See Church of Jesus Christ of Latter-day Saints, The
Moy, Merv 17, 25, 196
Mutton, Denise 13, 200
Mutton, Peter G. 13, 202

N

Naismith, James 1
Navy 219
netball 9, 54, 118
New South Wales 4, 6, 7, 16–17, 19, 22, 32, 36, 59, 127, 130, 143, 159, 166, 212–13
newspaper x, 3, 10, 14, 16, 19, 28, 49–50, 59, 62, 88–89, 94, 99, 111, 122, 166, 174, 244
Newton, Marjorie 19

O

OBI. See Our Boys Institute
Olympics xii, 2, 16–17, 20–28, 31–32, 43, 59–61, 81, 83, 86, 93, 97–100, 105, 110–12, 115, 121–22, 131, 133, 139–46, 152–54, 161–63, 171, 174–75, 180, 196–97, 214, 218, 226, 232, 241, 246–47, 256
Opperman, Hubert 3
O'Riordan, Dennis ix, 6, 18, 204
Our Boys Institute 12, 81–82, 109, 135, 195, 229

P

Pascoe, Allan 207, 274
Pearse, Neville 187, 209
Pedersen, Robert G. 33–36, 113, 211
Pemberton, Don 30–31, 214
Perth 31, 86, 154, 173, 175, 192–93, 253
Philippines 25, 100, 171
police 72, 243, 244
polygamy 12, 14, 35, 49, 99, 119, 122–123, 153, 168, 202, 220, 232, 254
preach 7, 46, 62, 95, 121, 212, 229, 235
prison 101
Prospect Branch 10, 22
publicity 4, 6, 10, 22, 28, 34–35, 41, 49–50, 62–63, 86–87, 89, 92, 99, 110, 113, 152, 159, 202, 216, 232, 250

Q

Queensland 5–6, 16, 19, 22, 32, 38, 42, 65, 117–18, 127, 159, 166, 183, 210, 212, 231, 239

R

radio 10, 16, 28, 35, 38, 49, 87–88, 94, 160, 171, 230, 244, 247
Rampton, James Richard (Rich) 36, 73, 213, 216–17
Reeb, Harold (Hal) 28–31, 173, 175, 214–15, 218
referee 108, 118, 137, 155, 171, 250
rink 12, 64, 82, 109, 220
Romney, Marion G. 19–20, 88, 151
rough 26, 111, 115, 205, 217
Russians 26, 60, 100, 105, 111, 140, 154, 171, 204
Ryan, Denis 186–87, 220, 233

S

Salt Lake City 1, 16, 18, 58, 70, 93, 112, 129, 157, 194
Seagulls 5
Second World War. See World War II
show 38, 41, 94, 240
shows 36
Skousen, Bob xii, 43–44, 112, 148–49, 184, 186, 209–10, 220–22, 224
smoking 30, 42, 56, 147, 215
South Australia 4, 10, 15, 19–21, 31, 124, 143, 159, 229
Sporting Globe All-Sport Magazine 24, 111
sportsmanship xii, 7, 15, 25, 50, 79, 118–19, 127, 144, 149, 164, 195, 207–8, 229, 234, 250, 257
stakes 44, 49, 98, 206
Stapley, Delbert L. 224
Steck, Robert (Bob) 10–11, 15–16, 56–57, 177, 228, 252
Steen, Raymond Arthur 233
Stringer, Keith 46–47, 236
Sydney xi, 4, 6, 16–19, 31, 32, 34, 36, 44, 58–59, 61–62, 68, 72–73, 75, 86, 91, 94, 97, 114, 126–28, 131, 146, 153, 157, 159, 172, 194, 196, 241, 252
Sydney Basketball Association 6

T

Tasmania 6, 19, 27, 31, 97, 140, 173, 180, 205, 218
television 32, 94, 153, 249
Thursday Island 44–46, 64–65, 165, 166, 188–89
Tingey Hall 5
Toowoomba 6, 7, 67
tour 18, 32, 33–36, 38–41, 43, 63, 71–72, 113, 117, 149, 153, 180, 213, 216, 239–40, 243, 245
tournament 1, 10, 31, 45, 56, 60, 65, 90, 93, 116, 121, 123, 139–40, 147, 166, 174, 182, 188, 228
Townsville 40–41
training 3, 24, 38, 46, 58, 63, 71, 134, 151, 185, 204, 206–8, 221
travel 15, 36, 38, 40, 45, 94, 110, 172, 179–80, 243, 252
Turley, Harold E., Jr. 38, 44, 52, 156, 239
Tuttle, Dell 39, 42, 242

U

University of Melbourne ix, 28–29, 31, 175, 214, 218
University of Utah 18, 22, 26, 32, 60, 73, 86–87, 94, 96–97, 137, 152, 155, 173, 179–80, 192, 216, 255
Utah State 22, 26, 87, 149, 152, 173, 180, 256

V

Victoria ix, 3, 19–23, 31–32, 48, 86, 88–89, 110, 142–43, 145–48, 150, 161, 173, 219
Victorian Basketball Association 4, 84
Volkswagen 34–36, 38, 113, 115, 216, 243

W

Walton, Garwood 4, 246
Watson, Ken ix, 21, 86, 97, 100, 143–44
Watts, Kay 47, 249
Watts, Stan 12, 178, 224–25
Weitzeil, Norman L. 11, 16, 252

West, Wilburn 255
Whyalla 171
Williams, Val 226
Word of Wisdom 3, 42, 45, 100, 115, 181, 189, 230, 236, 239
  drinking 31, 45, 147, 185, 189, 215, 236
  smoking 30, 42, 56, 147, 215
World War II 2, 4, 64, 70, 89, 91, 162, 248, 256

Y

YMCA 1–8, 12, 22, 32, 54, 82–84, 97, 105, 118, 121–23, 161–64, 196, 199, 214–15, 256
YMMIA 1

0 26575 10599 5